DATE DUE

The New Financial Capitalists

The New Financial Capitalists

Kohlberg Kravis Roberts
and the Creation of
Corporate Value

GEORGE P. BAKER

GEORGE DAVID SMITH

CAMBRIDGE
UNIVERSITY PRESS

THE UNIVERSITY OF CAMBRIDGE
nbridge, United Kingdom

CAMBRIDGE UNIVERSITY PRESS

The Edinburgh Building, Cambridge CB2 2RU, UK   http: //www.cup.cam.ac.uk
40 West 20th Street, New York, NY 10011-4211, USA   http: //www.cup.org
10 Stamford Road, Oakleigh, Melbourne 3166, Australia

© George P. Baker and George David Smith 1998

First published 1998
Reprinted 1998, 1999

Printed in the United States of America

Typeset in Sabon 10/13 pt. in Penta™ [RF]

A catalogue record for this book is available from the British Library

Library of Congress Cataloguing-in-Publication Data
Baker, George P. (George Pierce)
The new financial capitalists : Kohlberg Kravis Roberts and the
creation of corporate value / George P. Baker, George David Smith.
p. cm.
Includes bibliographical references and index.
1. Consolidation and merger of corporations – United States –
Finance. 2. Leveraged buyouts – United States. 3. Kohlberg Kravis
Roberts & Co. I. Smith, George David. II. Title.
HG4028.M4B335   1998
33.8'3'0973 – dc21   98-28007

ISBN 0 521 64260 4 hardback

For Lauren and Susan

Contents

Preface

GOOD ORGANIZATIONS HAVE STRONG memories. In the spring of 1994, George Roberts engaged the authors as consultants to help his firm, Kohlberg Kravis Roberts & Co., document the histories of its investments in systematic fashion. After some eighteen years in business, KKR was no longer just a small association of investors with a shared body of experience. It was important for the firm's senior partners to transmit both the details and the patterns of nearly two decades of experience to its younger generation of professionals and its widening circle of investors. For us – an economist (George Baker) and an historian (George Smith) – it was an exciting prospect. Though the project was strictly proprietary and intended for internal use, it gave us privileged access to the records and people of one of the modern era's most innovative and influential financial firms. We stood to learn a great deal about the private equity markets, and in particular the leveraged management buyout, a phenomenon that remained largely a mystery outside the rarefied precincts of high finance.

The project involved not just documenting the financial and structural parameters of each transaction KKR had done, but recording the post-transaction operating decisions, management and strategy changes, and operating performances of each of the forty-odd companies KKR acquired between 1976 and 1992. We combined extensive archival research (offering memoranda, SEC filings, internal budgets and memos, annual reports, and the like) with interviews of KKR principals and company executives. What concerned us were not only questions that could be answered by quantitative measures of leverage and operating performance, but also questions of business judgment, behavioral incentives, and the nuances of personal and professional relationships. Since much of the information we sought was qualitative and unrecorded, we relied heavily on the interviews to flesh out the history of each KKR investment.

As the record accumulated, we became aware of a rich history of financial innovation and organizational evolution. Much of what we learned in our research struck us as news. We learned a lot about what happened to corporate managers after they had undergone LBOs, how managerial behavior and operating performance changed as a consequence of leverage, management ownership, and active governance – not just in one or two firms, but in dozens of them. We were exposed to the thought processes of investors and managers as buyouts transformed the dynamics of owner-manager relationships. With the detail we had accumulated on how KKR's principals functioned as investment bankers, general partners, and board directors, we began to form in our minds a deeper, more textured understanding of the so-called LBO firm – its nature as an institution, its role in the economy – than had been possible for the most sophisticated financial economists to glean from the public record.

In the fall of 1995, we discussed with KKR's senior partners, Henry Kravis and George Roberts, the possibility that we might write a more complete history for public consumption. After some discussion, they concluded that some greater good might come from allowing more light to shine on KKR's history. They thus agreed to let us interpret and publish our findings, but only if *we* agreed to make any book that came out of the effort a serious study in financial history and policy. KKR had already been the subject of a body of popular business literature, which, with few exceptions, offered little insight into the historical and financial implications of the firm's business. Histories of the firm tended to be replete with trivial gossip and financially naïve. It was time, Kravis and Roberts agreed, for more serious consideration of the buyout as a financial technique and incentive system, for some assessment of its larger implications for corporate control and governance. These sentiments suited our interests perfectly.

Thus our engagement continued, but now with a public purpose. We developed an outline for a book that would be historical, insofar as we would attempt to understand KKR's story as a developing process, and to place it in its wider and longer-term social and economic contexts. We also wanted the book to be explicitly policy-oriented; we would present an argument for the leveraged buyout as an example of economically productive financial engineering. We wanted to explain what we had learned about the strengths and weaknesses of leverage, the need for more rigorous corporate governance, and the way in which KKR, in particular, had developed what we and other scholars believed to be a novel form of business organization. We wanted to assess what implications the management buyout had for the organization and management of corporations during a watershed era in the restructuring of the American business economy.

Under rules of engagement that have become accepted practice among scholars writing histories of firms, we requested that KKR give us complete access to its files and personnel. All choices of subject matter, themes, and interpretations were to be left to us alone. To ensure that a serious academic publisher would accept our work, there could be no censorship. We asked, and received, KKR's permission to publish any financial information that the firm shared with its limited partners. KKR released to us the rights in the manuscript in exchange for the following: We agreed that KKR would be able to review the text and have the opportunity to offer corrections of factual errors. We agreed to keep confidential proprietary information such as current competitive secrets or investment information. We agreed that interviewees could go off the record on sensitive issues so that we might at least benefit from important "background" information.

In the spring of 1997, we presented an outline to Cambridge University Press along with some drafts of a text for blind reading among academic experts. The three reports solicited by Cambridge were positive and critically useful. The readers were especially encouraged by our plan to explore KKR's more problematic and failed investments as well as its successful ones. One report, in particular, urged us to write for the intelligent lay reader, not just the specialist. To that end we have striven to eliminate unnecessary jargon and to be as clear as we can, without sacrificing rigor, in explaining the nature and transactions of the firm.

The product of our efforts is this volume, organized into half a dozen chapters covering KKR's activities from its founding in 1976 through the merger and acquisition boom of the 1980s. Each chapter is designed to be a more or less self-contained essay with its own thematic and interpretive structure, so that a reader may enter the book at any point depending on his or her interests. At the same time, we have designed the book so that it presents an integrated and overlapping set of themes regarding how financial structure relates to managerial performance in the pursuit of long-term value.

The first chapter is an overview of the leveraged buyout in its long-term historical and historiographical contexts. The second focuses on the highly leveraged transaction as both financing technique and incentive structure for realizing value (improving operating performance) in "undervalued" companies. The third takes up the issue of post-acquisition governance and management, with some in-depth case detail on the varied processes by which bought-out firms attempt to increase asset values. The fourth is a discussion of distressed buyout investments – the various causes and consequences of failure and how the buyout firm attempts to minimize and resolve serious problems. The fifth is a discussion of KKR as an institutional phenomenon. Here readers will encounter a firm that we believe to be an exception among small professional organizations, both in its formal management systems and in its style and culture. We also offer some hopefully useful correctives to the literature on the "LBO association," which we argue is a new and distinct form for organizing and monitoring corporations through critical phases of reform. Finally, in Chapter 6, we bring KKR's history up to date and summarize what we believe to be the larger implications of its financings for the governance and management of corporations.

We expect that the quantitative and narrative detail we provide in this volume will be useful to students of financial economics and history, to public policy makers, and to legal and financial practitioners. We hope that the insights we derive from our study of KKR's history will repay any nonspecialized reader's time and effort as well. The lessons readers will encounter are manifold, but four deserve highlighting. *Financial structure matters to corporate value creation.* In contrast with much of the theory of modern capital structure, we demonstrate that the way a company is financed affects not just the distribution of its cash flows, but also the way it is managed. *Value creation is, in turn, a long-term pursuit that requires hard work and constant vigilance.* Far from the conventional images that come to mind with the term "financial engineering," we find that the processes by which management and KKR create value following a buyout are far from short-term, formulaic, or guaranteed. *Aligning managerial and ownership interests leads to good results.* Some will find this the most obvious point in the book, but few will fail to appreciate the dramatic effects of turning managers into financial risk-bearing owners. *Flexibility in financing and adaptability to unforeseen events are crucial determinants of success.* Probably the greatest difference between a financial firm that completes many successful buyouts and one that founders in these treacherous waters is the former's consistent ability to structure transactions that can survive any number of unforeseen contingencies. Many parties – including investors, employees, and indeed society as a whole – suffer when financiers and managers ignore these basic lessons.

Many people have assisted us in the preparation of this work. A few deserve special acknowledgment. Davis Dyer of the Winthrop Group, Inc., provided substantial intellectual and writing assistance in the early phase of our documentation efforts. Elizabeth Neiva, Daniel Gross, Elizabeth Johnson, and Mark Samber were tireless and skillful research assistants.

Among our professional peers, each of us owes much to past colleagues, coauthors, and friends from whom we have learned and on whose wisdom we draw in this book. George Baker would like to thank Cynthia Montgomery and the Coordination, Control and the Management of Organizations teaching group at the Harvard Business School, including Carliss Baldwin, Kevin Murphy, Malcolm Salter, and especially Karen Wruck and Michael Jensen for years of conversation, joint thinking, and insights on these and related issues. (To Mike, in particular, I owe an incalculable debt.) George Smith would like to acknowledge the years of valuable collaboration with his consulting partners at The Winthrop Group, Inc., where he has learned to appreciate both the utility and the limits of economic and organizational theory. Countless hours of conversation with colleagues in the economics department at the Stern School of Business and with investment professionals Gene Dattel and Betty Sheets have deepened his knowledge of contemporary financial institutions. Most of all, thanks go to Richard Sylla, with whom he is writing a history of capital markets. (Dick, more than anyone, has nurtured my late-blooming interest in financial history.) We both also thank Lauren Jennings and Susan Gray, who, in addition to their criticisms and provocative questions about our work, have blessed us with their warm personal support.

While all members of the staff at KKR were invariably helpful and polite to us during our labors, we would like to thank particularly the following people. Jim Reynolds, who oversees the management of the firm's records in New York, and his staff were more than patient with our insatiable appetite for documentary information. Sal Bada-lamenti and his staff helped us to get the numbers straight. Lesley Harrison, Barbara Johnson, Sally Long, and Susan Smith cheerfully put up with our phone calls, impromptu visits, requests for meetings, and logistical problems, and they never missed a beat. Finally, we thank all the members of the firm, current and retired, who gave generously of their time and knowledge in our interviews.

1 | *The Rebirth of Financial Capitalism*

Economic progress, in capitalist society,
means turmoil.

– Joseph A. Schumpeter

I N *The Man in the White Suit*, Alec Guinness plays a mild mannered
industrial scientist who discovers a seemingly indestructible fiber.
Who could doubt what a boon that would be to society? His employer, a venerable, run-down British textile company, wants to sup-
press his invention. His coworkers are terrified by it. His friends turn
against him. His personal safety becomes endangered, and comic
chases ensue. All is well in the end – when the fiber turns out not to
work.[1]

Entrepreneurs seek profits by introducing new goods, services, organizations, and techniques. In doing so, they advance the economic
welfare of society. At the same time, their activities are profoundly
disturbing. Entrepreneurs are, after all, the agents of "creative destruction," as Joseph Schumpeter so aptly labeled the processes of
change they set in motion; their successes invariably upset existing
social arrangements, transferring wealth and power from old to new
sectors of the economy.[2] It is for that reason, throughout most of
history, that expansive empires and local tribal cultures alike have
tried to curb entrepreneurial behavior with political restraints and
social taboos, lest it upset the status quo.[3] Modern capitalist societies
depend utterly on entrepreneurship for their progress; but they too
remain ambivalent about its effects. In the United States, where the
individualistic pursuit of happiness flourishes as in no other country,
commercial invention and innovation have become the norm, encouraged by public policy and reinforced by cultural values that support progress, change, and social mobility. Yet even in the U.S., vested
interests have always risen up to protest, and otherwise resist, the

1

social and economic changes that entrepreneurship has brought about.[4]

Hence entrepreneurs are not always regarded with favor, and some are hardly regarded at all. Financial entrepreneurs, for example, are rarely held in high esteem by Americans. Few view history's more creative investors, such as Nicholas Biddle, J. P. Morgan, or Michael Milken, in the same way they do Thomas Edison, Henry Ford, Andrew Carnegie, or Sam Walton – people who either invented tangible goods or organized more efficient means for their production and distribution. The essential populism of American culture is uncomfortable with financial schemes, which have so often been associated with venal fraud and scandal, or worse, unfruitful labor. In the common caricature, the great practitioners of high finance have made their money without producing goods, extracting "paper profits" as if by sleight of hand, wringing fortunes from transactions that have no direct connection to anything productive. This view is hardly limited to the uninitiated; it is shared among highly sophisticated business people.

Yet even history's more infamous financiers deserve some credit for the positive impacts they have had on the nation's economic life. The quintessential nineteenth-century takeover artist, Jay Gould, was as greedy as they came. He was manipulative, dishonest, and could not run a railroad; but his ingenious raids on financially vulnerable lines compelled those who did know how to run them better. Turn-of-the-century banker Andrew Mellon was hardly a paragon of social sensitivity, but his ability to channel capital to new ventures spurred the development of important new technologies. J. P. Morgan's consolidations and restructuring earned him outsized fees and a largely deserved reputation as a monopolist, but he also saved poorly run railroads from bankruptcy and wrung gross inefficiencies out of industries suffering from excess capacity. In all such cases, creative financiers made it possible for those who managed the means of production to accomplish things they might not otherwise have been able to do.[5]

This book is concerned with a recent financial innovation: the leveraged buyout. The leveraged buyout was a classic entrepreneurial coup: its economic impact was great; its practitioners were accordingly respected and feared. Like so many of the more important innovations in economic life, it was developed outside the economic mainstream, in this case on the peripheries of high finance. Its invention is obscure, but it was quietly honed into a powerful financial technique in the back alleys of Wall Street during the 1960s and 1970s by the precursors of such now-famous specialty firms as Kohlberg Kravis Roberts; Forstmann, Little; and Clayton, Dubilier & Rice.

During the merger and acquisition boom of the 1980s, leveraged buyouts spurred a dual revolution in the American economy – one in corporate finance, another in corporate governance – that profoundly altered patterns of managerial power and behavior. They not only substantially improved the worth of specific firms, they also helped to change the ways in which business in general thought about debt, governance, and value creation. In order to succeed, they usually required drastic reforms in operations, reallocations of capital, and dislocations of personnel. They aroused the ire of numerous interests – from corporate executives to labor unions, from local communities to bondholders – whose power, status, jobs, and other economic interests were affected by the restructurings. It should be no surprise, then, that the leveraged buyout was denounced in many quarters as just another unproductive, dangerous financial scheme.

Among the so-called "LBO firms," Kohlberg Kravis Roberts (KKR) became the most successful, and the most notorious. Its organizational life began in 1976, when a restless trio of dealmakers left the investment bank Bear, Stearns, Inc., to found their own partnership. Jerome Kohlberg, Henry Kravis, and George Roberts opened two small offices in New York and San Francisco, from which they solicited funds from banks and individual investors, many of whom were familiar with their well-honed technique for buying small companies with debt. This would not have been particularly remarkable in the annals of financial firm startups. In the fragile institutions of investment banking, people constantly came and went, often abandoning the relative security of larger employers to establish their own shops. Because the survival of such ventures depended utterly on the stability and capabilities of their founders, most disappeared within a relatively short time. In this case, the small partnership of KKR grew from its modest beginnings to become one of the powerhouses in the history of big business finance, and remains today one of the more durable institutions on Wall Street.

Their success was based on the somewhat novel, if not unique, approach they had developed during eight years of collaboration at

Bear, Stearns. The trio would buy well-established, privately controlled companies with predictable streams of revenue and cash flow. In financing their acquisitions, they borrowed nearly all of the money. By employing high levels of debt, or *leverage*, they minimized the cost of buying the equity, which they shared with the target companies' managers. Assuming that the cash flows of the acquired businesses would be more than sufficient to repay the borrowing, their success depended on a combination of timely debt reduction and the promotion of longer-term efficiency. If all went well (typically within five to seven years), they resold the leveraged equity for substantially higher-than-average gains.*

What separated KKR from the pack of buyout specialists was its peculiar ability to adapt the technique to new opportunities in fast-changing economic and financial environments. KKR also proved adept at cultivating trust with debt and equity investors, on the one hand, and target companies and their managers, on the other. In the process, KKR drove the scale and scope of the leveraged buyout to unprecedented heights, culminating in 1988–89 with the $31 billion financing of RJR Nabisco, which was accompanied by an immediate overhaul of the company's management and projected massive divestitures and wholesale operating reforms. When that happened, KKR became almost a household word, appearing to the public as either one of the more progressive or malevolent forces in the nation's capital markets, depending on where one sat and whom one believed.

---

* KKR preferred to call these arrangements "management buyouts," but the term "leveraged buyout," often abbreviated as LBO, has stuck both in industry parlance and in the professional and academic literature. The terms *buyout*, *management buyout*, and *leveraged buyout* are used virtually interchangeably in this book, any subtle differences among them being clarified by context or explanation, where necessary.

KKR's history constitutes an important chapter in the larger progress of America's recovery from the economic doldrums of the 1970s. Following America's withdrawal from Vietnam, the nation's business system seemed likewise in retreat, its once-vaunted companies in disrepair, their management suffering from luxuriant decadence. The 1980s merger and acquisition wave was in good part a response to this situation, driven as it was by widespread opportunities to seek profits through the restructuring of the nation's corporations. KKR's activities were part and parcel of this larger process of reform.

The restructuring of American business in the 1980s had been conditioned by a longer history of merger and acquisition waves, each of which had contributed to the American business and financial system. Each preceding wave – there were three of major consequence – had been a response to structural problems in American business. Each had arisen at a time when both excess capacity was high and sources of funds for investment were abundant; each had run to excess; and each had prompted regulatory and legislative reforms that altered the motives and means for undertaking acquisitions. Each, therefore, had left legacies to which 1980s financiers, consciously or not, were responding.

Financial Capitalism

One of the most important of these legacies was an abiding question in U.S. corporate governance: how to reconcile the behavior of corporate managers with the interests of corporate shareholders. The roots of this problem extend back to the mid nineteenth century, when the first large corporations emerged to capitalize on the organizational efficiencies made possible by the industrial revolution. There was little to worry about in this regard among traditional firms, where managers owned and owners managed. Nor was there a problem in such pioneering big business enterprises as Carnegie Steel or Standard Oil, where ownership and managerial interests were closely aligned during the build-up phase of their industry.

A serious divergence of interests between shareholders and managers first became apparent in the infrastructure industries, where huge capital requirements led companies to make public equity offerings when their ability to finance expansion from retained earnings reached its limits. Board directors, who were bound to represent shareholder interests, and corporate managers quarreled over the use of profits. Managers who understood the great growth potential of new technologies bridled at constraints imposed on them by increasingly remote "absentee owners" who were inhibiting institution-building, long-term investment, and innovation. In 1885, Theodore Vail, the strategic genius of nineteenth-century telecommunications, quit his job as head of AT&T in New York, so frayed were his nerves from squabbling over resources with the hyper-conservative Boston Brahmins who controlled the company he had been hired to manage.

Systems builders in the young railroad industry found it difficult to persuade their boards to defer dividends in favor of building the kind of capital-intensive networks that would bring order, economies of scale, and stability to the nation's fragmented transportation infrastructure.[6] Such tensions between fragmenting ownership and systems-building management would become more commonplace, as big business evolved in virtually every major sector of the economy.

For their part, corporate shareholders had good reason to worry that their investments might be subject to managerial incompetence, opportunism, or corruption. Rational systems building, after all, could easily degenerate into managerial empire building. Lacking information and expertise in the technical and operating details of complex organizations, most shareholders had to rely on the integrity and skill of their hired managers and on the ability of boards of directors to monitor managerial performance.

That was certainly the situation at the time of the first merger wave, when financial entrepreneurs intervened to resolve some of the problems. During the years 1897–1904, some 4,277 American companies consolidated into 257 corporations. Most of these transactions occurred on the horizontal plane – that is, between companies that did the same things. (The Sherman Antitrust Act of 1890 was partly responsible for this outcome, as it prevented cooperation, but not combination, among competing firms.) As with subsequent waves, the profits earned from good deals stimulated bad ones; companies that had no economic reason to merge did so, only to come undone later. On the whole, however, the first merger wave was not merely a drive toward monopoly, it was a drive toward efficiency. The activities of the financiers who arranged the consolidations helped to rid the economy of chronic excess capacity, especially in such capital-intensive industries as railroading and steel.[7]

A new breed of investment bankers played key roles in promoting and financing these transactions, often with high levels of debt. The signature deal of the era, the 1901 amalgamation of eight steel companies into U.S. Steel Corporation, had a total capitalization of $1.2 billion – an astonishing amount equivalent to seven percent of the gross national product. It was financed by a syndicate headed by J. P. Morgan, the preeminent financier of his time, who had built his reputation by restructuring ailing railroads. With $550 million in 7 percent convertible preferred stock, $550 million in common stock, and $304 million in 5 percent gold bonds, U.S. Steel's capital structure was in effect 61 percent leveraged. The purchase price represented a premium to the sellers, but was low compared to the values the Morgan syndicate expected from U.S. Steel. Morgan then placed his partners on the new company's board of directors.[8]

This was typical of the larger financings of an era when investment bankers played a vital role in aligning the interests of owners and managers at the center of the nation's economy. Such intermediaries as J. P. Morgan; Jacob Schiff of Kuhn, Loeb; George F. Baker of New York's First National Bank, and their allies dominated the corporate boards of major public companies. As fiduciaries, they guarded the interests of both shareholders and bondholders, while providing informed advice on corporate strategy, policy, and financial structure. Such ongoing monitoring by the financiers who had restructured the businesses was the hallmark of what historians call "financial capitalism."[9]

Financial capitalism was already in retreat by the time of the second, longer wave of mergers and acquisitions, which began in 1916 and proceeded through the economic boom of the 1920s, before dying out in the aftermath of the 1929 stock market crash. Much of the activity involved the consolidation of newly constructed public utilities along with mergers in other basic industries that could benefit from reductions in capacity. Vertical mergers – that is, the combination of entities engaged in sourcing, production, and distribution – were more important in this era, helping regional companies expand their scope to serve national markets. Once again, investment bankers played a major role in promoting and financing mergers, and despite some grievous instances of fraud in a largely unregulated national securities market, the second wave was a generally positive development. Secondary markets for large corporate bonds and equities grew, as financial intermediaries became increasingly adept at channeling funds from smaller investors.

Yet even as finance became increasingly important to the nation's business life, financiers were losing their influence in the nation's boardrooms. Financial capitalism was giving way to managerial capitalism.

Managerial Capitalism

As their operations increased in scale and complexity, large corporations became increasingly dependent on a new kind of executive: the professional technocrat. In modern, complex corporations, managers typically became executives because of their strategic talents, technical expertise, and organizational experience rather than their familial ties or ownership stakes. In 1914, the social commentator Walter Lippmann noted that large-scale enterprise was now "managed by . . . managers [who] are on salary, divorced from ownership and from bargaining. . . . The motive of profit is not their motive."[10] He, like many others, thought this to be a highly positive development – a triumph of meritocratic bureaucracy. Expert management, free of rigid ownership constraints, proved vital to the progress of institutional capitalism through the mid twentieth century.[11] One would be hard pressed to argue with what is now well-documented history; but with the separation of management from ownership, control issues and bureaucratic problems inevitably surfaced.

Meanwhile, the bankers who helped finance corporate growth were growing less inclined to monitor managerial performance. This trend started before World War I, when Wall Street came under heavy criticism for its apparent concentration of control of the nation's productive assets. It would be furthered by New Deal regulations that would more explicitly limit the power of financiers to assert themselves in the boardroom. During the Great Depression, when public hostility toward business and finance was at its peak, the government sharply restricted bank holdings in corporations and reduced the financial incentives for financial intermediaries to sit on boards. The Investment Company Act of 1940 restricted the percentage of shares investment funds could invest in any one company. After that, money managers refrained from sitting on boards; and bankers, fearing liabilities, remained aloof from the governance affairs of companies to which they had loaned money. Investment bankers found that they could make plenty of money arranging transactions, while avoiding the liabilities and opprobrium associated with financial control of corporations.[12]

A price was paid for this outcome. With corporate ownership separated from control, and in the absence of strong intermediary representation on boards, the links between a manager's personal interest and corporate business interests were seriously weakened, if not altogether broken. Some observers found this outcome disconcerting. "If we are to assume that the desire for *personal profit* is the prime force motivating control," Adolf Berle and Gardiner Means wrote in 1933, in the classic treatise on the subject,

> we must conclude that the interests of control are different from and often radically opposed to those of ownership; that the owners most emphatically will not be served by a profit-seeking controlling group. In the operation of the corporation, the controlling group, even if they own a large block of stock, can serve their own pockets better by profiting at the expense of the company than by making profits for it.[13]

In other words, the modern corporation contained within it a heightened principal-agent conflict: the agents (the managers), who always had incentives to manage corporations in their own interests rather than in the interests of the principals (the owners), were now even less constrained by effective ownership control. What modern agency theorists call managerial opportunism – most often expressed in empire-building behavior – might prevail over more efficient, profit-seeking goals.[14] In economic terms, managers unchecked would be tempted to misallocate the corporation's free cash flow – that is, cash that ought to accrue to shareholders after all other corporate obligations have been met and all sensibly profitable long-term investments have been made.[15]

Even so, with managers in the ascendance, the doctrine that enterprise existed primarily for the purpose of creating wealth for shareholders remained the best discipline. We can consider why this would be so by looking at the ironic difference in outlook of two of the most important corporate managers of the twentieth century, Henry Ford and Alfred Sloan. Ford, who had always controlled his company's equity, liked to say that he was in the business of making inexpensive automobiles, and that making money was just an incidental by-product of producing good Model Ts. So annoyed was he with the explicit profit-seeking demands of his minority shareholders that he bought them out in 1920 so that he could conduct his business and allocate its resources as he saw fit. The problem was that without any authority but his own to challenge his thinking, he let the world pass him by, failing to respond in timely fashion to changes in demand and underestimating challenges from competitors. What had once been the most innovative automotive company in the world thus entered into a slow and steady decline; Ford's death in 1945 literally saved it from oblivion.

Sloan, the quintessential administrator, never forgot that he was in business to make money for his shareholders. With that objective foremost in mind, he reorganized General Motors, a once-struggling agglomeration of diverse assembly and supply companies, into a streamlined, coherent enterprise. When the demographics of demand changed, reflecting rising incomes and more elaborate tastes, Sloan segmented the market for GM cars, offering transportation for every pocketbook and preference. When success came, he kept his managers innovating. He exhorted them to revise their market forecasts, to redesign their products, to continuously improve their operations, to rethink their jobs. General Motors thus leaped past Ford within just a few years, and Sloan continued to make money for his shareholders during the depths of the Great Depression by constantly striving to make his company more efficient.[16] In 1946, Peter Drucker hailed Alfred Sloan's legacy in his famous book *The Concept of the Corporation*, in which General Motors became the very model of effective corporate governance and management.[17]

Managerial capitalism went on to enjoy its heyday during the "golden age" of American economic expansion following World War II, as equity investment expanded and ordinary householders came into the stock market in greater numbers. Shareholders had found that they could reduce their risks by diversifying their portfolios, while managers sought to reduce *their* risks by negotiating stronger employment contracts, increasing their own salaries and perquisites, weakening the monitoring power of those who could fire them, and ultimately by investing in more diverse assets. The strength of managerial capitalism was the discretion it afforded expert managers to invest in growth-seeking strategies. Its weakness lay in the temptation it afforded managers to build empires, and to allocate resources in ways that would not, over the long run, enhance shareholder value.

Breakdown in Corporate Governance

Succeeding generations of managers forgot Sloan's example, and this lapse would lead to a decline in corporate efficiency. After World War II, the trend was for the top executive managers of widely held corporations to anoint themselves chairmen and place their subordinates and friendly "outsiders" on their boards of directors. Internally, the ranks of middle managers swelled, as corporate offices grew to accommodate more and more managerial functions – few of which were eliminated when their usefulness diminished with changing circumstances. The structures of employment became ever more rigid, as managers bargained for labor peace. Unions won bigger shares of corporate revenues for their members, not only in wages but also in medical insurance, time off, retirement benefits, and automatic cost-of-living adjustments. More rigid work rules, grievance procedures, and seniority provisions also increased costs without guaranteeing increased productivity.[18] As labor costs rose, they also pushed up middle management salaries and perquisites.

During the 1950s and most of the 1960s, the U.S. enjoyed a towering military, political, and economic position in the noncommunist world. The aggregate U.S. market was so huge (nearly half the world's market in 1950) that there was little fear of foreign competition. Free in principle, domestic markets remained protected by virtue of foreign weakness, as virtually all of industrialized Europe and Japan struggled to recover from the devastation they had suffered during the war. Corporate profitability was high in this period, and the U.S. business system became the envy of the world. Consulting firms earned huge fees exporting American management theory and practice as the postwar dominance of the American economy reinforced the expansion and stature of managerial power.

In the late 1960s, two particularly influential books appeared, extolling the efficiency of the large American corporation: John Kenneth Galbraith's *The New Industrial State* and Jean-Jacques Servan-Schreiber's *The American Challenge*. Servan-Schreiber warned that the U.S., by dint of its superior organizational capabilities, might actually come to dominate world markets. Galbraith was a bit closer to the mark: worrying that the corporation had outrun society's ability to control it, he noted that corporate executives had certainly outrun the ability of shareholders to control them. But few American shareholders seemed to be aware of this problem, much less to care about it.[19]

The irony is that just when these books appeared, the American economy was already in trouble. The rapid growth of government indebtedness, due to the simultaneous swelling of domestic programs and the prosecution of the Vietnam War, was placing a heavy burden on the nation's economy. Once self-sufficient in almost every basic resource, the United States had become dependent on foreign oil to feed its insatiable appetite for energy. The price would come in the form of high rates of inflation and unemployment in the 1970s, which increased the cost of debt while dampening returns in the equity markets. Adversely affected by these larger economic problems, much of the nation's industry was also suffering from the untimely erosion of managerial competence.

By the mid-1970s, it became apparent to almost everyone that American business was in deep distress. Corporate profitability was in a long descent that would not bottom out until the recession of 1981–82 (see figure). The nation's steel and automotive industries, inextricably linked to so much of the rest of the economy, were under sharp competitive attack. Foreign producers, most notably but not exclusively the Japanese, were making products that were qualitatively better and less expensive. The Japanese had also stolen a march on the market for consumer electronics.[20]

Once-great American companies, such as General Motors, U.S. Steel, and RCA, went into decline. Mature industries at the center of the economy had become largely complacent oligopolies, in which the desire for stability took precedence over profit maximization and price competition. Labor relations had settled into industrywide patterns of collective bargaining by which increasing wages and benefits were built into the costs of goods and services. Corporate reward systems favored bureaucrats (who knew how to manage corporate politics) over entrepreneurial dissenters (who were more likely to provoke reforms). The widespread failure of boards of directors to hold managers of public companies to account exacerbated the problem. Had directors demanded accountability, managers might have striven harder to innovate, lower costs, and pay better heed to the changing needs of their customers.[21]

At the same time, a gradual change in the structure of the nation's equity markets was under way – a change that might offer some means to restore shareholder influence. For some years after the war, the typical equity holder of a public corporation was a wealthy, or at least upper-middle-class, individual or family. Now it was fast becoming the institutional investor. The stunning growth of pension funds, along with the growing popularity of mutual funds, began to

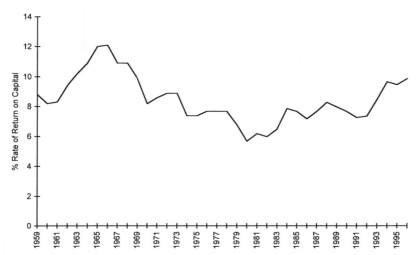

Corporate profitability, 1959–1996. Rate of return equals pretax income plus interest divided by tangible assets. Source: James Poterba, "The Rate of Return to Corporate Capital and Factor Shares," MIT and NBER Working Paper, March 1997.

reconcentrate the equity investments of small investors under the management of a relatively small number of sophisticated managers. This trend, however, did not lead directly to the restoration of shareholder influence, as government policies making it more difficult for unhappy shareholders to seek redress against bad management continued to multiply during the postwar era.[22]

Pre-war legislation and regulation had restricted mutual funds from owning more than 10 percent of any corporation's shares. In 1974, Congress passed the Employment Retirement Security Act (ERISA), which required a wide diversification of pension fund portfolios to preserve principal and minimize the risk of large losses. ERISA severely limited the ability of public pension fund managers to concentrate their influence in any one corporation. And since corporate executives generally maintained control over their companies' private pension funds, they could effectively limit any potential shareholder activism from those sources. Such provisions ensured portfolio diversification, but they attenuated whatever monitoring authority institutional investors might have over corporate managers. In sum, as the legal historian Mark Roe describes the situation:

Laws deliberately diminished the power of financial institutions to hold the large equity blocks that would foster serious oversight of managers. Banks . . . cannot own stock. Mutual funds generally cannot own large portions of a firm's stock. Insurance companies can put only a fragment of their investment portfolio into the stock of any one company. Pension funds own stock, but . . . face restrictions and are controlled by, and do not themselves control, managers.[23]

Thus, while managers routinely declared that their actions were based on their fiduciary responsibility to protect shareholder welfare, they were largely free – more than ever before – to act independently. Left to their own devices, executive managers of mature businesses acted bureaucratically, tending to favor routine over change, growth over efficiency. Too many managers overinvested in wasteful projects, acquiring assets simply for the sake of growth. Rather than return surpluses to shareholders, they were prone to invest instead in empire-building projects with little regard for their returns. Rank managerial opportunism was reflected in the erection of monumental corporate headquarters, the purchase of executive airplanes, stretch limousines, yachts and resorts, and the sponsorship of lavish trips and celebrity sporting events that did nothing to contribute to the bottom line. And some managers failed to invest enough in technologies and operating systems that would have enabled their companies to meet the challenges of changing markets, global competition, and deregulation.

Even when shareholders recognized managerial incompetence or opportunism, they had little recourse. The so-called "business judgment rule" of modern legal precedent helped to shield managers from charges of misappropriating corporate assets. Only in rare cases of financial crisis were outside directors with banking connections called upon to act. Captive boards of directors were disinclined to hold underperforming managers to close account unless conditions became so egregiously bad that the directors themselves could be held liable. Dissident minority shareholders could legally resort to costly proxy battles in order to install directors more friendly to their points of view, but such efforts were almost always unsuccessful.[24] Unhappy owners were left with the last resort option of selling their equity, which, as it occurred more frequently, enabled managers to argue that the increasing transience of shareholders rendered them uninterested in the long-term welfare of the enterprise.

This argument had merit if one could simply dismiss shareholders as absentee owners. Corporate shareholders, after all, *were not owners* in any conventional sense of the term; their rights were indirect. Shareholders, for instance, had no rights in corporate law either to manage or to dispose of assets represented by their shares. They had no right even to enter onto the physical property represented by their shares.

What they did have, however, was the right to elect boards of directors who in turn selected the executive managers, who ultimately bore a special fiduciary responsibility toward shareholders that they did not legally owe to other constituencies.

This responsibility was paramount, if only because it made perfect economic sense. As the residual claimants on corporate assets – that is, as those who would be last in line (behind vendors, creditors, and workers) to be paid in the event of liquidation – shareholders as a class had the greatest stake in the long-term health of the assets. Thus by striving to manage assets so as to maximize the welfare of shareholders, managers would necessarily be striving to maximize their efficiency, which over the long run would be the best economic outcome for society. Anything that weakened the sense of responsibility managers felt toward their shareholders could reduce the incentive to strive for long-term corporate efficiency, and increase the incentives for managerial opportunism.

Managerial Opportunism and the Conglomerate Wave

Managerial opportunism became grossly manifest in the nation's third merger and acquisition wave, which began to swell in 1963, and reached its peak six years later, when the number of announced transactions surged to 6,107 (see figure), the most in history until the record-breaking year of 1996. Once again, antitrust policy played a role in the particular form the merger wave took, but with a new twist. Heightened enforcement of regulations preventing anticompetitive mergers led expansion-hungry managers to seek new outlets for their surplus cash. (Increasing dividends was not a preferred alternative.) Financially sophisticated managers led the way, cobbling together companies in *unrelated* industries. For ten years after 1965,

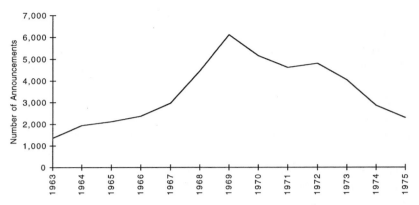

Number of mergers and acquisitions announcements, 1963–1975. Source: *Mergerstat Review*, 1989.

some 80 percent of all merger and acquisition activity involved such "conglomerate" mergers.[25]

In the peak years, conglomerate acquisitions were typically financed with stock, the value of which was generally rising in a bull market. Many conglomerate mergers were driven by cynical attempts to realize short-term stock price increases through the exploitation of wrinkles in the tax code and accounting manipulations, without any real attempt to improve the economic value of the underlying assets. The conglomerate wave subsided following a poor earnings report from one of the new conglomerates, Litton Industries; a downturn in the stock market; and the elimination of favorable tax treatments, all of which fueled growing market skepticism about the potential conglomerate strategies for increasing asset values over the long term. Nonetheless, conglomerate activity continued at a fairly robust pace; overall merger levels remained above 4,000 per year until 1974, when they fell off sharply in the wake of the international oil crisis.

Why did the conglomerate wave endure for so long? Conglomeration was in large part peer-driven, and like all business fads, it received affirmation from consultants, business writers, and executives. State-of-the-art management methodologies, it was argued, made it possible for skilled managers to engage in a variety of businesses. It was all too easy, in the absence of hard evidence, to rationalize conglomeration as a way to achieve "synergies," lower costs of capital, and economies of scope through a well-coordinated combination of highly diversified assets. Not everyone agreed: the historian Alfred Chandler shuddered at the phenomenon, bemoaning the tendency of senior managers "to grow through diversification – to acquire businesses in which they had few if any organizational capabilities to give them a competitive edge, [which] ignored the logic of managerial enterprise."[26] The logic of managerial opportunism prevailed, as the erection of conglomerate empires "justified" larger executive egos, salaries, and perquisites.

A few conglomerates managed to achieve consistently good long-term results – General Electric and Emerson Electric are among the more durable large-scale successes – but such long-term success generally came only in those cases where headquarters operated more like decentralized holding companies, restricting themselves to acquisitions, capital formation, and monitoring. Most conglomerate builders could not resist the temptation to "manage," weighing down their constituent companies with high overhead, bureaucratic red tape, and incessant interference with decision making. ITT's celebrated Harold Geneen was of this ilk. Believing he could control a mass of unrelated businesses with strong financial management, Geneen acquired some 350 companies around the world between 1959 and the late 1970s, enmeshing his operating managers in a confusing sprawl of responsibilities. ITT was characterized at every level by incessant meetings and countless reports. Before the ink was dry on Geneen's best-selling book, his conglomerate empire – bloated, inefficient, and corrupt – had begun to unravel, a feast for opportunistic buyers who picked it apart.[27]

Most conglomerate acquisitions proved financially disappointing.[28] That so many conglomerate mergers were misguided is evident from the massive wave of divestitures that eventually followed. Investors, initially enthralled, finally got the point. So inspired was the stock market by the news in 1983 that Gulf + Western's acquisitive and tyrannical CEO Charles Bludhorn had died, that investors bid up the company's stock price in eager anticipation of the spin-offs.[29] But other conglomerate architects were not so obliging, and there was little disappointed shareholders could do to force entrenched executives to reverse course.

One arena in which managerial opportunism was especially acute was the U.S. oil industry. The skyrocketing price of crude oil following the first and second oil shocks had coincided with the decreasing likelihood of finding (and increasing costs of exploring for) domestic reserves. This circumstance created an extreme temptation for major oil company executives to exploit their corporations' free cash flows. They had so much money flowing in, and so few productive investments to make in exploration and development, that their managers began to make acquisitions in unrelated areas. Most were of dubious value; Exxon's purchase of Reliance Electric and Mobil's acquisition of Montgomery Ward were two of the industry's more expensive mistakes. In 1984, when *Fortune* reported on the seven worst mergers of the preceding decade,[30] four were in the oil business, the industry where the so-called "market for corporate control" would first emerge.

The Market for Corporate Control

As the conglomerate wave began to ebb, a new vehicle surfaced for giving dissatisfied shareholders an opportunity to sell their stock in underperforming assets. The *tender offer* enabled buyers to bypass CEOs and boards of directors to appeal directly to shareholders. Typically, a tender offer gave shareholders the opportunity to sell their shares at prices substantially above the going market value, when a buyer, seeing the potential for increasing the value of the assets, was willing to pay a premium for them. In many cases, this would spell bad news for underperforming managers, who were likely to be replaced by the new owners. In other cases, buyers might retain managers, but under newly restructured agreements or understandings about how the assets would be managed. Most often, the tender offer was associated with a corporate raid, or "hostile" takeover attempt – that is, one resisted by the target company's board of directors.

Neither the unfriendly takeover nor the tender offer was new. In the nineteenth century, Jay Gould made a number of raids on vulnerable railroads. The tender offer had already been perfected in the United Kingdom when it caught on in the U.S. during the 1960s as a means for acquiring small firms. The fact that tender offers were employed mainly in unwanted bids led to the passage of the Williams Act in 1968, which regulated their use by requiring purchasers of equity to announce their holdings and intentions when their accumulations reached 5 percent of a company's stock. For a twenty-business-day period, a bidder's offer to purchase a controlling interest would remain open, while shareholders decided. The act had two effects that made tender offers – generally regarded as disreputable – more attractive. The mere fact of regulation effectively legitimized tender offers in the eyes of bankers who had formerly shunned them. It also provided target company boards time to mount takeover defenses, or else to solicit higher offers from friendlier "white knights," which almost inevitably raised the premium to exiting shareholders.

In 1973, the tender offer came to life in the U.S. as a vehicle for acquiring large companies when the International Nickel Company acquired ESB Corporation in a hotly contested struggle for control that gave the "hostile takeover" its name. The acquisition turned out to be a poor investment, but it helped to inspire similar gambits. Two years later, Harry Gray of United Technologies mounted a successful raid on what he identified as a seriously undervalued cash-rich company, Otis Elevator Company. Otis benefited from a change in management and quickly turned out to be a good investment, a productive cash generator for its conglomerate parent. After Colt Industries took over Garlock Industries in an extremely bitter contest, the hostile takeover became commonplace.[31] So did corporate takeover defenses – "shark repellents," "poison pills" – that substantially increased the costs or reduced the value of target companies.* Investment bankers and corporate lawyers, who could earn handsome fees on either side of such battles, increasingly became sources of information on prospective targets for likely suitors. As takeovers gained in popularity, they inspired other kinds of stock-price-enhancing speculation for "undervalued" companies, such as stock arbitrage and "greenmail." Combined, these activities formed part of a new market for corporate control in which the process of transferring ownership could be used to dislodge otherwise entrenched managers.

> * Companies employed an array of "defenses" against hostile takeovers, ranging from litigation and other forms of delaying tactics to more formal "shark repellents," such as corporate charter provisions that set terms for "fair prices," financial restructurings, board membership elections, and supermajority voting provisions. "Poison pills" were defenses that managers could employ without formal approval from shareholders that would reduce the value of the company to potential acquirers in the event of a change in control. Examples of this tactic were sales of assets triggered by takeover attempts or so-called "shareholder rights plans" by which a target company would declare common stock dividends in the form of rights to purchase additional stock at a discount in the event of a takeover.

Among the first to grasp the potential for systematically improving share prices by using the market to contest managerial control was T. Boone Pickens, who launched a series of raids on major oil companies. Pickens recognized that the industry's companies were essentially in liquidation, depleting their oil reserves faster than they could replace them. In doing so they were releasing a flood of cash, which managers then tried to spend largely (and wastefully) on exploration and development and unrelated acquisitions. The stock market responded by "undervaluing" oil company equities, anticipating the managers' waste of free cash flow to the extent that the value of proven reserves often exceeded the total value of the companies listed on the New York Stock Exchange. It was a common joke at the time that one could buy oil more cheaply on Wall Street than in the "oil patch."

Pickens's proposed solution was to restructure the oil companies with what he called a "royalty trust." This was a device through which an oil company could spin off its reserves directly to its shareholders, who could then directly receive the profits from liquidating the reserves on a far more advantageous tax basis than if they realized their profits after the assessment of corporate taxes on income. More significant than the tax advantages, Pickens's proposed structure would deprive oil company managers of much of their accustomed cash, forcing them to run their other operations, including their refining and retail gas distribution businesses, without the cross-subsidy that they had been getting from liquidating oil reserves. Royalty trust reorganization would therefore force managers to wean themselves from the free cash flow that their businesses had been generating and to manage them in a more disciplined and efficient way.[32]

Pickens never succeeded in getting any of the major oil companies to adopt his structure, but his hostile runs at Cities Services, Gulf Oil, and Unocal had some of the desired effects. In each of these cases, his targets wound up being acquired by "white knights" – that is, buyers preferred by the boards of the target companies. The companies that ended up owning the assets, including the oil reserves, had to take on large amounts of debt to finance their acquisitions, which always required huge cash payments to preexisting shareholders at prices that had been driven up by the intervening bidding process. The payments were financed by liquidating the reserves, and thus served much the same function as the royalty trust, the underlying motive for which – the channeling of free cash flow to the shareholders – was the same as that of another technique for realizing value: the leveraged buyout.

U.S. merger and acquisition announcements, tender offers, and contested tender offers, 1974–92

	M&A Announcements	Tender Offers	Contested Tenders
1974	2861	76	12
1975	2297	58	20
1976	2276	70	18
1977	2224	69	10
1978	2106	90	18
1979	2128	106	26
1980	1889	53	12
1981	2395	75	28
1982	2346	68	29
1983	2533	37	11
1984	2543	79	78
1985	2001	84	32
1986	3336	150	40
1987	2032	116	31
1988	2258	217	46
1989	2336	132	28
1990	2074	56	8
1991	1877	20	2
1992	2574	18	2

Source: Mergerstat Review, 1994.

Pickens and other corporate raiders inspired yet more takeover activity aimed at liberating free cash flows and improving equity prices in undervalued companies. The time was ripe. Knowledgeable enough to know when particular companies were not performing up to potential, many institutional shareholders were nonetheless limited in their power to influence management. The stakes they could hold in any one company were limited by both regulatory and fiduciary requirements, and they did not – or could not, for fear of conflict of interest – sit on boards of directors. At least the tender offer and the corporate raider showed them how they could sell out for a premium.

Hostile takeovers were never a large portion of the total number of mergers and acquisitions (see table, above), but they were characteristically undertaken against large corporations, and the mere threat of them inspired an increase in preemptive friendly mergers and buyouts. As the market for corporate control gained momentum after 1981, the device of aligning managerial and shareholder interests through the leveraged buyout had not yet been applied to large corporations. KKR's 1979 acquisition of Houdaille, a $380 million financing of a public company, hinted that this might someday happen. Houdaille's experience convinced many fearful CEOs (and their investment bankers) that the leveraged management buyout might be a friendly alternative to a hostile bid. And there was another outcome, even more important from a historical perspective: if the basic principle of the management buyout could be applied to other large public corporations, then financiers could reassert themselves in the boardroom in highly constructive ways. Once that occurred, the pendulum could then swing back toward financial capitalism, which would limit managerial discretion in favor of more rigorous exploitation of corporate resources.

KKR and the Fourth Wave

KKR came of age in the fourth merger and acquisition wave, which began just as the U.S. emerged from the recession of 1981–82. Global competition had laid bare the weaknesses in the traditional American center industries. In many cases, changes in markets and technology had resulted in obsolete assets and redundant personnel. The progressive deregulation of airlines, trucking, telecommunications, and banking would also reveal excess capacity in those industries. The conglomerate boom had saddled corporations with unwieldy, inefficient, or undermanaged operations. Massive shifts in investment away from manufacturing to services, along with energy shortages, high inflation, rising interest rates, and falling employment had all further contributed to the most serious crisis of confidence in the American business system since the Great Depression. Postwar corporate profits were reaching a low point, and many of the nation's biggest companies were suffering from low productivity and a widely perceived loss of managerial competence.

Completed U.S. mergers and acquisitions, leveraged buyouts, and KKR Fund leveraged buyouts, 1981–90

	M&As	LBOs	LBOs as Percent of M&A	KKR Fund LBOs	KKR as Percent of all LBOs
1981	2,328	99	4.3	7	7.1
1982	2,299	164	7.1	0	0
1983	2,395	131	9.6	3	1.2
1984	3,176	254	8	6	2.4
1985	3,490	255	7.3	4	1.6
1986	4,471	339	7.6	2	0.3
1987	4,037	279	6.9	3	1.1
1988	4,049	381	9.4	3	0.5
1989	3,766	371	9.9	1	0.3
1990	3,663	224	6.1	0	0

Sources: Mergers and Acquisitions, Almanac and Index (1987, 1991); KKR files.

Many of these problems were addressed by the merger and acquisition wave of the 1980s. Changes in the macroeconomic environment provided the impetus. In August 1982, the Federal Reserve reversed its credit tightening policy adopted in 1979 to stem high rates of inflation. As the long-bond rate declined, debt financing became more attractive. Antitrust policies were also changing, as the Justice Department and the Federal Trade Commission signaled, through both policy decrees and their handling of specific cases, that they were less inclined to act against mergers unless they were likely, according to rigorous economic analysis, to result in less efficient outcomes.[33] At no time did the number of transactions approach the levels achieved during the 1968–74 period (see table), but the fourth wave was different from previous ones in that both hostile takeovers and leveraged buyouts played a significant role, stimulated by aggressive investment bankers, corporate raiders, and heightened shareholder activism. The fourth wave was also characterized by increasing foreign participation, especially following the relative decline in the value of the dollar and the reduction of federal taxes on capital gains in 1986. The wave was stalled by the stock market crash of October 1987, and then rebounded briefly before ebbing and then finally foundering on the shoals of financial scandals, banking and real estate crises, political intervention, and the collapse of the so-called junk-bond market. By 1990, it was effectively over.

Domestic U.S. merger and acquisition, leveraged buyout, and KKR Fund leveraged buyout average and median values, 1981– 91 (in millions of dollars)

	M&A Average Value	M&A Median Value	LBO Average Value[a]	LBO Median Value[a]	KKR Fund LBO Average Value[a]
1981	154	22	N/A	N/A	270
1982	83	15	N/A	N/A	0
1983	58	14	78	38	285
1984	99	15	213	72	849
1985	173	45	206	55	1,311
1986	212	66	394	129	6,765
1987	183	50	397	145	2,776
1988	188	50	297	131	1,273
1989	171	30	458	83	31,430[b]
1990	108	18	187	42	0
1991	79	11	94	25	315

[a] LBO values are stated in terms of acquisition transaction costs.

[b] The transaction value of RJR Nabisco, which does not include KKR's investment in the K-III Communications Corporation "leveraged build-up." RJR Nabisco's acquisition began in 1988 and was completed in 1989.

Note: Overall LBO value data for 1981 and 1982 are too unreliable to report. Moreover, this and the LBO data in the previous table are constructed from different databases, which vary greatly in their reporting from year to year. The tables are not, therefore, meant to be consistent with each other; they are merely intended to illustrate trends over time and relative orders of magnitude among categories. In particular, multiplying the average transaction values in this table by the number of transactions in the previous table grossly overstates most estimates of aggregate transaction values.

Sources: Securities Data Company, KKR 1996 Fund Memorandum.

Nevertheless, as chaotic as things may have seemed, the American economy in 1990 was showing strong signs of resurgence: inflation was under control, and the stock market was buoyant, having already achieved the longest bull run in history. America's entrepreneurial resilience was no longer in doubt; and at the traditional center of the economy, even the nation's scaled-down "rust-belt" corporations were reviving from their torpor, regaining much of the vitality they had lost during the decades following World War II. Some of the corporate excesses, including unproductive conglomeration and bloated payrolls, had been brought to heel. "What accounted for the turnaround?" asked the National Bureau of Economic Research. "The tendency in many . . . corporate control transactions was to transform fat conglomerate frogs into sleek princes – firms focused on just a few core businesses."[34]

KKR's success in this larger story depended on its ability to build on a cumulative track record for extracting value from underperforming assets. From 1977 through the 1980s, the firm engineered a string of buyouts that generated extraordinary returns through changing economic conditions. In the process, the firm elaborated the basic techniques of leverage in a wide range of industries, while tapping new sources of funding, including larger and larger pools of equity capital, through highly variable market conditions. As its credibility with lenders increased, so did KKR's ability to raise equity funds, enabling KKR to surge ahead of a growing pack of specialty firms and the newly established buyout departments of the investment banks.

As experience accumulated, innovation increased. KKR's purchase of Wometco in 1984 was the first billion-dollar leveraged management buyout; it was followed by the first known *friendly* tender offer in the leveraged buyout of a public company, Malone & Hyde. Then, in its acquisition of Cole National Corporation, KKR entered into what would become a profitable alliance with Drexel Burnham Lambert. Drexel's unmatched ability to sell high-yield securities, or "junk bonds," enabled KKR to develop more elaborate debt structures for even larger-scale buyouts. When in 1986 the firm acquired the struggling conglomerate Beatrice for $6 billion, it became clear that even big corporations could be acquired through leveraging techniques previously thought to be limited to small and medium-sized concerns. By mid-1988, relying on Drexel's debt-raising capabilities, KKR had bought five more companies, at prices ranging between $1.4 billion and $4.7 billion (see Appendix), all of which solidified KKR's reputation as the leading player in the art of leveraged buyouts. Later in the year, KKR won out in a closely contested competition, as it assembled the financing for the $31 billion acquisition of RJR Nabisco.

KKR bought the tobacco giant with more than 90 percent debt, much of it in the form of subordinated "junk" securities.

High leverage notwithstanding, KKR could not afford to treat the buyout market as a high-stakes gambling casino. To so regard it, especially during the early years when buyouts were little understood, would have made it impossible to convince such conservative institutions as pension funds and educational endowments to participate in buyout equity pools. Nor would so many institutions – commercial banks, insurance companies – have come to the table to buy the debt. As the general partner for its buyout funds, KKR had to persuade investors that the risks would be managed from the first glimmering of an investment opportunity to the last day of ownership. The inherent risks of a leveraged buyout could be reduced only through careful selection of companies and managers, due diligence, price discipline, and cautious, if not conservative, structuring of the acquired company's balance sheet.

KKR won investor confidence not merely by virtue of its dealmaking skills, but through its reputation for trying to build *long-term* value in companies. Each buyout's initial financial structure mattered, but even more important was what happened after an acquisition closed. KKR continued to oversee the executive and financial performance of its acquired companies on a close and continuous basis. As board directors, KKR partners monitored their companies far more rigorously than did conventional corporate boards. They managed corporate financings and subjected managers to ongoing review. When companies ran into trouble, they assumed responsibility for solving the problems, providing consulting assistance, replacing executives when necessary, and maintaining faith with creditors. When managers presented plans for investment in research and development, new capital equipment, marketing or acquisitions, KKR generally supported them so long as they were consistent with protecting prior obligations. In sum, KKR strove to achieve a regime of tight budget controls without unduly limiting managerial creativity.

KKR's buyouts represented only a small fraction of leveraged buyout transactions, which in turn were only a small portion of all merger and acquisition activity (see table, p. 24). But their impact was disproportionately great. In 1989, the value of the firm's one completed acquisition amounted to about two-fifths of the value of all the nation's 371 leveraged buyouts. To put it in perspective, just after the

RJR Nabisco buyout, KKR oversaw nearly $59 billion worth of corporate assets in thirty-five companies, with just six general partners and eleven professional investment associates supported by a staff of forty-seven. Only four U.S. corporations among the Fortune 500 – GM, Ford, Exxon, and IBM – were larger, and their headquarters were staffed by employees numbering in the thousands.

The Reaction to LBOs: Images in the Press

KKR's financings had been reported regularly in the media since the 1979 Houdaille buyout. They were emulated by a growing number of competitors, and tracked studiously by financial economists. KKR's influence in the rarefied world of high finance was already substantial when it acquired RJR Nabisco. The 1986 Beatrice acquisition had got the attention of virtually all large company CEOs, and its shock waves had since reverberated beyond the boardrooms into the halls of Congress. But RJR Nabisco brought the firm public notoriety. Even though the company had been "put in play" by its own CEO, and even though its board of directors had welcomed all comers, the deal was widely and incorrectly reported as a hostile takeover. Having completed the largest single acquisition in the history of business enterprise, KKR became virtually synonymous with the era's megadeals, hostile and friendly alike. The firm moved from the business pages to the front pages, and became engulfed in a media firestorm.

There was plenty of drama in the air. Hordes of takeover specialists, arbitrageurs, and junk-bond traders were terrorizing corporate executives, striking fear in the hearts of employees, and arousing the ire of politicians. All this was grist for the literary mills not only of journalists, but also of playwrights, screenwriters, and novelists. If there were emblematic characters of the 1980s they were the luminous *anti*-heros of finance – the Michael Milkens and Carl Icahns of real life, and the Gordon Gekkos and Sherman McCoys of movies and fiction. "Corporate raiders," "greenmailers," and "takeover artists" were the stuff of modern morality tales. Their apparent avarice and insensitivity to other people's lives and jobs went far to explain the widespread anxiety caused by the "gales of creative destruction" sweeping through the economy – the inevitable dislocations associated with changing technology and global competition.

Many recent practitioners of high finance had rightfully earned their reputations as greed-driven rascals – inside traders and stock manipulators like Ivan Boesky and Dennis Levine, who went to jail after highly publicized plea bargains. New York's soon-to-be-mayor Rudolph Giuliani built a popular political career as a federal district attorney, thrilling tabloid and *New York Times* readers alike by arresting, handcuffing, and prosecuting both real and imagined white-collar felons. Other financiers who were engaged in merger and acquisition activities, though hardly criminal in their dealings, were tainted as well – widely regarded as crass dealmakers who cared little about what happened to the assets or the people they affected.

Consider Larry "The Liquidator" Garfinkle, protagonist of Jerry Sterner's *Other People's Money*, an extremely clever play that spoke to the nation's ambivalence toward high finance. Larry had taken a position in an "undervalued" diversified manufacturing concern – a "bear hug," in Wall Street parlance – designed to persuade management to sell out. The plot then revolved around his attempts to complete a hostile takeover. He would, he explained to his quarry, "get rid of the wire and cable division [the company's traditional core business], a financial cancer." By disposing of plant and equipment, laying off redundant workers, and then liquidating the pension fund, he could nearly double the value of the firm's remaining assets, from $14 to $25 per share. Addressing the undecided stockholders, the firm's gentlemanly chief executive excoriated the unmannerly raider as a heartless vulture who would pick the bones of a business that had survived "numerous recessions, a great depression and two wars," only for the sake of extracting paper profits. "At least the robber barons of old left something tangible in their wake," he cried. All sympathy was on the side of management, but reason lay elsewhere. Larry's appeal to the pocketbooks of the stockholders, many of them old friends of the beleaguered CEO, won out. Sleazy, greedy, and manipulative, Larry would undoubtedly do better for the company's owners – whose investment, he reminded them, had been squandered by well-meaning but incompetent managers. He would pay them a premium over the current values of their shares. It was hard, reason aside, to like Larry; he was enriching greedy owners at everyone else's expense.[35]

Or was he? Economists could argue that the firm was misallocating resources that would be better invested elsewhere. In real life, respected financiers like Warren Buffett earned a measure of popular respect by taking control of undermanaged assets and improving them. Buffett and other buyers of "undervalued" companies did not simply acquire, strip, and sell assets; they explicitly fostered improvement in the long-term values of the assets they controlled. That almost invariably meant increasing capital investment, employment, and productivity, if not in the short run, then over the medium and longer term. Buffett became a popular hero and the subject of a cottage industry in popular books on his life and investment techniques.[36] The fact that management buyouts achieved much the same kind of result was lost on most people.

As public concern over the effects of the merger wave increased, the main sources of information on the phenomenon were journalists. Financial economists and legal scholars undertook more systematic analyses, but their studies were published in specialized journals and expressed in language and equations that were difficult to translate. It would take a few years before their findings would percolate up to the mass media.[37] That left public opinion at the mercy of superficial reportage that for the most part failed to distinguish the leveraged buyout from the larger phenomena of which it was a part.

Not all journalists saw only problems. Many, particularly in the more sophisticated corners of the business press like *Barron's* or *The Economist*, hailed the cleansing effects of corporate takeovers and buyout restructurings.[38] KKR generally received high marks for its creative leveraging techniques and its run of successful investments. Reports focused on returns, but tended to overlook the longer-term effects of buyouts on corporate structure and managerial behavior.[39] Journalists reflected what they heard, including the perpetual drumbeat of worries that the debt markets were spinning out of control or had been distorted by corrupt forces.[40] One would expect that in day-to-day reportage; but as journalists turned to the manufacture of instant history, they found it difficult to elongate their perspectives.

A plethora of journalistic books documenting the excesses of Wall Street appeared toward the end of the 1980s. Some were, of course, far better than others; but in most of them, financiers became villains awash in greed, corruption, and corporate intrigue. At center stage were the swashbuckling pirates, including such newly minted household names as Boone Pickens, Carl Icahn, and Sir James Goldsmith, three prominent and outspoken corporate "raiders." On the fringes were the corrupt and greedy gnomes – Ivan Boesky, Dennis Levine, Martin Siegel, and even the *Wall Street Journal*'s Foster Winans, who used his position as columnist to gather, and then help his friends trade on, inside information. Of Wall Street's major players, Michael Milken was the most mysterious, and hence became the leading player in the drama of corporate restructurings – a renegade of sorts who could somehow raise huge sums of debt financing and then channel them to the aggressors on the battlefields of corporate takeovers. His firm, Drexel Burnham, loomed as the evil empire of high finance – brash, unconventional, alienated from Wall Street's more prestigious bankers, the bane of corporate CEOs. When authors fixed their sights on buyout practitioners, they scrutinized them through much the same lens, focusing on the minutiae of personalities while missing the larger significance of the economic behavior. Jeremiads on the social evils of greed substituted for more considered reflection on the causes and consequences of wealth creation in a capitalist society.

Oddly enough, despite its prominence and its novelty, KKR was hard to peg for most journalists in pursuit of juicy stories. Perhaps the firm was simply uninteresting. Its partners, with the exception of Henry Kravis – whose limited but high-profile social life was followed closely in the press – remained largely anonymous, even by Wall Street's reticent standards. Aside from RJR Nabisco, KKR's corporate acquisitions were hardly swashbuckling affairs, and its deals, though exotic, had no hint of impropriety attached to them. As the era's numerous insider-trading stories broke, KKR proved to be a dull venue for rumor mongering. Connie Bruck's *The Predators' Ball* and James B. Stewart's *Den of Thieves* (two of the genre's typically sinister titles) found leveraged buyout deals everywhere amid the scandals that brought disgrace to the likes of Milken, Boesky, and Levine. KKR's partners, however, stood clear of those who illegally profited from the firm's deals. Drexel's youthful star Martin Siegel confessed in 1989 to piling up riches for himself and his friends on inside information while serving as an outside advisor to KKR on several of its buyouts. Recounting the story of Siegel's plea bargain, Stewart, ever-alert for wider conspiracies, relegated one telling point to a footnote. Facing years in prison if he did not cooperate, Siegel had no qualms about naming his coconspirators, but he was unable to give zealous prosecutors one of the heads they hoped for the most – Henry Kravis. There was nothing wrong there, Siegel explained.[41]

The press could not accuse KKR and its sister buyout firms of such illegalities. Instead, journalists criticized them on broader ethical grounds. The tenor of this attack is clear in Michael Lewis's often hilarious autobiographical glimpse into Wall Street, *Liar's Poker*, published in 1989, in which he spares the LBO specialists the cutting ridicule he unleashes so effectively on others (especially his former colleagues at Salomon Brothers). If anything, the masters of the leveraged buyout were entirely too clever to be ridiculed. While collecting huge fees, they managed to lay off most of the risk of their deals onto their limited equity partners, institutional holders of debt, and ultimately the taxpayer (who was shortchanged by the exchange of non-taxable debt interest payments for taxable stock dividends). In Lewis's work, as in most of the contemporary popular literature on Wall Street, buyout firms, junk-bond dealers, corporate raiders, and even more conventional financial intermediaries were lumped together as a despoiling horde of mythic proportions.

Each succeeding journalist who took the time to "investigate" the buyout movement treated it with muckraking disdain, denouncing the social dislocations caused by the corporate sell-offs and layoffs linked to the leverage in the deals. Susan Faludi's feature article on the aftermath of the Safeway buyout, published in the *Wall Street Journal* in 1991, quickly became a staple of business school ethics courses with its affecting personal stories of workers whose livelihoods and psyches had been shattered by post-buyout corporate restructuring.[42]

In the wake of the RJR Nabisco buyout, three books on KKR, all written by *Wall Street Journal* reporters, sped into production. Two book-length profiles of KKR appeared almost simultaneously in 1991, one far superior as a reliable documentary record of the history of the firm. Sarah Bartlett's angry and gossipy account in *The Money Machine*[43] was quickly displaced by George Anders's more sober, better-researched story, which presented considerable evidence of the value-creating effects of the firm's deals and did a credible job of detailing the evolution of KKR as an institution. Anders wrote in the populist mode, admiring the creativity of his subjects while condemning their success. His conclusions were as dire as his title, *The Merchants of Debt*, would suggest. According to Anders, the high levels of debt employed in KKR's deals helped to enrich the firm and its limited partners via the exploitation of tax loopholes and radical corporate downsizings, which, by implication, came at the expense of taxpayers and workers.[44]

Unfortunately for Anders, his efforts had been "scooped" by one of the most commercially successful books of the genre, *Barbarians at the Gate*. Appearing in 1990, it provided a narrower but far more lively and memorable impression of KKR. The authors, Brian Burrough and John Helyer, skillfully dramatized the frenzied struggle for control of history's biggest acquisition prize in remarkable faux-detail. In their fascinating fly-on-the-wall account (the authors painstakingly reconstruct conversations as if they had been privy to every negotiation, business dinner, telephone call, and intimate party), KKR emerges not merely as the victor but as the one rational, albeit amoral, player in an otherwise seamy tale of corporate mismanagement, financial greed, and social insensitivity. Everyone involved in their story is scrambling to make money at the expense of a great corporate enterprise and its employees.[45]

Barbarians captured the essence of the wheeling and dealing quite well, but failed to make its larger case that something terrible had gone awry in the corporate economy. What the authors, perhaps unwittingly, demonstrated, according to former SEC Commissioner Joseph Grundfest, was that the real barbarians were *inside* the gates. As the financial economist Michael Jensen observed:

[W]hat emerges from the 500 plus pages – though the authors seem to fail to grasp its import – is clear evidence of corporate-wide inefficiencies at RJR-Nabisco, including massive waste of corporate "free cash flow," that would allow KKR to pay existing stockholders $12 billion over the previous market value for the right to bring about change.[46]

The Political Debate

Wall Street scandals and related stories of financial arrogance and intrigue simply confirmed what people on Main Street had always suspected: people tempted by large sums of money will often succumb to greed. What mattered more to Main Street were jobs, security, and a sense that the outcomes of economic upheavals were more or less fair. What mattered in the political arena was whose ox was being gored. The political fate of highly leveraged transactions was part of this larger public policy question: what should be done, if anything, to reconcile the conflicting interests of those affected by the transfers of wealth and power caused by the ongoing financial revolution?

Congressional hearings on mergers and acquisitions, hostile takeovers, and highly leveraged transactions bloomed like hardy perennials in the late 1980s, generating reams of testimony from virtually every constituency affected by corporate restructurings. From 1987 through 1989, critics and defenders of corporate take-overs and leveraged buyouts flocked to the witness chairs. Labor leaders, CEOs of large corporations, prominent bankers, business journalists, lawyers, and economists expressed their anxieties over the rising tide of corporate merger and acquisition activity. They cited the potential dangers to the nation's economic stability brought on by high levels of debt financing and the destabilization of corporate morale and finances caused by hostile takeover attempts. Some of these concerns were expressed by objective parties; most were the more typical arguments of interest group representatives.

In the spring of 1988, the bankruptcy of the drugstore chain Revco, the first large leveraged buyout to run aground, spiked fears that the economy was overleveraged and that buyouts fueled by junk bonds were the primary culprits. Edward J. Markey, chairman of the House Subcommittee on Telecommunications and Finance, spoke for this increasingly popular view to an audience of academics and policy-makers at New York University. Markey said the country was "awash in corporate debt" and that "the annual accumulation of . . . often low rated, questionably backed debt cannot be swallowed endlessly without choking." He warned that the pressure was mounting on Congress to consider eliminating deductions on debt payments by companies whose debt-to-equity ratios exceeded government specified norms.[47]

Though most economists – or congressmen, for that matter – would not have advocated such a measure, the proliferation of highly lever-aged transactions was a serious concern from a macroeconomic per-spective. Federal Reserve Chairman Alan Greenspan, appearing before the Senate Finance Committee in early January 1989 amid the tumult over the RJR Nabisco buyout, offered a tempered view of lev-eraged transactions. "[S]o far," he testified, "various pieces of evi-dence indicate that the trend toward more ownership by managers and tighter control by other owners and creditors has generally en-

hanced operational efficiency." Still, he warned that heightened levels
of corporate debt posed a "broad based risk" for the nation's welfare
in the event of an economic slowdown or a spike in interest rates. He
did not advocate regulatory changes other than some possible tinker-
ing with the tax code to reduce the relative attractiveness of debt.[48]

Financial experts, though varied in their views, were generally sympathetic to buyouts, as were legal experts. The Subcommittee on Labor Management Relations in 1989 heard testimony on the role of
pension funds as equity participants in corporate takeovers, providing
a forum for those who saw that leverage had salutary effects on corporate managers. Dean LeBaron of Batterymarch Financial Management, for example, contended that managers were forced by such
deals to pay more attention to their shareholders, like it or not. "Today," he observed,

it is widely understood by managements completely, that their only protection from a merger or acquisition, or for that matter an LBO – which in
most cases they don't want, because they want to manage their companies
– is a higher stock price.[49]

Corporate executives who testified for the most part demurred. In
1987, executives from Gillette and Goodyear had testified to the hor-
rors they experienced as targets of unwanted takeovers, arguing that
their defenses had been costly and their options narrow.[50] A particularly complicated picture was painted by William Reynolds, the
CEO of GenCorp, Inc., who testified before Congress in February
1988 in support of the Business Roundtable's position on legislation
to limit hostile takeovers. GenCorp had owned and operated a curi-
ous mix of businesses in commercial airlines, aerospace and defense
products, industrial plastics, tires, movie studios, radio and television
stations, and soft drink bottling. In the third year of his tenure, Reynolds had been implementing what he called a long-term plan designed
to improve shareholder value when his company was attacked by
AFG Industries. This, he said, was nothing more than an attempt to
"manipulate the capital markets so as to capture the increase in
value" of GenCorp's stock price. In defense, GenCorp put in place
an expensive poison pill, and sold off assets to pay for it. By the end
of 1987, GenCorp had shrunk from a $3 billion company to one
about half that size. Gone were the tire, movie, and bottling businesses, which, Reynolds said, he would have sold in good time. The

corporate headquarters had been forced to lay off personnel, and people's lives had been disrupted.

What especially irked Reynolds was the "massive transfer of wealth" embodied in the transaction fees paid to "the financial community" – the lawyers and investment advisors who arranged the sales – and the profits that had gone to unworthy raiders, whose initial purchases of stock had been increased in value by expectant arbitrageurs (and, of course, GenCorp's own restructuring). Stock values had been enhanced, from $81.58 to more than $118 per share within a month. (What was the implicit value of the assets if broken up? Reynolds did not say.) But the increase in value came at a high social cost to the corporation's other important constituencies – "employees, customers, suppliers, plant communities, and governments" – all of whom might have been better served had GenCorp been allowed to proceed with its own plan. The high debt levels required to defend against a takeover, he complained, "reduce the flexibility of management to respond to social values." GenCorp's forced restructuring had been "a traumatic event in all the places where our corporation touches the social fabric."[51]

In his complaint, Reynolds echoed the "stakeholder" theory of corporate governance as advanced by the Business Roundtable, a major policy forum for the nation's large corporations.[52] Outside the halls of Congress, big business was lobbying heavily at the state and federal levels for some relief from the assaults of financial capitalists. Corporate takeovers and leveraged buyouts were the topics of the day. Corporate speechwriters cranked out position papers on these issues, most of which reached the same conclusion. Soon after the RJR Nabisco buyout, John Smale, Procter and Gamble's CEO, rhetorically asked his audience at the Kellogg School of Management: "Is maximizing shareholder value the primary responsibility of directors? . . . I think the answer is clearly no. The primary obligation of management and of the board of directors should be to the corporation and its successful continuation."[53]

It would not be easy for politicians to dismiss pleas from major corporate CEOs for social responsibility. In this the CEOs were supported heartily by lobbyists for organized labor. The AFL-CIO's Thomas Donohue warned that employment stability was imperiled by "the dynamics of a changing economy" and that leveraged buyouts were undermining any attempt to achieve that stability.[54]

Throughout the public debate, distinctions were seldom drawn between buyouts and mergers, between friendly and unfriendly takeovers, between highly leveraged and more conventionally financed transactions. Only a decided minority questioned whether inefficient companies should be allowed to sustain the high costs of excess capacity and personnel or whether some companies might not be better off shrinking than growing. What seemed of most concern was that corporate assets were fast changing hands with unsettling results.

Among KKR's allies, Don Boyce of Idex, the successor company to Houdaille, was the only CEO to appear before Congress, in large part to defend his company's record against a critical book by the journalist Max Holland entitled *When the Machine Stopped*.[55] Boyce had to parry Holland's contention that the overhang of buyout debt and obsession with profits had caused Houdaille to forgo investments in plant and technology that would have saved its machine tool business from the onslaught of foreign competition.[56] This was just one variant of the argument against buyouts posed by other economic and business experts who appeared before Congress asserting that American management was increasingly driven to short-term thinking at the expense of long-term organization building. In faster-growing economies like Japan's, argued the economic historian William Lazonick, in what was then a fashionable comparison, companies thrived largely because they did *not* have to respond to shareholder pressures.[57]

Executives who had participated in buyouts of their firms were vulnerable to yet another criticism, this one from the other end of the interest group spectrum. By participating in buyouts, it was argued, equity-seeking managers put themselves into a conflict of interest with pre-buyout shareholders and bondholders. The premiums normally paid to exiting shareholders in buyouts may not be high enough, if one assumed that managers had a stake in keeping the value of the shares relatively low compared to what they could expect to earn if the buyout went well. (It was management, after all, who controlled the information on which third-party "fairness opinions" were based, and on which the buyers would ultimately rely.) Bondholders, too, would be hurt by the dilution of the quality of their securities by the issuance of large amounts of low-grade debt. That the interests of shareholders and bondholders could be harmed by buyouts just added more fuel to the political fires that had erupted in the market for corporate control.

Feeling they had little to gain from public exposure, KKR's partners, along with the principles of other buyout firms, were conspicuously absent from the congressional hearings. They chose instead to lobby members behind closed doors, hoping to fend off legislative attempts to curtail their ability to continue doing highly leveraged deals. KKR entered written testimony in the form of a report on the positive economic effects of its deals. The report responded to congressional concerns over whether buyouts adversely affected corporate productivity and employment, and whether LBO firms gained unfair advantages by exploiting favorable tax treatment of debt financing.[58]

Assembled by its accounting firm, Deloitte, Haskins & Sells, KKR's data showed that its buyouts had resulted not only in substantial increases in the market values of companies and potentially higher tax revenues, but also in generally increased employment, capital investment, and R&D expenditures of assets that remained under KKR's control. These findings were tentative and vulnerable to criticism,[59] but a revised tabulation of the accounting histories for the seventeen KKR buyouts between 1977 and 1989 for which enough time (at least three years) had passed to accumulate significant data showed the following results.[60]

In aggregate numbers, employment increased from 273,000 in the first year to 311,000 three years later, during the period when the companies were operating under the most intense leverage pressures.

Aggregate capital spending (which normally dipped in the first year after a buyout) increased over a three-year period from $1.02 billion to $1.29 billion.

Research and development expenditures likewise increased from $85 million in the first year of the LBO to $103 million three years out.

The Emerging Academic Consensus

In his testimony before Congress, labor leader Tom Donohue lamented that "nobody has accurately assessed the damage that the LBO craze is doing, not only to the companies involved, to their employees, to their stockholders, but [also] to the communities and to the nation's power to produce and compete in a world economy."[61] In fact, there had been a large accumulation of empirical studies on mergers and acquisitions, and by 1990 a clear consensus was forming among academicians: leveraged buyouts were more effective in cre-

ating shareholder value than mergers, and they were good not only
for shareholders, but also for the other stakeholders in the corporate
economy.

The most significant empirical research on leveraged buyouts had
been undertaken by a loose network of financial economists and others strongly influenced by "agency theory." Agency theory had scholarly roots in Berle and Means, and had been more recently resurrected
in legal scholarship by Henry G. Manne in the 1960s, and in financial
economics by Michael Jensen and William Meckling in the 1970s.
Manne, inspired by the recent developments in small-company tender
offers, argued that the stock market – if only regulatory constraints
were relaxed – could efficiently solve problems of managerial opportunism through the easy transfer of corporate control.[62] As two scholars recently summarized his conclusion:

In unfettered markets, corporate managers would be disciplined by a simple
rule: a decline in market value below the replacement cost of the firm would
induce outsiders to bid for control with the intention of enhancing their
wealth by the liquidation or reorganization of the acquired business. . . .[A]
perfectly fluid system would allow discipline to be imposed on inefficient
managers and firms [in] a perfectly competitive environment with recon-
tracting for all managerial talent with short-term contracts.[63]

The problem with Manne's ideal market for corporate control was
the same that would plague many hostile takeovers in reality. It did
not allow for the difficulty of replacing executive managers. Nor did
it allow for the basic sense of security and confidence that most managers needed in order to focus on their jobs and do them well. But
his ideas inspired further work in agency theory, which saw the executive manager's key job as one of allocating income among various
constituencies to which companies were obligated. The general agreement among agency theorists was that managerial and shareholder
interests had become woefully disjointed. What the buyout – in particular the *management* buyout – offered was an opportunity to provide managers the security they needed while at the same time making
them substantial equity holders, so that divergent interests could be
brought back into alignment.

Intrigued by what they saw unfolding in the buyout market, financial economists and legal scholars tracked its development. By 1990,
an academic consensus was forming that leveraged buyouts had gen-

erated substantial gains to both pre- and post-buyout shareholders. As to other long-term social benefits, the evidence was still tentative, but the empirical findings failed to provide strong support for the economic arguments against leveraged buyouts. Among the scholars, Michael Jensen became an early and consistently forceful advocate of the market for corporate control, and of the LBO in particular, as the salvation of shareholders from the excesses of managerial capitalism. In a landmark *Harvard Business Review* article in 1989, he went so far as to predict the "eclipse of the public [managerial] corporation."[64]

Some buyouts fared better than others. The evidence provided by KKR for its buyouts – increased employment, research and development expenditures, and capital investment – was hard to generalize. Many industrywide studies regarding the short-term effects (usually two years out) of buyouts showed little or slightly negative effects in those categories, although the evidence improved as years progressed.[65] The academic studies did confirm, however, that pre-buyout shareholders had sold out at premium prices, and that preferred shareholders and convertible bondholders also did extremely well. One important study addressed one of the more controversial public policy concerns, the impact of clever buyout accounting on taxes. It showed that tax revenues deferred by buyout partnerships through interest and depreciation deductions were more than offset by capital gains taxes on exiting shareholders and, eventually, on selling shareholders when companies went public once again. The increased earnings of the more efficient buyouts also generated government revenues, as did taxes paid by lenders on their interest incomes.[66]

If scholars made public policy, the debate would have been settled in favor of letting the market work. As more data accumulated, more positive academic findings on the buyout restructurings of the 1980s would be reinforced and extended. The cumulative evidence confirmed that leveraged buyouts generally had resulted in improvements in the post-buyout performance of the assets that remained in the buyout partnerships' control.[67] Evidence also mounted casting doubt on the long-term value to acquiring shareholders of more conventional, "strategic" mergers, in contrast to the more successful buyouts.[68] When economic and legal histories of the 1980s market for corporate control began to appear, they agreed with Jensen that the legal and institutional structure of the leveraged buyout represented a new corporate form with the potential to correct long-standing problems in corporate governance.[69]

But politicians made policy, and what the academic studies could not resolve for them were issues of perceived fairness. The shock therapy that the leverage in a buyout's capital structure imposed on a company could sometimes be much like that of a hostile corporate takeover, especially in the first year or two following the acquisition. Restructurings of assets, retrenchments in employment, replacements of personnel, and divestitures upset individual lives and careers and sometimes brought hardship to local communities. The resolution of affected interests, including those of some powerful antagonists, would be left mainly to legislatures and the courts.

Hostile takeovers were the main concern. Corporate managers and labor unions enjoyed more success with state legislatures than they did with Congress. In the late 1980s, laws designed to blunt the effects of hostile takeovers proliferated, most importantly in Delaware, with its large number of big corporations. Federal and state courts supported these laws and upheld the legality of various takeover defenses. Also strengthened were state antitrust laws, which could be invoked to prevent some mergers, especially in cases where the not-so-hidden political agenda was avoiding layoffs. These actions helped to bring the 1980s merger wave to an end. Other legislative and regulatory actions aimed at controlling leverage would have even more direct impact on the kinds of friendly management buyouts undertaken by KKR and other specialty LBO firms.

Ebb Tide

The decline of leveraged buyouts occurred amid circumstances that adversely affected the broader climate for mergers and acquisitions and, in particular, hostile takeovers. There were also specific factors at work that affected the attractiveness of highly leveraged deals. In the macroeconomy, problems had been mounting, particularly a fast-growing national debt, which deflected savings away from the private sector, and decreased liquidity in the nation's banking system. Commercial banks were suffering from massive defaults on loans to Third World countries. An even more serious crisis erupted in 1987, as failures in the savings and loan industry became widespread due to a collapse in the nation's commercial real estate markets.

Meanwhile, prices for corporate assets had been increasing with the demand for them. New entrants into the buyout market made the bidding for target companies more competitive. Banks grew more stringent in their requirements for senior debt, while subordinated debt financing in the form of high-yield securities also drove up acquisition costs. Buyouts financed after 1984 were shakier propositions – higher priced, more expensive to finance, and ultimately yielding lower returns as a group.[70] In the fall of 1989, as news of problem deals began to increase, UAL (United Airlines) failed to secure financing for its proposed buyout, which presaged a crisis in the junk-bond market.

That same year, in response to the banking crisis, Congress passed the Financial Institutions Reform, Recovery and Enforcement Act (FIRREA). The law required banks to increase the ratio of their capital to outstanding loans and to otherwise reduce the risk in loan portfolios. FIRREA also required that savings and loan institutions, which had amassed seven percent of all outstanding high-yield securities, divest them by 1994. Only a handful of S&Ls were involved, but as confidence in the market for high-yield securities weakened, the S&Ls unloaded their holdings and triggered a panic. Other institutional holders of high-yield securities quickly followed suit.[71] This, in turn, undermined Drexel Burnham's ability to maintain an orderly market. Already badly wounded by the disarray caused in its junk-bond operations following Michael Milken's indictment in October 1989 for securities violations, Drexel would file for bankruptcy in early 1990. The principal market maker for high-yield securities was suddenly gone.

Drexel's demise would also hurt what had been a good system for arranging out-of-court settlements of debtor claims whenever highly leveraged companies it had helped to finance defaulted on their debt payments. Drexel's powerful position in the junk-bond market had given it the authority to help financially distressed companies and their creditors work out informal, relatively inexpensive reorganizations in preference to more costly bankruptcy workouts. LBO partnerships gradually learned to play that role as well, until a federal court ruling in January 1990 limited the value bondholders could expect from informal exchange offers. That ruling, combined with new tax penalties legislated by Congress on out-of-court reorganizations, effectively increased the number of bankruptcy filings by highly leveraged companies.[72]

These factors combined to reduce the confidence in highly leveraged transactions, which never fully recovered their popularity. Leveraged buyouts had peaked in numbers (381) in 1988 and in value ($70 billion by some measures) in 1989.[73] In the 1990s, the numbers remained well below those for the mid-1980s. Signs of an economic slowdown that would continue into 1993 did not help. In 1996, there were about 150 completed leveraged buyouts valued at about $33.5 billion, in an otherwise brisk merger and acquisitions market of more than 6,000 transactions[74] that generally relied on much lower levels of leverage than had been common in the 1980s.

Financial Capitalism Redux

As the millennium approached, it was clear that many of the basic principles of the leveraged management buyout had permeated the corporate economy. Just what those principles were, and how they were put into practice by the leading practitioner of buyouts, is the subject of the rest of this book. In its essence, the buyout was a method for creating long-term shareholder value. In KKR's hands, value creation was achieved through the creative uses of debt, managerial equity participation, and close monitoring by a dynamic board of directors. Having demonstrated that its basic principle and practice in buyouts could be applied to large corporations, KKR showed that shareholders could reassert themselves in the boardroom in highly constructive ways.

In some superficial respects KKR's activities harked back to the turn-of-the-century Morgan deals, but they were more in tune with a modern trend toward the democratization of capital. Buyouts empowered institutional investors who managed money for millions of ordinary citizens. In controlling its constituent companies, KKR also fashioned a novel and highly effective form of corporate organization – the so-called LBO association, which comprised KKR, its fund investors, and the managers of its constituent companies. The LBO association was neither a corporate nor a conglomerate headquarters, nor was it a holding company, even though it performed many of the functions of each. Each of its constituent companies was organized and funded by a separate investment partnership, each of which remained independent of the other companies' operations. Through its unique structure, KKR could coordinate the collective interests of institutional investors – shareholders and debtholders alike.

Most important, KKR's buyout regime guaranteed that the interests of owners and managers were kept in alignment. In 1976, the idea that shareholders would be, or could be, restored to power in the governance of corporations was obvious neither to their managers nor to their shareholders – nor, for that matter, to Wall Street's more prominent financiers. But during the 1980s, the mere specter of the corporate takeover was prodding more and more executives to undertake internal reforms – in some cases for no better reason than to defend against unwanted buyers, in others because they had been inspired by example. A few big company executives, such as Jack Welch of General Electric, overhauled their companies and then encouraged ongoing reforms without waiting for external shocks to drive them to change. Some boards of directors grew more active, taking action to replace executives before looming crises turned into disasters. By 1993, the boards of General Motors, American Express, Kodak, and IBM had done exactly that. As more companies began to link managerial compensation to shareholder value creation, more managers were inspired to respond in kind, increasing corporate productivity, profits, and market values.

As the 1990s unfolded, U.S. business enjoyed a financial and managerial renaissance, in no small measure because of what corporations had learned from the leveraged buyout. The managerial corporation did not in fact disappear,[75] but institutional shareholders became more active, and boards of directors more attentive. Executive compensation became more tied to equity performance. Boundaries separating the interests of managers and owners, of shareholders and other stakeholders, began to blur in both the rhetoric and outlook of corporate managers. With the apparent success American business was having after some fifteen years of structural reform, even European and Japanese companies began tying managerial performance more closely to incentives to improve shareholder value. "In that sense," wrote the financial economist Steven Kaplan in 1997, "we are all Henry Kravis now."[76]

2 | Recasting the Role of Debt
Creative Leverage and Buyout Financing

Financial leverage is not just a tool of quick-
footed opportunists and scoundrels. It can,
and does, produce very beneficial results . . .
– Roy Smith, *The Money Wars*

"HE THAT GOES a borrowing goes a sorrowing," warned Benjamin Franklin's Poor Richard. Generations of schoolchildren have been taught to heed this advice. Yet even in Franklin's day, time and season said otherwise. To be able to borrow in the eighteenth century was vital to any farmer who had to pay for seed, tools, and labor before the harvest, to any merchant who wished to conduct distant commerce, to any tradesman who wanted to set up his own shop. Still, debt remained in Revolutionary America what it had been throughout the history of Western civilization: a moral problem. For many, to take on debt may have been necessary; but it was not a good thing to be in debt.

Preindustrial America was still very much a traditional society; and in traditional societies, to be in debt was to be in thrall, often to lenders who might set exorbitant terms for the use of their funds.[1] Neither individuals nor communities ought to be in debt, according to Thomas Jefferson, the icon of American republicanism. The national debt, if not extinguished, would lead inevitably to "corruption and rottenness," Jefferson said, worrying about the power it gave to banks and governments alike. He made it his policy as president to retire the modest federal government obligations that his political arch-enemy Alexander Hamilton had incurred in the name of stimulating national credit, taxes, and fiscal policy. That Jefferson, like so many of his peers among the Virginia planter class, was chronically indebted no doubt kept him awake many nights. Year after year, his financial obligations mounted in tandem with his spendthrift habits, leaving him in a more or less constant state of default, from which only his monumental prestige spared him the consequences. Jefferson was typical of the conflict that Americans through the generations have experienced between their private behavior and public attitudes toward debt.[2]

Ambivalence toward debt was based not simply on populist fears of power and corruption, or simply on aversion to risk, but also on abiding notions of personal sin. From Biblical times, usury – the practice of lending money at interest above a notional "just price" – was considered vile, and those who made their livings lending money were held in contempt. Reckless or unfortunate borrowing was not much better; default on a loan could land the borrower in the poorhouse, or worse, in prison. Though borrowers valued the opportunity that debt afforded them to improve their fortunes, they dreaded the constraints it placed on their freedom. Lenders, seeking income-producing outlets for their savings, were always left to worry about repayment.

As the industrial age unfolded, the governments of developing nations supported institutional means by which surplus private capital could be channeled into productive uses. Industry not only increased the demand for credit, it stimulated new ways of thinking about credit and new ways of providing for it. Gradually, people in business grew more comfortable with the idea that debt could do more than simply tide them over through shortfalls – that it could be structured and managed to create capital and increase wealth.

The Paradox of Debt

Artfully managed, debt could accomplish wonders, as some keen observers of the changing order recognized. British pundit Walter Bagehot, founder of *The Economist*, explained in 1873 just how the "chronic and constant borrowing" that pervaded the world's first industrial economy had fueled "the increasingly democratic structure of commerce." For the timid, debt remained a tyranny; for the bold it could mean upward mobility, a means by which aspiring capitalists could fulfill their dreams. Debt enabled upstarts to inject competition into an otherwise static world, to disrupt the comfortable "routines" of entrenched elites; in this case the risk-averse, change-resistant "merchant princes" of the British commercial establishment. In the scramble to build wealth, high leverage was a useful tool.

To illustrate the point, Bagehot cited the small businessman whose debt to asset ratio was 80 percent debt. He could actually exploit the equity he had in the business more profitably than the more conservative merchant who was reluctant to put his capital at risk. Debt, to use the British term, "geared" the rising entrepreneur's investments, and made him work harder. It was at once constraining and liberating. To the proper gentleman this might seem a "rough and vulgar" process, driven by what Bagehot in mock irony called a "dirty crowd of new little men." Yet it was these new men who were more likely to establish more innovative and efficient ways of doing business.[3]

Debt was at the financial core of the industrializing United States as well. In the first half of the nineteenth century, borrowing made it possible to organize textile production to efficient scale and scope. The nation's canal, railroad, and telegraph systems would have been impossible without the bond issues that channeled foreign and domestic investment into those vital infrastructure enterprises. Inability to obtain credit for borrowing could make a crucial difference to fulfillment of individual aspirations – as ambitious African American sharecroppers and tradesmen, for example, discovered to their detriment after the Civil War. But in general, changing laws and practices had made debt easier and safer to obtain for entrepreneurial purposes. Chartered banking and insurance institutions had become well established by the latter part of the nineteenth century, along with specialized investment intermediaries who packaged and placed long-term debt instruments, usually backed by real estate or other tangible assets. The price of credit became less subject to custom or regulation, fluctuating according to prevailing relationships between the supply and demand for money. Legal contracts replaced less formal agreements, and debtor prisons gave way to the more orderly processes of bankruptcy protection, which removed some of the stigma, and reduced the risk, of debt transactions.

By the time big business exploded on the scene in the late nineteenth century, debt had become institutionalized, if not yet entirely respectable. Of course, debt remained risky, always at the peril of unforeseen events. It was still no better than a destructive vice whenever imprudent lenders loaned to reckless borrowers. In 1889, the American political economist Richard Ely observed: "Our entire land is strewn with the ruins of business wrecked by men who have mismanaged the property which unwise credit gave into their hands."[4] This was an age when the failure of a single large bank or insurance company could trigger a transcontinental panic. On the occasion of every major bankruptcy, critics inveighed against the evils of indebtedness, as if it were a potentially fatal vice like drinking or gambling.

In the emerging corporate environment, debt financing made it possible for industrial organizers to assemble the assets required for grand undertakings. Debt fueled the capital-intensive requirements of steel mills, oil refineries, electric power generators, and auto companies, which in turn swept away the agrarian world. It became normal, by the time of World War I, for even the most well established corporations to carry long-term debt on their balance sheets – to rebuild and expand capital equipment, to make acquisitions, and to fund innovation. And even when businesses ran into trouble, strategic use of leverage could help salvage and rehabilitate failing enterprises, as J. P. Morgan's railroad and industrial refinancings proved. Morgan's merger of eight large companies into U.S. Steel showed how huge amounts of debt from many lenders could be used to restructure an entire industry.

Not all such deals were successful, even in the hands of the most sophisticated investors. What may have been history's first substantial leveraged buyout was a flop: Morgan's heavily leveraged (86 percent) assembly of the International Mercantile Marine Company in 1902, which quickly foundered on changes in trade patterns and political conditions. Years later, in a daring move to rid himself of minority shareholders, Henry Ford "took his company private" in a spectacular purchase of shares at a heavy premium, all financed with short-term bank debt. When the sharp depression of 1920–21 imperiled his ability to meet his debt service, Ford crammed his inventories down the throats of his dealers to raise desperately needed cash, angering many of them just as his company came under attack by the General Motors Corporation. Such highly publicized transactions were object lessons in the downside consequences of risk – that leverage could punish as sharply as it could reward. Few dared tread in the shoes of Morgan and Ford, or their bankers.[5]

Nevertheless, giant corporations by that time routinely financed their longer-term plans not only through the issue of asset-backed securities, but also through such "unsecured" devices as convertible bonds, debentures, and the debt-equity hybrid known as preferred stock. The variety of long-term debt instruments enabled lenders to invest in accordance with their specific risk and reward preferences, and borrowers to finance big projects under strict and enforceable terms of agreement. As lending institutions became more skilled at fashioning terms, and credit-worthiness became subject to more adept scrutiny and analysis, it became possible to match lenders and borrowers with greater precision, less risk, and lower cost. The lender's "covenant" (a biblical term signifying the deep obligations of the borrower to the lender) gave institutional lenders a greater sense of security and power – power to set limits on corporate spending and to establish conditions for managerial behavior.

Meanwhile, debt among ordinary people had migrated from the farm to the city. Credit facilities helped the U.S. transform itself into a modern consumer society, as individual households became increasingly habituated to consumer credit, buying stocks on margin, and borrowing to finance education. By the mid twentieth century, despite memories of the punishing years of protracted depression and the ensuing wartime austerity, individual wage earners discovered that they could smooth out their income and consumption patterns over time, financing current expenditures with debt covered by future earnings. Household mortgages became the common person's version of the leveraged buyout. Government helped by making interest payments deductible from income taxes. What had worked for business, now worked for everyone. Still, risk was always present, as was the traditional ambivalence toward debt.

Ambivalence toward debt also pervaded the nation's executive suites. In the boom years following World War II, growth-obsessed corporate managers still harbored memories of the Great Depression, and deemed it prudent to keep their leverage ratios as low as possible. In the oligopolistic center of the economy, value creation was equated with growth, and was best achieved through the reinvestment of profits. It is hardly a caricature of corporate executive thinking of that era to put it this way: debt, with all its tax benefits, may be useful for acquisitions, but it threatens managerial freedom. Too much debt on the balance sheet invites inflexible covenants, interferes with long-term development, and discourages innovation.

In the late 1960s, when earnings per share came to be the standard gross measure of corporate performance, financially adventurous managers of some mature corporations discovered that they could expand their empires and improve their price/earnings ratios by acquiring growth companies outside their core businesses. These conglomerateurs used debt liberally. But since the risk of debt was largely a function of the skills of lenders and borrowers and the purposes to which it was put, that risk increased with an excess of hubris. The collapse of too many conglomerate strategies – dramatized by Ling-Temco-Vaught's inappropriately leveraged acquisition of the struggling steel giant Jones & Laughlin – simply reinforced the aversion that most people felt toward highly leveraged transactions.

The idea that business could well support far more debt than it did was validated by a new generation of financial economists. In the 1960s, Franco Modigliani and Merton Miller published several seminal papers in which they argued that a company's capital structure was irrelevant, except insofar as debt was tax-advantaged relative to equity financing. Their theory suggested that companies ought to lever up as much as possible in order to capture the tax advantages of debt, so long as the cost of financial distress was kept to a reasonable level. Michael Jensen and William Meckling went so far as to ask: "Why don't we observe large corporations individually owned with a tiny fraction of the [equity] capital supplied by the entrepreneur . . . and the rest simply borrowed?" Their answer – that such high debt levels would encourage managers to take excessive risks – did not anticipate the role that deal organizers would play in cultivating long-term relationships with lenders, and so came just shy of predicting what would become the leveraged buyout movement.* Meanwhile, other academics, like Edward Altman, were just developing their now-familiar quantitative techniques by which investors could more accurately assess the bankruptcy risk of corporations under various conditions.[6]

As mainstream corporate America slipped into the doldrums in the late 1970s, theory met practice in the back alleys of Wall Street. Emerging buyout firms like Kohlberg Kravis Roberts & Co. were per-

* Michael Jensen and William Meckling argued that the "agency costs of debt" in companies with highly leveraged capital structures would be excessively high, since managers with little equity in their companies (and thus very limited downside) would be tempted to take on overly risky projects. This in turn would lead lenders to charge exorbitant interest rates to compensate for the downside risk. The early LBO sponsors overcame these problems by setting up governance systems that prevented this sort of managerial behavior, and by becoming repeat players in the market for debt. Lenders knew that if a sponsor allowed managers to take excessive risks and his deals went bad, the sponsor's reputation and his ability to do future deals would be destroyed.

fecting their craft, matching increasingly fine techniques of debt analysis to the ambitions of small company executives willing to labor under heavy leverage in order to acquire more control of the assets they managed. The paradox of debt was evident in each of these deals: while the debt covenants and heavy interest payments constrained managers' actions, they also freed them from their former owners, giving them almost total authority within the constraints imposed by the buyout's capital structure. In this way, the buyout firms served to challenge conventional assumptions about debt. Leverage could be usefully employed not only to make acquisitions, but also to create value by stimulating improvements in operating performance. Leverage could liberate management, even as it constrained its prerogatives.

Up by the Bootstraps

The leveraged buyout – for which the name is a recent one – has a long pedigree. Though hardly new under the sun, so-called "bootstrap" acquisitions – typically involving assets from a few hundred thousand to a few million dollars – became more common after World War II among small businesses in England and the United States. The investor's idea was to acquire the equity of target companies, and usually to take them private, putting as little as feasible of the buyer's own money into the transaction. The investor would normally seek out a company with strong cash flow characteristics and would most likely have to pay a premium above its market value, if a public company, or above its perceived value by owners, if already privately held or owned by a parent corporation. In any case, the buyer had to see potential for strongly improving the assets – that is, for pulling the company "up by the bootstraps," out of debt and into more efficient performance. Otherwise the leverage in the investment would not be worth the trouble.

Each bootstrap deal contained one or more of the components of modern leveraged buyouts. All bootstraps were financed by using a company's own assets or cash flow to secure high levels of debt financing. They generally involved large payouts to the pre-buyout owners, either outside investors or incumbent owner-managers, who wanted to liquidate their holdings. Typically, the new investors would team up with incumbent owner-managers who wished to stay on, or with hired hands who wanted to gain ownership control of the assets they managed. (The beauty of high leverage was precisely that it shrank the equity investment required, so that managers of modest means could become owners.) In its most common form the bootstrap entailed using large amounts of debt to provide executive managers with the opportunity to become substantial shareholders. In some cases, the sponsor of the bootstrap took on a board-level governance role after the deal was closed.

One successful version of the bootstrap was employed by a young American investment banker, George Ohrstrom. After World War II, Ohrstrom tapped British investors to support buyouts of small, well-managed, proprietary American manufacturing companies in stable markets. He bought these companies "with their own cash," employing generous portions of debt to acquire assets from their owner-managers in order to merge them into a public entity. There were two vital prerequisites to such acquisitions: the predictability of cash flows at levels sufficient not only to meet the debt service but also to effect a rapid paydown of principle; and the continued loyalty of existing management. The latter was perhaps even more critical than the former in financing the transaction, since in the eyes of the lenders, only good management of the assets could ensure reliable repayment. Before his untimely death in 1955, Ohrstrom employed this technique to good effect in assembling two successful industrial conglomerates, Carlisle and Dover corporations, which then grew in large part by continuing to acquire companies consistent with Ohrstrom's original design and monitoring them closely thereafter.[7]

The firm Dyson-Kissner-Moran also began during the 1950s to build a modest portfolio of companies acquired with high levels of debt. Sometimes individual or family investors, such as Henry Hillman in Pittsburgh, bought 100 percent of the equity of small companies on a highly leveraged basis, leaving their managements to run the businesses. It was also possible, but more difficult, to bootstrap companies without involving current management in post-transaction plans. That approach was taken by Carl Hess at AEA Investors, who organized a small network of retired executives to invest in management-starved companies; and by Laird & Company, another early institutional player in the buyout field, whose strategy was to muster a cadre of potential CEOs and then help them find and finance acquisitions they could manage. The strategy did not always work, and Laird eventually disappeared, though not before incubating a number of buyout specialists who would start up the well-known firms of Gibbons, Green and van Amerongen and Clayton, Dubilier & Rice.[8] It was in 1978 that Clayton, Dubilier, initially a "crisis management team" for troubled companies, entered the field, ready to provide its own management talent for bought-out companies. Its success in doing so remains something of an anomaly in the modern LBO industry.[9]

Bootstraps ran athwart of two conventions of corporate financial management. First, the feasibility of any bootstrap had to be measured not by a company's profitability in the traditional sense, but rather by its cash flows, which would have to be sufficient to pay down debt without debilitating operations.* Thus the favored targets for buyouts were "mundane" and "mature" businesses. Second, since it normally took years, not months, to improve performance to the point where the sale of equity would yield a high return on the original investment, bootstrap investors had to forgo dividends, looking forward to capital gains commensurate with the risk of their original investment. They had to be patient. The strategy worked only if assets could be sold at a high price after the debt had been paid down, which was not likely if the company were managed for short-term profits.[10]

* The cash flow of a company is typically measured as earnings before interest and taxes (EBIT). This can be refined to include the adding back of noncash expenses, such as depreciation and amortization, in a measure often presented in accounting reports as EBITD, EBITDA, EBDIT, EBDITA, or simply "cash flow from operations."

Experience came with development of professional buyout firms, which began to surface in the late 1960s. The buyout firms of the 1970s and 1980s elaborated on the basic characteristics of the bootstrap, elevating an ad hoc procedure to a practice. KKR's Jerome Kohlberg has often been credited with establishing the modern buyout as a specialized practice during his tenure at Bear, Stearns. In a retrospective newspaper interview, he explained how he "refined" the traditional bootstrap deal "by adding the role for management as owners."[11] (There was some precedent for that in other transactions, including the highly leveraged buyout of Anderson-Pritchard Oil by its own management in 1961.)[12] Kohlberg's greater contribution was to adopt as a principle a vital governance role for the financiers in all the buyouts he would do at Bear, Stearns and later at KKR. Managers managed, but the financier-dominated boards of directors did more than own; they became engaged fiduciaries – active partners, in effect, with management.

Kohlberg's first leveraged buyout was serendipitous. In 1964 he and an associate, Walter Luftman, encountered the seventy-one-year-old H. J. Stern, head of a small Westchester-based gold refining and dental supply company called Stern Metals. Stern had no confidence that his children could run the business, and he wanted to convert his equity into cash in order to provide his family a liquid inheritance. There was a catch, however. Stern loved his business, and adamantly refused to sell it to a corporate buyer, who could ruin all he had built. He also wanted his money – and soon. After puzzling over the problem, Kohlberg and Luftman hit upon a plan to sell the company for $9.5 million to the Stern family and a small group of outside investors, including the dealmakers. The equity investors put up just $1.5 million, and the rest was borrowed. The business was small, had a steady market, and churned out cash, and so it was not difficult to find takers for the debt. Citibank provided some bank credit, while most of the debt financing was "junior," a tranche of subordinated securities sold to the Mass Mutual and Paul Revere insurance companies, who also received an "equity kicker."*[13]

> * In many LBO transactions, debtholders were granted options or warrants to buy stock in the new company at a future date at a price equal to or higher than the stock price at the time of the buyout. These so-called equity kickers served two purposes: they enhanced, or "sweetened," the deal for potential debtholders, and by giving creditors an ownership interest, they reduced potential conflicts of interest between debt and equityholders should the company suffer financial distress.

What made the Stern acquisition unusual was that it was more like a traditional exercise in "merchant banking." Merchant banking – in which the financiers themselves became "principal investors" in the companies for which they arranged financing – was more common in Europe. It had largely disappeared in the United States, where investment bankers served more commonly as intermediaries, earning their money from percentage fees on the transactions they arranged. As a boy, Kohlberg had been impressed by a friend's father, a British merchant banker. "He had a nice roll-top desk," Kohlberg recalled. "He was his own boss, which appealed to me. So I called what we started to do 'merchant banking,' because we prospered or fell on what we did as opposed to working for a fee."[14]

The Stern deal closed in the summer of 1965, just in time for
George Roberts, a summer employee, to witness the event. Within
eight months the company was able to offer stock, priced originally
at $2.50 per share, to the public for $11.75. But this was not to be
a quick hit. The dealmakers stayed invested, using proceeds from the
sale of stock to pay down debt. The business grew under new management (who had also bought equity), began making acquisitions,
changed its name to Sterndent, and four years later was sold at a
price eight times the original cost. The apparent ease by which the
original investors increased the value of their equity struck many as
Wall Street legerdemain. This was certainly not the last leveraged buyout that would attract suspicion and adverse publicity, but it was the
first of many successful deals that Kohlberg would do.

Kohlberg arranged three more small leveraged acquisitions by the
end of the decade. He had set himself on a path to become a dedicated
leveraged buyout specialist when he took on Roberts full time in
1969. Roberts was the son of a Houston oil broker and the nephew
of Ray Kravis, an Oklahoma petroleum engineer and friend of Cy
Lewis, who was then Kohlberg's boss. Roberts had recognized the
high profit-making potential of leverage from the moment he saw it,
and in the following year he persuaded his cousin and friend Henry
Kravis, with whom he had attended school at Claremont College, to
join him and Kohlberg in their unusual and lucrative financings.[15]

At the beginning of their association, the trio had no special name
for what they were doing. They did "financings," for which they happened to employ a lot of debt. The term "leveraged buyout" – Kohlberg still used the term "merchant banking" – would not appear until
the latter part of the 1970s. Later, when asked why he and his partners had chosen to disregard conventional wisdom and build their
careers around using debt to buy companies, Roberts would say, "because we couldn't afford them any other way." In fact, as we shall
see, there was a lot more to it than that.[16] Meanwhile, it took time
to establish the practicality of doing leveraged transactions as a specialized, ongoing business. Information on small private firms was
hard to come by. ("The main sources were Dun & Bradstreet reports
and direct contacts with companies," Roberts recalled).[17] Conglomerates were snatching up companies with stock (the fad was in full
swing by the late 1960s), so it was hard to find cash-rich companies
ripe for debt-financed acquisition. And it was not easy to bring lend-

ing institutions to the table for highly leveraged transactions of substantial size. They had simply not achieved the kind of "legitimacy" that experience and volume would bring.

Bear, Stearns – which by contemporary Wall Street investment banking standards was a crude backwater – was not particularly supportive of Kohlberg's activities. Its corporate finance specialists preferred to spend most of their energy on more "mainstream" transactions. Buyouts were "lockups," in the jargon of the group, and during the lean years of 1973–75 especially, the idea of locking up money in such relatively long-term investments was almost anathema in a culture of traders. "Their idea of long term investment was overnight," Kohlberg complained. Still, he was a partner in the firm, and his small buyout team was generating income; so he was left to his own devices. Kravis and Roberts soon became partners, too, and learned a lot – prospecting, cold calling on investment brokers and companies, getting to know and understand managers. They analyzed countless income statements and balance sheets, doing calculations with a pencil on a yellow pad. "Then there weren't the computer programs that you could just crank out," recalled Kohlberg.[18]

Some of their education came from bad investments, such as the acquisition of Cobblers, Inc., a shoe manufacturer that fell apart when its CEO committed suicide, and the purchase of a broadcasting school that lurched into bankruptcy. But more often, the Bear, Stearns buyouts met with success, generating good fees at the time of the deal and yielding high returns in the longer run. As George Roberts explained, "our early buyouts were in principle no different than what they are today. We were going to buy a company and the manager was going to invest with us. We were going to have a governance function and going to be an investor for five to seven years and eventually sell our shares and get capital gains."[19] It was also established early on that after each buyout closed, each company would continue to float on its own bottom. There would be no mergers, no Ohrstrom-style holding companies, no attempts to create conglomerate "synergies," no cross-subsidies.

As Kohlberg's leveraged transactions began to increase in size, they became more varied. The Bear, Stearns buyout portfolio came to include such diverse entities as Thompson Wire, Boren Clay Products, Barrows Industries (a jewelry manufacturer), and Eagle Motor Lines. When the conglomerate boom soured, an important category of larger buyout candidates came onto the market – the so-called "orphans." For example, Vapor Corporation was purchased in 1972 from the conglomerate Singer Corporation, despite considerable misgivings on the part of the parent company and its lawyers about the leverage in the transaction;[20] and then Incom International was bought from Rockwell International. Incom was a small enough subsidiary that it did not get much attention from its parent company. But, at a $92.5 million purchase price, it was big enough to make the front page of *The Wall Street Journal*. (Most of the team's other investments had been in the $10 to $20 million range.) As with Vapor, Incom was blessed with managers who could be motivated by greater authority and equity participation. "All of a sudden they were owners," said Henry Kravis with his characteristic vividness. "Off came the shackles and they were off to the races!"[21]

Equally important, the team began to solidify its relationships with debt managers at insurance companies and with bankers (particularly at Prudential, First Chicago and Citibank) who would come to specialize in leveraged buyouts. Their participation on a deal-by-deal basis was supplemented by the participation of such family and individual investors as M&T Associates (William Towne) and Wilmington Securities (the Henry Hillman family). Such relationships enabled the buyout team to assemble debt and equity financing on a more reliable and timely basis, a critical factor in a competitive market. They befriended deal brokers and investment bankers. They established what would become durable relationships with accountants, attorneys, and their institutions. The services of trusted individuals such as Thomas Hudson at Deloitte Haskins and Sells, Richard Beattie at Simpson Thacher & Bartlett, and John McLoughlin at Latham & Watkins, would prove invaluable to them over time.

What the trio could not do was raise an equity fund – that is, pool a substantial sum of money from would-be equity investors for which the buyout specialists would serve as investor and general partner. This would have given them more flexibility, not only to seek out acquisition opportunities but also to act on them more quickly. Speed was often essential to winning a bid and to keeping a price within reasonable bounds. But the corporate finance department at Bear, Stearns was not interested in supporting such a move. Jerry Kohlberg and his two young partners were still marginal players. They were also probably the best in their business; and after a decade of accumulated experience they had learned most of what they would later need to develop and hone their own business.

Over time, the three partners had derived a set of fundamentals that would become the basis for the KKR-style buyout. First, the target company had to have good cash flow characteristics – if not steady, at least predictable. It had to have clear potential for substantially decreasing debt levels, and thus increasing equity values, within three to five years; and a good CEO had to be in place or at least in the offing. The prospective buyout had to be acceptable to the target company's board of directors (there would be no coercive "raids"), and managers had to be persuaded to participate. Early lenders to buyouts, though few in number, became ardent supporters of the Bear, Stearns buyout team and were helpful in making the case to managers of target companies. Bankers at First Chicago, for instance, helped Kohlberg, Kravis and Roberts persuade the management of Vapor Corporation to go forward.[22]

Calibrating the price for a prospective buyout was a delicate matter. In order to convince prospective (and often reluctant) sellers, premiums had to be paid over the current share prices; but the success of any buyout required that buyers not overpay. Balancing these conflicting pressures required enough discipline to walk away from very tempting prospects that were even slightly overpriced based on *conservative* forecasts of what the projected debt service would require. Then, too, one had to assess the degree to which the post-buyout risks could be controlled. The financial structure of the buyout – including the types, levels, and terms of debt – had to be tailored as precisely as possible to the likely ability of the company to meet interest and principal payments.

Fundamentally important, the executive managers of a company undergoing a buyout had to agree to invest a *substantial* portion of their own net worth in the equity portion of the transaction. As owners, managers might then go the extra mile, seeking out and unlocking "hidden values" in assets in which they now had a major stake. Whether managers regarded that prospect as one of tyranny or liberation was perhaps the most important indication of whether they were up to the task. For their part, the dealmakers would have to commit themselves to long-term engagement in working with the managers following the buyout. They could not afford simply to walk away like common intermediaries. The terms of the debt financing imposed a discipline on all concerned. In order to meet the obligations set forth by the financing, the company would have to operate differently – generate more cash, husband resources more efficiently, and invest more wisely. The very structure of the buyout demanded such changes. The combination of debt constraints and management equity ownership would impel managers to meet performance expectations, and more.

Thus sponsors and managers had to set clear expectations at the outset. "The deal" was far more than simply a financial transaction: it was a set of expectations and an agreement between the managers, creditors, and sponsors as to what the company intended to achieve over the next five to seven years. Again, those expectations were locked into the financial structure, in the form of payment schedules and debt covenants, encapsulating a virtuous circle of debt discipline, equity ownership, and high standards for performance.

Venturing KKR

Kohlberg, Kravis and Roberts extricated themselves from Bear, Stearns in 1976. They took some of their investments and most of their good will with them, despite their former employer's attempts to forestall their efforts. They opened shop on May 1, 1976, and after two months of seemingly fruitless prospecting, Henry Hillman came forward with unexpected support for a $25 million equity fund the trio was trying to raise. As Kravis related the story:

We had tried to explain to Hillman who we were and what we were trying to do. He said, "I'll be back to you in two weeks." After six or seven days, his associate Wes Adams called. "Did you not like us?" he asked. "What are you talking about?," I said. He said, "I haven't heard anything from you." "But, Wes," I explained, "I thought you'd be back to us in two weeks." He started laughing. "The minute you walked out of the door we made our decision. Our decision is, we'd like half the fund." I literally jumped. He was going to take $12.5 million![23]

When they went out to talk to other people, Hillman's imprimatur in hand, they encountered some obstacles. Other potential investors had fixed ideas about what acquisitions to make and how to structure them. Some suggested that KKR form a board of directors to oversee the investments. Kohlberg, Kravis, and Roberts wanted more freedom than that; they wanted passive investors. They changed their plans and went back to a small group of friends with a fresh proposal for covering KKR's overhead for five years – time enough, they thought, to test whether their firm could succeed. They persuaded eight parties to pledge $50,000 a year for five years – $400,000 in all. (The three partners would contribute an additional $100,000 annually.) In return for their pledges, the outside investors would have the right, but not the obligation, to examine and participate in every investment the firm made. The firm would put up one percent of the equity in each, and take twenty percent of the profits, which became a precedent for all KKR investments. Henry Kravis's father, Ray, came in; Jerry Kohlberg brought along two of his friends; and three other individuals subscribed, including William Graham, a drug company executive in Chicago. First Chicago Corporation's venture capital group was the one institution to pitch in. Hillman, displaying his confidence in the venture, pledged double the asking price of admission, thus rounding out the eight units of investment KKR had been seeking.[24]

KKR had completed its first three investments with this group when Graham called Kravis to say: "Henry, I want to go into all your deals, since I'm not smart enough to pick and choose. You should really go out and raise a fund." The three KKR partners warmed to the idea. In 1978, they raised the first of their equity funds, a $30 million limited partnership based on the venture capital model for "blind pools." The fund investors, as "limited partners," entrusted a fixed contribution of cash to experts, the "general partners," who assumed all the liabilities and who decided where and how the money should be invested within a defined period of time – in this case, six years. The general partners, who put up one percent of the equity, assumed all the liabilities, but also received a healthy share – in KKR's case, 20 percent – of the profits. This, the first LBO equity fund, attracted such institutions as Allstate and TIAA, along with venture capital from Citicorp, Continental Illinois, and Security Pacific Banks. Out of gratitude to its original investors, whose personal resources were small by comparison, KKR agreed that they could continue to invest in all future deals at their discretion without paying any additional fees.[25]

Defining the Buyout Framework

Though there was no formula, as such, for financing leveraged buy-outs, some rules of thumb had been worked out – a basic framework within which future KKR buyouts would fit. In its pro forma plans, KKR would buy companies with about 10–20 percent equity and 80–90 percent debt.[26] Of that, senior bank debt was to have fairly short (five-year) repayment requirements, while subordinated debt typically carried somewhat longer terms. A typical plan for a KKR buyout would show the company repaying the acquisition debt within five to seven years.

The key to high equity returns was the recognition that company growth was not necessary to value creation. The leveraged financing allowed reforms in management – sometimes radical, sometimes no more than mundane operational "blocking and tackling" – to be converted into capital gains. To see how this works in general terms, imagine an all-equity company that is bought for $100 million. Before the acquisition, this company generates $10 million in cash flows, just enough to give shareholders a 10 percent return. The acquisition is financed with $90 million in debt and $10 million in equity. The company is then able, through improved operations, superior asset utilization, and careful capital investment, to increase cash flows from $10 to $20 million per year, *without either increasing or decreasing the value of the assets.* By paying no dividends, and by using this $20 million in cash flow strictly for debt service, this company can pay down the $90 million of debt (at an interest rate of 10 percent) in about 6 years. At the end of that period the company would still be worth $100 million, but it would now be all equity. In other words, the original $10 million equity investment has been transformed into one worth $100 million, for a 47 percent compound annual rate of return![27]

Within the basic buyout framework existed a myriad of possibilities. Each financing was crafted to fit the perceived situation. Each took into account the preferences of lenders as well as the needs and capabilities of the company involved. As former SEC commissioner Joseph Grundfest said, "the perception that many contemporaries had that leveraged buyouts were mere cookie-cutter transactions was much more fiction than reality."[28]

The firm's first half-dozen buyouts between 1977 and 1980 illustrate just how varied the possibilities were. A.J. Industries was a suffering conglomerate, albeit with a vital core business and a dogged chief executive. L.B. Foster was a family business ready to liquidate. Like U.S. Natural Resources (USNR), which followed, it had less-than-certain cash flows in cyclical businesses. Houdaille was a public corporation, a diversified manufacturer of basic products for niche markets. Sargent Industries depended largely on national defense markets – a low technology, "boring but beautiful business," said KKR partner Bob MacDonnell, but well managed with plenty of excess cash flow. Most unlike the others, F.B. Truck Line Company was a service provider, a regulated common carrier.

One thing all these companies had in common was their "undervalued" stock. It is important to bear in mind that undervalued assets were not normally a function of an inefficient public market nor of ignorant sellers of privately held assets. So-called undervalued assets were more likely evidence of undermanagement. In the nation's large corporations – in an environment that stressed growth in assets over value creation, that encouraged often-wasteful spending at the expense of dividends – poor incentives often led to widespread, systematic destruction of value. The same problems plagued smaller companies as well, often even more severely.

In the family firms and small public companies of the late 1970s, budget and income projections tended to be highly elastic and speculative. Even in "well run" companies, performance in terms of asset utilization and return on investment was rarely subjected to rigorous examination. In smaller businesses, the most intelligent, well-intentioned managers were rarely trained in state-of-the-art business technique. If they themselves were not owners, they had few direct incentives either to manage costs carefully or to pursue new opportunities aggressively. Or managers could simply lack the resources to fund projects that would maximize longer-term effectiveness and profitability. While this broad characterization may not have been universal, there were plenty of smaller companies that fit the profile. And many of them could be expected to have "good" managers who would rise to the opportunities and challenges of ownership.

KKR's first investment, A.J. Industries, acquired in April 1977, had a perfectly good manager with far more potential than he had yet realized. It was small, requiring just $25.6 million in financing; yet it proved difficult to raise the money. The offering price of the stock was twice A.J.'s current public market value. The still-wary debt markets of the time made it difficult for KKR to persuade even those lenders who had worked with them successfully at Bear, Stearns to take a chance by imposing high leverage on A.J.'s awkward jumble of businesses. A.J. fit perfectly within KKR's general concept of the kinds of companies it was then seeking – "mainly manufacturing businesses, 'metal benders' with good management and decent cash flows."[29] But it was hard for others to fathom the prospects of a company that made suspension systems, heavy-duty brake drums, carburetors, in-flight refueling systems, fuel and infrared heating systems, metal furniture, metal castings, and precious metal mining. (The firm also held unimproved and industrial real estate.) And it was hard to accept KKR's bet on the intrinsic quality of A.J.'s management. The critical blow came when Prudential Insurance declined to lend money for the transaction, making it impossible to secure the subordinated debt financing KKR had hoped to obtain from insurance companies that usually participated at the "mezzanine" level. KKR was forced to fund the entire debt portion of the buyout with $17 million in bank debt. On the basis of the perceived risk, the banks lent the money in the form of a secured loan. (The difference between the bank debt and the common equity investment, which amounted to less than 8 percent of the total financing, came in the form of preferred stock subscribed to by a small group of investors, along with A.J.'s cash balance of $1.6 million.)[30]

> * Throughout its history, KKR has been loath to use secured financing. Other buyout firms routinely relied on secured debt financing, but the terms of the associated covenants impaired what KKR valued most in the initial structuring: flexibility. A.J.'s debt-to-asset ratio was just two-thirds at the deal's closing, not all that high by leveraged buyout standards. But the lack of flexibility associated with the secured financing (the diminished bargaining power with lenders and the inability to sell assets in the face of cash shortfalls) was a source of concern. As George Roberts, who had scrambled to put A.J. together, asked: "Which would you rather have: low leverage with no flexibility or high leverage with flexibility?" The question was purely rhetorical.

Fortunately, A.J. was blessed with Raymond O'Keefe, an ebullient character with infectious enthusiasm who thrived under the new regime. O'Keefe seized upon the freedom KKR gave him, and in the face of heavy debt repayment obligations worked almost nonstop to make his budgeted targets. Within just two years, A.J. was restructured and healthy, throwing off enough cash to justify refinancing all the bank debt on an unsecured basis.*

L.B. Foster, a $94.2 million transaction completed in August

1977, was structured far more to KKR's liking. Based in Pittsburgh, L. B. Foster was a finisher and supplier of steel pipe for the oil and gas industries; it also made products for industrial, railroad, and construction markets. It was a private company with solid management, attractive growth prospects, and a strong reputation. One concern was that most of L.B. Foster's sales were cyclical, which could jeopardize the company's ability to meet fixed repayment requirements. Henry Kravis, who led the financing effort, believed that KKR was buying "at the right turn in the cycle," especially in the company's major oil and gas markets. If so, the cash flows were predictable for the near to medium term, and it appeared that the business would generate enough cash to pay down most of the short-term debt without resorting to dramatic changes in operations or the sale of assets.

In this case it was easier to persuade lenders, and L.B. Foster's buyout capital structure fit more closely with the general pattern in KKR's deals into the early 1980s. A revolving bank credit facility, provided by five institutions, represented only 23 percent of the financing. Institutional lenders, led by Prudential, provided nearly $66 million in senior and junior subordinated debt, which came with two classes of preferred stock. This sort of "strip" financing, in which debt investors also held some equity, was another technique to provide flexibility in case of financial distress. Because they had some upside participation through equity, creditors would be less likely to push for premature debt repayment if the firm failed to meet an interest or principal payment. In the event, such flexibility proved unnecessary: when L.B. Foster went public in 1980, having paid down a quarter of its debt, the 1.7 million shares sold for $17 each, compared to an original value of $1.43. The company's performance had exceeded the most optimistic projections at the time of acquisition, mainly through rigorous control of administrative costs and aggressive marketing.

That L.B. Foster was temporarily whipsawed by a downturn in its core markets in the early 1980s recession did not belie the basic financial strategy, though it did provide a lesson on the risk of leverage in cyclical businesses. The Washington-based USNR likewise operated in cyclical markets. A manufacturer of heavy-duty equipment for the forest products industry, it also operated coal mines; sold rock, sand, and gravel; and distributed industrial products. In 1977 it was trading well below its book value, despite its rising fortunes after several bad years. The company's management and board put it up for sale and it quickly attracted a number of potential buyers. KKR won the bidding with an offer of $8.25 per share, much higher than the stock's most recent high of $5.60, for a total price of $22.2 million.

In making its bid, KKR had undertaken what would become a characteristic blend of analysis and qualitative judgment. First there was the usual due diligence: the careful assessment of the company's accounts, credit history, assets, tax position, markets, and management. But George Roberts acknowledged the ultimately speculative nature of any buyout, arguing that

> you wind up bidding what you can afford to pay and finance and still get an adequate return. We just figured that if we could make three or four times our money in five or six years, it would be a good investment. We didn't rely on twenty pages of computer printouts with all the numbers and all the balance sheets. A lot of it was by the seat of our pants.[31]

USNR performed well under its highly motivated management, who had bought 20 percent of the equity. After seven years the company had delivered a 40 percent annual compounded rate of return on the original equity investment by the KKR partners,* through a deft combination of asset sales, new acquisitions, and day-to-day operating improvements. In 1985, KKR helped the management team finance a leveraged "buyback," making them majority owners of the firm.

These first three buyouts, all successful, reflect the basic framework that KKR was developing. Each relied on solid management of assets, judicious divestitures and acquisitions, and modest organizational growth, which, when combined with leveraged financing, delivered very high equity returns. It was now time to see whether KKR's model for leveraged buyouts could work on a larger scale.

---

* Unless otherwise stated, returns on KKR investments are reported to reflect the change in the full economic value of a company's equity from the time of acquisition. Returns to KKR's limited partners after deducting for KKR's "carried interests" (20 percent of profits) and fund management fees (1.5 percent of funds committed) are accounted for in the Appendix.

Breakthrough: Houdaille Industries

It was the acquisition of Houdaille Industries – the first modern leveraged buyout of a mid-sized public company – that woke up everyone on Wall Street. Though far from qualifying as a large
corporation, Houdaille was a blockbuster by the standards of the
time. Few – not even the investment bankers at the prestigious firm
of Goldman, Sachs, who were shopping the company – initially believed that the company could be bought out profitably. Though not
as highly leveraged as most buyouts, the complexity of Houdaille's
debt financing, with its creatively engineered, multilayered web of securities, became an object lesson for dealmakers, corporate management, and the SEC alike. Perhaps more than any single transaction,
Houdaille set the stage for an explosion of leveraged buyouts during
the 1980s.

Houdaille had brought to market the first hydraulic shock absorber
in 1929, and had begun to diversify its business in the mid-1950s
when automotive companies began assembling more of their components in-house. Its first acquisitions were construction firms in New
Jersey and Florida. In 1957, Houdaille acquired a machine tool company and soon afterward expanded its investments in machine tools
as well as in pumps and other industrial products. By 1977, pumps
represented 58 percent of the firm's sales and 68 percent of its profits.

With $55 million in cash and only $25 million in debt, the company
was ripe for a takeover. In a July 7, 1978, article entitled "Takeover
Hope and Houdaille," columnist Robert Metz told *New York Times*
readers why Houdaille might be a good buy. At 67, Houdaille's CEO,
Gerald C. Saltarelli, was past normal retirement age. The company was
rich in cash, and carried little debt on a very conservative balance sheet.
It had some $55 million in pretax profits, and was thought to be worth
$35 to $40 per share to any potential suitor, compared to its then-
current market price, which hovered around $14.25. The news at-
tracted the interest of several potential buyers, and Houdaille was soon
beset by an unwanted suitor, the Jacobs family of Buffalo, New York,
who began acquiring blocks of the company's stock.

Saltarelli had been with the company since 1948, and feared for
his subordinates and all they had worked to build. He was determined
not to turn Houdaille over to a hostile raider. His only alternative
now was to seek out a more "friendly" buyer, one who might be

willing to work with the company's existing management. Goldman, Sachs was given the job of putting the company up for auction in hopes of finding such a buyer, perhaps in a merger. Jerry Kohlberg and Henry Kravis knew Goldman's Peter Sachs was Houdaille's banker, and asked Sachs to arrange a conversation with Houdaille's management. Initially reluctant, Saltarelli agreed to meet Kohlberg and Kravis at the company's new Fort Lauderdale headquarters in August 1978. Saltarelli, who had a meticulous sense of detail (he was trained as a lawyer) and an intuitive fear of debt (his brother had lost a construction company during the Depression), initially considered KKR's proposal preposterous. He had, in accordance with his generation's "sound" business doctrine, kept Houdaille nearly debt-free throughout his entire fifteen-year tenure as CEO, and was not inclined to change that policy.

In August 1978, Saltarelli and his three principal lieutenants – Thomas Bainbridge, Philip O'Reilly, and Donald Boyce – met with Kravis, Kohlberg, and their associate Don Herdrich. The managers listened to KKR's discussion of cash flows "absolutely in disbelief," said Kravis. Herdrich wondered how anyone could come up with the financing for so large a transaction. KKR encouraged the managers to make projections for Houdaille on a worst-case basis; and Kravis told Herdrich sotto voce, "If they say they'll do the deal, we'll figure out how to raise the money, somehow."

Don Boyce recalled that "after a lot of crunching" – in which Houdaille's managers "kept redoing the numbers" to see how it worked with different levels of debt, preferred stock, and dividend and interest rates – "we determined that a leveraged buyout could work." Still, Houdaille kept KKR at bay until October, when Saltarelli, under pressure from other prospective buyers, came back to the table. It had been a luxurious waiting period. No one else had entered the arena with a formal offer. Houdaille's main businesses were booming, and the second Middle East "oil shock" was as yet unanticipated, so interest rates, though high by historical standards, were still moderate enough. Nevertheless, the market for conglomerate buyout financing was very skeptical, especially at this scale of effort; and Houdaille, with eighteen distinct operating units, looked like a very complicated tangle of interests. In the meantime, O'Reilly and Boyce had been laboring to appease their boss's fear of debt. It was Peter Sachs who finally persuaded the CEO to listen to KKR's offer, by appealing to

Saltarelli's sense of fiduciary responsibility to obtain the highest possible price for his shareholders. Sachs also explained that Goldman was unlikely to find any prospects for a merger.[32] As Jerry Kohlberg remembered it, Saltarelli said, "I'm too old to have that [debt] burden on my shoulders." Nonetheless, "he felt that this was a good thing for his company and his people."[33]

When it finally became clear to Saltarelli that KKR was serious about respecting Houdaille's plan for management succession (with the understanding that Saltarelli and Bainbridge were about to retire), the parties came to an agreement in principle. On October 26, KKR announced its tentative merger agreement offering $40 per share for common and $50 for preferred stock. The common stock had been trading for under $10 per share prior to the rumors of a buyout, and after the announcement the stock moved up to the high 20s, peaking for a time at $31 per share. Forty dollars began to look very good to Saltarelli, whose concerns about his shareholders were allayed.

By then KKR and Houdaille's younger executives had worked out a detailed plan. "We looked at it pretty simplistically," Roberts explained. Houdaille was a powerful cash generator with some good businesses and some poor ones. According to Boyce, there were plans for selling off businesses in construction materials and in automotive products.[34] The company's highly profitable business in chrome bumpers was to be phased out, because its products did not meet new regulatory standards. Indeed, the management already had good ideas about buyers for some of the less desirable pieces; the buyout would provide the incentive for making the appropriate divestitures. What would remain, mainly, was a core set of businesses in machine tools and industrial products. No one foresaw the debacle in store for the U.S. machine tools industry, as its share of the domestic market would be cut by more than two-thirds within the coming decade by Japanese and other foreign competition.

As George Roberts remembered it, when KKR announced that it intended to acquire Houdaille, "everybody called up and said, 'how are you going to do this?' I remember saying: 'We don't start what we can't finish.'" Though he immediately regretted the bravado, it would come to stand KKR in good stead. One call came from a less skeptical quarter: Michael Tokarz, a young and hungry lender from Continental Illinois, was casting about for companies with undervalued stocks and strong cash flows. He read about KKR's intentions during his five a.m. commute to work and called both the Houdaille and KKR offices, "just letting the phones ring for about two hours." When Kravis finally answered, Tokarz committed his bank for $30 million. Others quickly followed suit.[35]

Anticipating some $60 million in bank loans – from Continental Illinois ($30 million), Bankers Trust ($15 million), and Manufacturers Hanover ($15 million) – and having lined up what they thought was a reliable ally, Prudential, for a large share (as much as $150 million) of the senior and subordinated debt, KKR began to raise funds for the roughly $380 million in financing. The equity portion would be a relatively small part of the total and could be managed largely through the newly raised 1978 Fund. But Prudential turned out to be a less certain participant than anticipated. Former New Jersey Governor Robert Meyner, who sat on the insurance company's board, opposed the buyout. Henry Kravis knew that without Prudential's imprimatur, the deal would founder. It took some time for Prudential's lending officers to bring their company into the fold, and afterward there was still a problem of assembling what would be a wide array of relatively small debtholders. It was not until May 1979 that KKR was able to complete the transaction, and then only after some complicated financial engineering.

Houdaille's management, in the meantime, had prepared its plants for visits from a variety of would-be lenders. There was no "road show" of the mid-1980s variety – no formal, glitzy presentation to a roomful of would-be investors eager to spend their institutions' money as fast as they could. It was an arduous sell; lenders had to see for themselves. In all, KKR managed to line up seventeen different institutions to subscribe to three classes of debt securities, some with warrants attached, and preferred stock. After Prudential (which took $74.8 million of the total senior notes and $40 million of senior subordinated notes), the largest participant was TIAA (which took approximately $25 million, spread across three classes of debt). The remainder, mostly insurance companies, took much smaller bites. Management, principally O'Reilly and Boyce, were encouraged to subscribe to equity in the company on the same terms – at $2.52 per share – as the KKR partners.[36]

Houdaille Industries: sources of financing

		Dollars Invested ($000)	Percent of Total Financing	Percent of Fully Diluted Equity
Excess Cash		$ 26,000	6.8%	
Bank Revolving Credit		60,000	15.8%	
Senior Notes		140,000	36.8%	
Senior Subordinated Notes		75,000	19.7%	10.0%
Junior Subordinated Notes		31,500	8.3%	
Preferred Stock		23,500	6.1%	
Common Stock		24,946	6.6%	
	Management			10.0%
	Preferred Holders			24.4%
	Jr. Note Holders			25.2%
	KKR & Investors			30.4%
Total Financing		$380,946		

In addition to setting a new standard for the size of leveraged buy-outs, Houdaille demonstrated how creative financial structuring could both increase cash flow and enhance deal returns. As KKR assembled investors for the transaction, Thomas Hudson, the head of the Greensboro, North Carolina, office of Deloitte, Haskins & Sells, proposed an idea to reduce Houdaille's tax burden and to generate more cash to meet debt service. Hudson had passed many pleasant hours with his colleague, Michael McCormick, brainstorming creative solutions to just such tax problems.

We would get in a room sometimes, just the two of us and a flip chart, and we would start drawing diagrams of the structure and playing "what if" games. "What if we did it this way? Where would you have to place the layers of financing? What were the exposures as you moved from step A to step B to step C?" We would play these kinds of war games, trying to figure out a structure that would work.[37]

They were now in a position to put their ideas into practice. With his courtly manner and soothing voice, Hudson would lead the KKR partners through intricate passages of the tax code. He laid out for Kravis in exquisitely fine detail just how Houdaille was carrying its plant, equipment, and inventories far below full market value. He was confident he could legitimately add $100 million to Houdaille's book value by *revaluing* all the assets, including intangibles. Most of Houdaille's factories had been purchased before high inflation set in. Those assets were carried on the books at very low nominal valuations. Hudson's complex calculations – which took into account everything from plant and equipment and inventories to such intellectual property as patents, drawings and other software – revealed that the resulting "step-up" in depreciable assets would enable Houdaille to reduce its likely tax bill during the first few critical years by an additional $15 million.

All this could be done only if certain technicalities in the prevailing tax laws were followed. The acquisition had to be for Houdaille's stock, not assets, which would then be followed by a liquidation of the acquired company. In this way, the purchase price would serve as the cost basis for tax purposes; the seller would not have to pay taxes on the gain created by the step-up; and the buyer could get the tax benefit from the increased depreciation. The procedure would require setting up shell corporations to arrange the borrowings and to execute Deloitte's strategy for purchase and liquidation on a tax-free basis to the exiting shareholders. This could be done, so long as the liquidation, as specified by the so-called General Utilities Doctrine, was carried out within a twelve-month period. George Anders has provided a colorful description of Henry Kravis convening a meeting of one of the shells, HH Holdings, on March 5, 1978:

What followed was out of *Alice in Wonderland*. . . . Kravis was furiously busy. He proposed eighteen resolutions – covering everything from the official corporate seal to the company's role in the Houdaille buyout. He wrote down each resolution, and approved them all, in a unanimous 1–0 vote. A few days later, Kravis did the same thing for [another of the shells] HH Acquisition.[38]

The elaborate tax strategy, along with the scale and complexity of the Houdaille financing, added to the delay in getting the deal closed. The intricacy of the transaction puzzled Houdaille's lawyers, who were deeply concerned to shield Houdaille's directors from any legal risk. The prospective transaction also invited nearly microscopic scrutiny from the SEC, which had recently raised its standards for disclosure on transactions involving public companies. The details passed muster, and Houdaille finally closed on May 4, 1979, after KKR had done all it could to satisfy the lawyers, regulators, and Houdaille shareholders with a virtual blizzard of documents. Houdaille's prospectus, which included an intricate and nearly incomprehensible diagram of all the relationships among the corporations involved in the proceedings, became a hot item in Wall Street accounting circles (see figure, pp. 72–3).

The impact of the tax savings on Houdaille was substantial, and its financing involved the kind of tax-accounting sophistication that earned Deloitte a place in KKR's durable constellation of service providers. Asset revaluation techniques, the employment of tax shelters, the use of "mirror subsidiaries," and the like, were becoming vital parts of KKR's acquisition repertoire.* Even though such tax and accounting strategies would have little impact on overall returns (high returns were expected through improved management of the assets), they could be decisive at the margin, allowing KKR to outbid other firms. But it was imperative to remain innovative if KKR were to sustain its advantage. There were "mirrors" – but no smoke, no trade secrets, no proprietary

* Mirror subsidiaries were a useful means for achieving a low-tax or tax-free acquisition of entities whose book values were low compared to their market values. In concept, mirrors worked like this: Consider that the acquisition target has some assets which the acquirer intends to spin off. Under prevailing tax law, the acquirer could organize a parent company for the acquisition, which would then set up two subsidiaries, which we shall call S1 and S2. The acquirer could then endow each subsidiary with cash, the amounts equal to the fair market value of the unwanted assets and the wanted assets respectively. S1 and S2 would then jointly buy the new company, after which, through a series of tax-free intercompany transfers, all the unwanted assets would be held by S1, and the wanted assets by S2, in direct proportion to the value of the subsidiaries created in the mirrored holding companies. Since the value of S1 was calculated for tax purposes as the cash put into it at the time it was organized, its assets could be disposed of at their anticipated higher market value without paying taxes on the difference between this value and the lower book value. Before mirrors were outlawed in 1987, this technique would help KKR reduce tax liabilities in large acquisitions such as Beatrice and Walter Industries.

techniques. Every new wrinkle in tax accounting and financial structure was transparent. Every new idea would transfer quickly to other firms, as increasingly sophisticated dealmakers jumped on the buyout bandwagon. The firm had to continue to develop new techniques to stay ahead.

Houdaille would struggle for a time. Soon after the buyout its man-

$60,000,000
Bank Revolving
Credit Agreement (1)

Three Banks

Not purchasing any Common Stock,
however, a venture capital subsidiary of the
bank holding company that owns one of
the banks will purchase 10% Senior
Cumulative Preferred Stock and Class B
Common Stock

2,350,000 shares of 10%
Senior Cumulative Preferred
Stock at $10/share
($23,500,000)

Six Institutional Investors
(mostly venture capital
subsidiaries of bank holding
companies) (4)

Also purchasing 972,400 shares of Class A
Common stock at $2.52/share, 1,716,000
shares of Class B Common stock at
$2.52/share, in addition three of such
institutional investors will purchase
841,803 shares of Class B Common Stock
at $2.52/share pursuant to separate
purchase agreements, will pay $8,896,11[...]
in the aggregate for Common Stock
constituting 32% of Common Stock, 13%
of the voting Common Stock (2) (5)

$140,000,000 principal
amount 10¾% Senior Notes
$75,000,000 principal
amount 12% Senior
Subordinated Notes

Sixteen Institutional Investors
(consisting primarily of
insurance companies)

Also receiving 1,100,000 shares of Class A
Common Stock in consideration for
making the loans but at no additional cost,
constituting 10% of the Common Stock,
15% of the voting Common Stock (2)

$31,500,000 principal
amount 12% Junior
Subordinated Notes

Ten Institutional Investors (3)

Also purchasing 1,725,593 shares of Class
A Common Stock at $2.52/share, 924,000
shares of Class B Common Stock at
$2.52/share, will pay $6,676,974 in the
aggregate for Common Stock, constituting
24% of the Common Stock, 23% of the
voting Common Stock (2)

---

(1) Houdaille will also have available to it $15,000,000 in Bank Lines of Credit after the Merger.
(2) The shares of Common Stock shown under these three captions in the aggregate equal the amounts shown under the cap[...]
    "Twenty-three Institutional Investors."
(3) Of such ten institutional investors, eight are also purchasing Senior and Senior Subordinated Notes and two are affiliates of b[...]
    holding companies acting for their own account or in a fiduciary capacity.
(4) Of such six institutional investors, one will purchase Junior Subordinated Notes, an affiliate of one will purchase Senior and Se[...]
    Subordinated Notes, and an affiliate of another will purchase Junior Subordinated Notes for trusts administered by it.
(5) In circumstances relating to a failure by Holdings to pay dividends or make certain mandatory redemptions, such purchasers [...]
    also be entitled to receive warrants to purchase up to 1,000,000 additional shares of Class B Common Stock at $2.52 per s[...]
    (subject to certain adjustments).

THE FINANCING

$306,500,000 in debt to be issued by Acquisition and assumed by Houdaille at the Effective Date of the Merger

$448,000 in equity to be issued by Holdings at the Effective Date of the Merger (11)

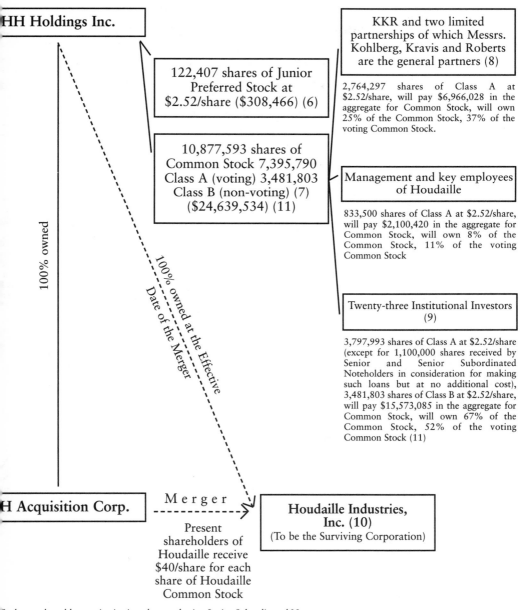

HH Holdings Inc.

100% owned

122,407 shares of Junior Preferred Stock at $2.52/share ($308,466) (6)

10,877,593 shares of Common Stock 7,395,790 Class A (voting) 3,481,803 Class B (non-voting) (7) ($24,639,534) (11)

100% owned at the Effective Date of the Merger

KKR and two limited partnerships of which Messrs. Kohlberg, Kravis and Roberts are the general partners (8)

2,764,297 shares of Class A at $2.52/share, will pay $6,966,028 in the aggregate for Common Stock, will own 25% of the Common Stock, 37% of the voting Common Stock.

Management and key employees of Houdaille

833,500 shares of Class A at $2.52/share, will pay $2,100,420 in the aggregate for Common Stock, will own 8% of the Common Stock, 11% of the voting Common Stock

Twenty-three Institutional Investors (9)

3,797,993 shares of Class A at $2.52/share (except for 1,100,000 shares received by Senior and Senior Subordinated Noteholders in consideration for making such loans but at no additional cost), 3,481,803 shares of Class B at $2.52/share, will pay $15,573,085 in the aggregate for Common Stock, will own 67% of the Common Stock, 52% of the voting Common Stock (11)

H Acquisition Corp.

Merger

Present shareholders of Houdaille receive $40/share for each share of Houdaille Common Stock

Houdaille Industries, Inc. (10)
(To be the Surviving Corporation)

To be purchased by one institution also purchasing Junior Subordinated Notes.

Class B Common Stock will be exchangeable, subject to certain restrictions relating to the regulatory status of the holder, into Class A.

See "Information Concerning KKR, Holdings and Acquisition" for certain fees to be paid to KKR by Holdings and Houdaille.

The institutions purchasing or receiving Common Stock are also purchasing Senior and Senior Subordinated Notes, Junior Subordinated Notes, 10% Senior Cumulative Preferred Stock, or a combination of such securities, in the amounts indicated elsewhere in the table.

Book value per common share $20.18 on December 31, 1978.

Amounts shown do not reflect the accounting treatment of the 1,100,000 shares of Common Stock to be issued to the Senior and Senior Subordinated Noteholders in consideration for making loans to Acquisition. See "Capitalization."

agement cut costs and improved cash flows, in part by selling off underperforming assets, and its operating profits rose through 1981, when the roof fell in on the machine tool business.[39] The company reeled and almost went under, but recovered by 1984 when it acquired the Warren Rupp Company, an industrial pump manufacturer. That year, KKR arranged a recapitalization of Houdaille, which allowed impatient investors to cash out while increasing KKR's and management's percentage ownership in the firm. Soon after Houdaille's restructuring, the British holding company TI Industries made an offer for the company. What TI coveted was John Crane, a large and successful Houdaille subsidiary that made packing seals.[40] KKR thus exited, having realized for its 1979 Fund a 33.9 percent annual return on the deal. But the story was not over: TI was quite satisfied to have netted its prize, and within weeks of the transaction it agreed to sell the rest of Houdaille back to KKR. It became the basis for a new corporation, Idex. KKR invested $7.3 million in Idex at $0.06 per common share, which traded in 1997 at around $40 per share.

The Houdaille deal had long since transformed the market for leveraged buyouts. When Houdaille's prospects for a takeover were trumpeted in the *New York Times* in July 1978, its shares, which had been trading in the $20–$25 range for about three months, moved up to more than $30 before plunging to less than $21 in October 1978. After KKR announced its $40 bid in late October, the stock moved up to only around $36 in late February 1978, so skeptical were arbitrageurs that the deal would close at the announced price. At no time before KKR closed the transaction did Houdaille's market value reflect KKR's confidence in its bid for the company (see figure). That would not happen again.

Houdaille's successful financing attracted a horde of new institutions into providing financing for leveraged deals, as an increasing number of corporations presented themselves or their subsidiaries as candidates for leveraged buyouts. In 1981 – a year in which KKR did six deals – just short of 100 buyouts were recorded nationwide, despite double-digit inflation and soaring interest rates. In the recession year of 1982 the overall number swelled to 164. Then, after former Treasury Secretary William Simon's firm, Wesray, parlayed a $1 million LBO equity investment in Gibson Greeting Cards into $70 million over a sixteen-month span, even more would-be buyout specialists entered the arena. By the end of 1983, 230 buyouts had

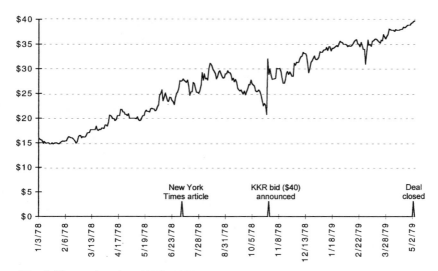

Houdaille stock price, 1978–1979.

closed in the United States, amounting to $4.5 billion in total financing. From then until the first great buyout wave came to an end in 1990, the average annual number of leveraged buyouts rose to more than 300 per year. Throughout the period, KKR focused its efforts on relatively few, but large, transactions.[41]

The increase in buyouts was attended by an increase in competition, especially for the higher-quality prospects. In time, even mainstream investment-banking houses like Morgan Stanley, trading firms like Salomon Brothers, and brokerage giants like Merrill Lynch organized their own buyout departments. As volume increased, however, so did the temptation to make riskier investments. KKR would have to maintain its discipline, just as it would have to continue innovating, if only to be able to offer competitive prices under conditions that would reasonably assure that debt financing could be repaid.

Fashioning the Debt Constraint

Throughout the 1980s KKR was the leader, in both the scale and variety of its investments, of what would become a virtual industry in leveraged buyouts. Flexibility remained the key to its continuing success in dealmaking. Each company KKR decided to pursue (out of the scores screened by its growing staff of professionals) presented a different set of opportunities and problems. It was never enough to ascertain that the company's stock was undervalued; it was important to form a clear picture of where and how value could be unlocked. James Greene, who joined the firm in 1986, learned just how specific each buyout transaction was, and just how much had to be settled in the minds of everyone concerned before the financing took place.

> It was a matter of understanding at the outset, before we bought anything, what the company's objectives were, how its management thought it was going to attain those objectives, what kind of capital they needed to spend, what kind of investment in R&D, people, equipment, software, and so on. Then we structured the balance sheet and leveraged the company appropriately . . . [42]

With that kind of preparation, KKR could design organizational and capital structures uniquely appropriate to both the existing and the projected longer-term circumstances. In some cases the circumstances required an acute understanding of the best means by which to increase value in assets. In others, they called for creative approaches to financing for acquisitions that might not otherwise be feasible. In all cases, it was crucial to structure both the leverage and the equity in the transaction in order to focus managerial efforts on maximizing strategic and operating efficiencies.

A basic precept of the leveraged buyout is that value creation does not necessarily come from growth. Norris Industries, a $420 million financing that closed in December 1981, was an early example of how leverage could help improve value in a company, even as assets decreased. Norris was a good company to begin with – well managed and well endowed with strong products. Before its buyout by KKR, many product lines in Norris's array of businesses in automotive components, building products, military ordnance, and home appliances had been battered by cyclical downturns in their markets. The nearly 88 percent leverage in its buyout capital structure anticipated a reversal of those cycles, and was based on the assumption that the company's management would continue to perform well enough to cover debt service. Jack Meany, the company's CEO, reduced capital expenditures, sold off his weakest operations, and offered 6 million shares of common stock to the public, using much of the proceeds to help retire debt.[43] As it turned out, good fortune in the economy lifted sales, and the debt was paid down much more rapidly than expected.

In just two years Norris cut its debt by more than half, while eliminating all the nearly $40 million worth of subordinated debt on its balance sheet. In the last quarter of 1984 KKR arranged for the sale of Norris to Masco Industries for $460 million plus the assumption of debt, on a book value of assets that in the intervening five years had declined from $560 million to $491 million. The equity value, however, had soared. KKR realized a better than 85 percent annual return on its original investment.

Financial structures could be tailored in highly precise ways to encourage specific managerial reforms. Consider the case of Fred Meyer, Inc., which operated 65 retail stores, mostly in the Pacific Northwest. It sold a wide range of general merchandise and food items and operated a dairy, bakery, photo finishing plant, pharmaceutical plant, and a central kitchen to process products sold primarily through its stores. Fred Meyer required $533 million in financing, which was effected by acquiring the company's real estate holdings in a partnership separate from the one established to purchase the retail operations. This division of assets enabled two new entities, each with different financial characteristics and prospects, to shoulder the debt burden more effectively. The acquisition prices totaled $304 million for Fred Meyer Real Estate Properties Ltd., and $229 million for the Fred Meyer Acquisitions Corporation (the retail operations).

It was George Roberts who had proposed raising money for the Fred Meyer buyout by splitting the company into two separately financed entities, after ascertaining that the undervalued part of the company consisted primarily of its real estate, including the land under many of its stores. Many of the stores had been leased under fixed terms that were below their current market values. If the real estate assets and leases were revalued upward to reflect true market rates, then the real estate partnership could finance a large portion of the total acquisition price. Then, if necessary, real estate could be sold to raise more cash.[44] By renegotiating the real estate leases with the operating company to reflect market rates, KKR eliminated previously hidden cross subsidies that the retail operations had been enjoying. This, in turn, changed the way the managers of the operating company behaved. Seeking better use of the assets, they shifted their priorities, curtailed spending on expansion, closed some stores, and focused on improving the profitability of existing properties. The two-pronged financial strategy thus prompted precise changes in behavior required to make the buyout more successful than it would have been with less creative financing.[45]

Just how a financial structure could be crafted to make an otherwise impractical deal worthwhile is evident in KKR's buyout of Union Texas Petroleum (UTP), the firm's first joint venture. UTP produced oil, natural gas, and hydrocarbon products, and was owned by the Allied-Signal Corporation. In 1983, at an institutional investors conference, Allied's CEO Edward Hennessey approached George Roberts and Henry Kravis about putting UTP up for sale. KKR won the opportunity to acquire the business with a proposal that was priced nominally less than a competing offer, but that was structured to provide greater tax benefits to the seller. As the parties negotiated it became clear to KKR that the volatility of the oil markets (oil was selling at around $35 a barrel in 1984) made the deal too risky to finance as an ordinary LBO. By partnering with Allied, KKR could reduce its risks, not simply by cutting its investment but also by cushioning its position, in this case by half. For its part, Allied wished to participate in what might be a substantial improvement in UTP's value.

In the ensuing recapitalization, UTP took on about $1.2 billion in debt, the proceeds of which were then distributed to Allied-Signal. UTP also issued $300 million in preferred stock to Allied-Signal. Then KKR and Allied each invested $250 million in common equity in the joint venture. (UTP's management bought an additional $4 million in equity.) The terms of the investment were structured so that KKR could further minimize its market risk. Under the joint purchasing agreement, Allied's preferred stock would lapse if returns to KKR investors fell short of a 28 percent annual return over five years. In addition, the agreement provided a way for cash flows to remain relatively stable, even if oil prices declined sharply. Allied agreed to an additional investment in UTP of up to $200 million in exchange for more preferred stock, should UTP's cash flows fall below targeted levels. The agreement turned out to be prophetic: within nine months of the closing of the transaction in July 1985, oil prices plunged to $10 per barrel. The very terms under which the acquisition had been structured thereby ensured that under suddenly adverse market conditions, UTP's management still had access to enough cash to cope with its debt burden.[46]

By the mid-1980s the leveraged buyout, originally aimed at making good companies better, was becoming a tool for turning troubled companies around. KKR's acquisitions began to include companies whose undervaluation did not result from prior circumstances or suboptimal operating disciplines, but from more fundamental mismanagement – bad strategies and outmoded structures. This was certainly true in the case of the largest corporations for which KKR mustered buyout financing. Indeed, the two largest LBOs of the 1980s – Beatrice Companies in 1986, and RJR Nabisco three years later – departed from this and other traditional buyout models. Neither Beatrice nor RJR Nabisco depended upon the cooperation of incumbent CEOs, and both relied heavily on a new source of debt financing: the subinvestment-grade, high-yield securities commonly known as "junk bonds."

Scaling Up

The scale-up of KKR's business was determined in part by the firm's evolving relationships with debt and equity investors. As the 1980s progressed, KKR raised progressively larger equity pools and remained ever alert to alternative ways of leveraging deals, as bigger companies became candidates for buyouts. As confidence grew in the efficacy of leveraged buyouts, it became easier to bring institutional investors into the fold. The 1984 acquisition of Wometco – an unwieldy conglomeration of broadcast and cable television stations, Coca-Cola bottlers, food service companies, movie theaters, amusement parks, and real estate – was the first billion-dollar buyout. With the advent of junk-bond financing, it became possible to source even more layers of unsecured debt to increase the funding of transactions once considered impossible. The 1988 buyout of RJR Nabisco required an astonishing $31.4 billion in financing, and could not have occurred without years of intervening experience and accumulated good will.

From 1980 onward, KKR devoted increasing internal resources to raising new and larger equity pools. In 1982, the firm attracted an important new class of investor: the pension fund. The firm's leveraged buyouts had achieved enough respectability to become an outlet for the small percentage of conservative money-fund managers interested in "alternative investing." The first of the pension funds to participate was the Oregon Public Employees' Retirement System (OPERS), whose head Roger Meier had been wooed by George Roberts during KKR's acquisition of Fred Meyer. (Oregon was among an increasing number of states lifting prohibitions on pension fund equity investing, prohibitions that had restricted those funds' ability to earn market rates of return.) OPERS committed $178 million for the acquisition, despite sharp criticism from the state treasurer's office and other political quarters; other pension fund managers took note. When KKR assembled a $316 million equity fund in 1982, the pension funds of the states of Washington and Michigan signed up.[47] Also signing up was Harvard University's endowment fund, which helped to attract other educational institution fiduciaries. Successive KKR funds in 1984, 1986, and 1987 included more and more varied institutional investors, including public and private (corporate) pension funds, banks, and insurance companies. The 1987 Fund also attracted seven foreign banks – five of which were Japanese – along with a Japanese insurance company. At each turn, KKR's success attracted larger pools of equity, which in turn increased the firm's ability to raise debt, which then enabled the firm to craft even larger and more finely elaborated financial structures.

In debt financing, there were two major institutional developments. In the early 1980s, it appeared that KKR would lose some of its flexibility in structuring buyouts as the insurance companies, believing themselves indispensable in the placement of subordinated debt, began to demand higher fees and more equity as the price of their participation. As part of the May 1981 financing of Marley Company, a water systems manufacturer, KKR had to offer the insurance company participants most of the equity. After that, KKR turned increasingly to bankers, who had come to know the firm well enough that it could avoid so heavy a reliance on the insurance companies. The 80 percent leveraged acquisition of Lily-Tulip, a paper and plastic container company bought in 1981, was closed without any insurance company participation at all.[48] Continental Illinois and Bankers Trust provided the bulk of the $120 million debt financing for Lily-Tulip. (In the far larger Houdaille deal, banks had put up only $60 million.) For the next three years, KKR structured nine acquisitions that would rely principally on banks for debt financing, enabling its fund participants and partners to retain most of the equity. An ancillary consequence was that the leverage ratios of KKR's buyouts dropped significantly; they would not rise consistently above 80 percent until 1986 (see figure).

That circumstance would change radically with the application of

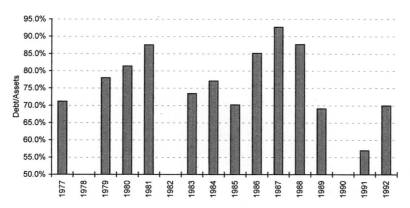

Average leverage ratios for KKR buyouts, 1977–1992.

high-yield bonds to buyout financing. It was in September 1984 that KKR first tapped this relatively novel source of debt with the help of Drexel Burnham Lambert and its brilliant bond specialist, Michael Milken. Cole National Corporation was a diversified retailer, selling optical wear, cookies and breads, gifts, knickknacks, and toys. Drexel had first pursued a relationship with KKR in 1981, but the KKR partners had harbored doubts as to Drexel's ability to place large amounts of subordinated debt quickly and reliably. By 1984 the time seemed right for a trial. Drexel seemed able to raise the money, to do it without a lot of covenants, and to do it quickly. It was not inexpensive – "they charged a lot to raise the money," said Paul Raether, who led the Cole National buyout, "but it was available." At $330 million, the deal seemed manageable enough to make it worth a trial.

Before Jeffrey Cole, the company's CEO, traveled to Milken's office in Beverly Hills to make his presentation, KKR had prepared him carefully for a grueling critique from Drexel's buyers. He could expect, he was told, a rigorous meeting with a half-dozen or so people, including analysts armed with lists of pro forma questions. The first meeting took place before just one of Drexel's more reliable buyers of high-yield securities, Fred Carr of Executive Life. As the story goes, five minutes into Cole's well-honed exposition, Carr stopped him cold, saying, "I don't want to hear anymore. I know your presentation is canned. I'm sure it's going to be wonderful. Why don't you just sit down in the chair, and let me start asking questions." After fifteen minutes of spontaneous discussion, Carr declared himself ready to invest.[49] No such meeting would have been conceivable with the likes of TIAA, Prudential, or Northwestern Mutual. KKR had just stepped into a remarkably unbureaucratic universe of debt financing: Michael Milken's network.

The Cole National transaction set a pattern for future buyouts in which KKR would call upon Drexel to help with the financing. It took time for KKR to get used to Drexel's informality and become convinced of its reliability. In 1985, when a recently recruited KKR associate, Saul Fox, ran into resistance in the mezzanine-level debt markets in his attempt to finance a buyout of the underdeveloped Motel 6 hotel chain, he wanted to turn to Drexel. He was sharply dressed down by George Roberts, who was skeptical of Drexel's ability to place the proposed high-yield securities. In the end, Fox was given leeway to proceed and raised $132 million in senior and junior subordinated "junk" debt, as part of more than $330 million in financing.

Drexel's money became a key element [Fox maintained]. If we didn't do it this way, we'd have had to pay a lot more and have had to rely on a much more complex, unwieldy structure, relying on insurance companies. We would have been so bound up with covenants that we never would have been able to do all the things we did at Motel 6.[50]

Jerry Kohlberg later said that the price for Motel 6 may have been too high.[51] The deal involved a more serious turnaround than anticipated when revelations that some of the chain's executives had been engaged in systematic fraud required KKR to overhaul the company's top management and involve itself more than usual in day-to-day decisions.[52] But the junk bonds had given KKR a flexible base from which it could proceed with aggressive new building and facilities upgrading, which were essential to the ultimate success of the investment. In the first year after its buyout, Motel 6 built twenty-two new motels, tapping funds from a financing subsidiary that KKR organized for the purpose. Capitalized with seed equity of $25 million and $60 million of revolving construction loans (secured bank debt), the subsidiary operated on a "credit card" principle. As KKR took out mortgage loans on the new properties, it repaid the bank debt with the proceeds, thereby replenishing the revolving loan, as Motel 6 continued to build. Capital improvements were likewise financed so that Motel 6 did not have to pay down its net debt as it kept building.[53]

In 1986, KKR converted Motel 6 into a nontaxable master limited partnership along the lines normally employed for tax shelters in the natural resource industries. Such partnerships avoided the double taxation of dividend distributions, and could issue units for new investment on advantageous terms that could be traded in the secondary markets.[54] Since Motel 6 generated healthy cash flows, this arrangement gave the company the ability to distribute cash to investors and still accelerate its expansion programs. In 1990, a run-up in lodging valuations offered a timely opportunity to sell the much larger and vastly improved chain. Motel 6 was sold for $2.5 billion, a 37.9 percent annual equity return.

Throughout the second half of the decade, junk bonds became a staple of KKR buyouts. The firm's relationship with Drexel proved helpful in its ability to win and leverage such large transactions as Storer Communications ($2.4 billion), Beatrice ($8.7 billion), Owens-Illinois ($4.7 billion), and others. By 1989 Drexel's "highly confident letter,"* though not a guarantee, had become virtual assurance to the markets that the debt for any transaction in which it participated would be placed.

With Beatrice and RJR Nabisco, the leveraged buyout penetrated the lofty parapets of big business. Beatrice Companies, Inc., was the twenty-sixth largest company on the Fortune 500 list in October 1985, when KKR announced a bid for what would be by far the largest buyout in history. The century-old diversified food, consumer, and industrial goods conglomerate had grown far beyond its original dairy business, largely through a series of well-executed small-company acquisitions beginning in the early 1950s. In 1975, *Dun's Review* named Beatrice one of the five best-managed corporations in America. A decade later it was a mess. Following the retirement of the architect of its diversification strategy in 1976, a series of boardroom brawls, along with a disastrous change in strat-

> * In 1985, Drexel Burnham Lambert's Michael Milken began the practice of issuing assurances (just short of hard contractual commitments) that he would be able to raise the "junk-bond" financing necessary to close a merger or acquisition transaction. These assurances took the form of "highly confident letters." "The pronouncement would seem, for a time, almost talismanic in its power," wrote Connie Bruck in her biography of Milken. "One after another, multibillion-dollar tender offers were launched on the power of . . . two words uttered by Drexel. It became an article of faith for Milken that once he said he was 'highly confident' that he could raise a given amount of financing for a bid, he would never renege or cut back on the terms." *The Predators' Ball* (New York: Simon and Schuster, 1988), p. 166.

egy, significantly weakened the performance and reputation of Beatrice. In 1979, a new CEO, James Dutt, went on an acquisition binge, buying large public companies for which the "fit" was dubious. The ill effects of his misconceived strategy were exacerbated by inappropriate organization. Attempts to centralize administration set the scene for a disastrous attempt to centralize marketing programs, as well.[55]

Early in 1983 Donald Kelley of the Chicago-based conglomerate Esmark made a run at Beatrice. It came to naught (Beatrice bought back Esmark's shares at a premium), but the episode reportedly irked Beatrice's CEO. When Kelley proposed in May 1984 to do a leveraged buyout of Esmark with KKR, Beatrice overbid KKR and bought Esmark for $2.8 billion. This marked the beginning of the end for James Dutt, who was widely criticized for the price paid for Esmark. Dutt's notorious autocratic management style did not help matters either. Top management turnover during his tenure had been brisk, and in the summer of 1985 Dutt's own demoralized management team went to the Beatrice board to demand his head. In a specially called meeting on Saturday, August 3, James Dutt was forced out, to be replaced by board member William Granger, who was himself a retired Beatrice manager.

When the markets opened the next Monday morning, Beatrice's stock price shot up by 7 percent to $32.25. Lying in wait, KKR crafted a proposal to acquire Beatrice in September. Since management had not requested that KKR make an offer, a letter was sent to the Beatrice board offering $45 per share for the company, in KKR's first use of a "bear hug" takeover strategy. The response was surprisingly swift and positive. Still, KKR had never put together a buyout proposal without top management's participation. Fortunately, the firm was able to tap Don Kelley, the former Esmark chairman, to help with its bid for Beatrice. This proved a major advantage for KKR, as Kelley and his former Esmark team, along with former Beatrice managers recruited by Kelley, knew a good deal about large segments of the business.

KKR's initial $45 offer was made up of $42 in cash and $3 in preferred stock. The Beatrice board tried to solicit other offers, but found no takers. On October 29 KKR raised its bid to $47 per share, and later to $50 per share. After some fine tuning, prompted by the revelation that Beatrice had more tax exposure than the due diligence examination had shown, KKR's offer of $40 in cash and $10 in stock was accepted in February 1986.[56] Raising financing for a leveraged buyout this size was unprecedented, and would be made more difficult by unfortunate circumstances. In addition to the approximately $6.2 billion for Beatrice common stock, KKR had to finance nearly $2 billion of Beatrice indebtedness. More than $3.5 billion in bank debt would have to be raised for the nearly $8.2 billion financing, and since KKR was between equity funds, it did not even have the $400 million in equity ready when it first made its offer.

The arduous labor it took to put together the financing – KKR partners working on the transaction recall that it was excruciatingly difficult – was almost belied by its speed. The bank loans and the equity were assembled after KKR contacted each of the fund investors and asked whether they wanted to put in additional money to participate in the Beatrice buyout. These "overcommitments," along with $50 million from Coca-Cola Company, made up the equity fund for the transaction. This fund bought 80 million shares at $5 per share, and warrants for 8 million shares, for the total investment of $402 million. Management put in an additional $7.1 million. Michael Milken so deftly arranged the mezzanine financing, placing $2.5 billion in Beatrice junk bonds,[57] that the deal closed in early March, barely two months after the Beatrice board had given KKR the green light.

With more than 95 percent leverage and a heavy overhang of bank debt, Beatrice's management had little choice but to proceed with radical pruning.[58] The entire post-buyout strategy for shrinking the headquarters, decentralizing marketing, and selling off unmanageable operations was forced by the deal's capital structure. Bank covenants demanded the sale of $1.5 billion in assets within eighteen months of the closing. More than $100 million in unnecessary overhead was also cut within a few months. As it turned out, with all of the assets sold in a series of divestitures ending in 1990, Beatrice staged the largest corporate sell-off in history. Within five years Beatrice shed numerous operations, packaged in eleven mid- to large-sized companies, five of which were structured as management buyouts.[59]

The Big Deal

Unprecedented though it was, Beatrice paled by comparison to RJR Nabisco. The story of the struggle to win the tobacco and food giant has been often told. Of interest here is the financial structuring that made the complex, two-step buyout possible. The peril in the buyout's capital structure will be discussed in Chapter 4; but the very fact that the deal happened showed that there were no longer any limits, of scale or imagination, to applying the leveraged buyout principle.

KKR first became interested in RJR Nabisco in 1986, when Henry Kravis approached its CEO, Ross Johnson, about a possible deal. Johnson rebuffed him, but the idea stuck. In late 1988, Johnson made headlines when he announced his intention to take the company private, and enlisted the investment bank Shearson Lehman to help him orchestrate a $17 billion (or $75 per share) leveraged buyout. The announcement put the company – widely considered to be poorly managed, awash in waste, and hence undervalued – in play. Less than a week after Johnson's announcement, KKR submitted a $90 per share bid, which made Johnson's initial offer smack of greed. In the month following KKR's bid, RJR Nabisco became the object of an auction between several eager potential buyers. KKR stayed in as the bidding escalated, largely because its continuing and deepening analysis showed that RJR's enormous cash flow could support substantial leverage. "RJR just generated so much cash that we felt that we would not have any problems paying the debt down," said Henry Kravis. "We saw a lot of waste that could be cut, and an enormous opportunity to reorganize the company."[60]

On November 30, 1988, the fifth and final round of bidding came to a close. KKR's bid of $109 per share was nominally lower than Shearson's $112 per share. But RJR Nabisco's financial advisors and board decided that KKR's proposed financing structure, which included $6 billion of high-yield securities, had a much greater likelihood of bringing investors 100 cents on the dollar than Shearson's proposal. KKR's final offer also came with "intangibles" that the company's board thought would benefit equity holders and employees. Not the least of these intangibles was the growing publicity surrounding Ross Johnson's past disregard of shareholder welfare. His excessive management perks appeared greedy, if not symptomatic of a more fundamental and widespread misallocation of corporate assets.[61]

KKR's winning bid (in this case KKR led a syndicate that included Merrill Lynch, Morgan Stanley, and Drexel Burnham) of $109 per share broke down into three large categories for RJR Nabisco shareholders. The offer for each outstanding share of stock, on a blended basis, consisted of $81 in cash, $18 in PIK (pay-in-kind) preferred stock, and $10 (with an $8 face amount) in PIK converting debentures.[62] The shareholders would carry off a premium of more than 90 percent[63] over the pre-buyout value of their equity.[64] KKR would also assume the company's debt of some $5.2 billion. The buyout was accomplished in stages, in a finely elaborated series of moves.

The first stage, a tender offer for 74 percent of the company's outstanding equity, was consummated on February 9, 1989, through a hierarchy of entities set up for the transaction. The funds for the tender came from numerous partners in KKR's equity pool; from leading banks the firm had dealt with in previous transactions; and from new participants around the world, including Japanese, Canadian, and European banks. Other sources of revenue included a $1.5 billion equity investment by the KKR equity fund, $5 billion in "increasing-rate notes," and $500 million in debt securities issued by KKR to a common stock partnership organized by the firm for the buyout.

The second stage, in April, was the financing of a merger to complete the acquisition for approximately $24.8 billion in cash and securities.[65] KKR paid off the short-term credit facilities for the tender offer, reducing much of the expensive senior debt used for the purchase of RJR Nabisco stock by substituting less costly short-term bank loans that were to be paid off quickly, by 1991.[66] Most of the increasing-rate notes were redeemed with a variety of longer-term subordinated debentures and common stock warrants, known in the aggregate as the "permanent debt securities."

The so-called permanent debt securities comprised a formidable mix of high-yield instruments, which were key to getting the deal done. The sheer variety of junk bonds for the transaction seemed tailored to fit every conceivable preference of junk-bond investors. Four billion dollars' worth of the increasing-rate notes were redeemed (the remainder would be redeemed in 1990) through the cash proceeds from private placements of five distinct types of junk bonds along with warrants that would amount to 14 percent of fully diluted equity.[67] When the dust settled, KKR had provided RJR Nabisco's new senior management team with a 6 percent share of the company's stock, as well.

In effecting the world's largest buyout, KKR had been forced to go to the limit in making its bid, and the anticipated cash flows were expected barely to cover the cost of debt service. Moreover, in pursuing the company KKR had necessarily deviated from its traditional practice of trying to work with existing management. Ross Johnson was not only the competition in this instance, he and his management team were the core of the problem that made RJR Nabisco so ripe for a takeover. KKR would have to replace most members of a weak team of managers with new blood.

KKR harbored no preconception as to whether RJR Nabisco would become a larger or smaller company. The Nabisco division chief, John Greeniaus, had identified several underperforming food brands for which the parent company could expect attractive prices. Proceeds from such sales would immediately be applied to debt reduction. The broader managerial mandate for the first few years was conceived more simply as the unglamorous business of "blocking and tackling" – improving the company's overall financial performance by making operations more efficient, division by division, department by department, employee by employee.[68]

Thus the new RJR Nabisco CEO, Louis Gerstner, arrived to find a plan that was already embedded in the financial structure. It was not a plan he had helped devise, but he bought into it (literally) with the purchase of a large block of stock and the pledge of a multiyear commitment. KKR had anticipated that the company would continue to develop new product lines in its food business, while also expanding its international tobacco business. The initial emphasis of post-buyout activity, however, would be on cost reduction, made all the more urgent by the sheer weight of the debt, which included a heavy dose of bank loans that demanded rapid repayment. Once the initial round of divestitures and cost reductions was completed, Gerstner would have to devote his energies to the more systematic tasks of achieving higher productivity and lower overhead through continuous improvements in day-to-day operations. In this basic respect – that the leverage in buyout was intended in large part to re-direct management priorities – RJR Nabisco was typical of the KKR buyout.

The Importance of the Debt Constraint

The shock waves that RJR Nabisco sent throughout corporate America prompted new debates about how much debt financing the corporate world could stand; yet there was no doubt that in all but a very few cases, leveraged management buyouts had worked significantly to improve the performance of assets. In crafting the leverage for each buyout, KKR relied upon a mélange of tax, cash flow, financing, and management incentive considerations. Taken together, they amounted to a major innovation in the financing and management of modern corporate organizations.

In each buyout, form followed function. The capital structure at the closing was based on a detailed understanding of the company's *potential* for higher cash flows. At that moment, everyone – the firm, the equity partners, and CEOs alike – had literally "bought into" a basic debt-driven strategy and objectives for the first two or three years. The incontrovertible debt covenants between the company and the lenders *required* improvements in performance and economic efficiency in order to work. Repayment contracts would *force* the managers of the bought-out company to adhere to strict, results-oriented budgeting. The deal's projections thus became imperatives, and virtually locked in the budgets at every level of operation.

Though the imperatives were clear, results were never predetermined. As we shall see, post-acquisition management was not simply a machine put in motion by the constraints embedded in the leverage. The ultimate success of every buyout investment was contingent on a set of dynamic, human factors, chief among them the relationship between the KKR board of directors and the company's chief executive. As principals in the investments they made, the KKR partners had every incentive to stay engaged. As general partners of equity funds, moreover, they bore a fiduciary responsibility to all equity investors. And as repeat players in the market for debt, they had powerful reasons to look to the interests of the debtholders as well. In other words, the same KKR partners who became famous for their ability to assemble and finance complicated deals within weeks, looked forward to years of uncelebrated work: monitoring, advising, and possibly even restructuring the companies for which they were responsible.

For at the consummation of every deal, after KKR – along with a battery of lawyers, accountants, investment bankers, and others – collected their fees, the real money was yet to be made.[69] A financing in and of itself was of no good consequence if KKR's judgment of a company's prospects proved to be mistaken, if the leverage proved too costly, or if unforeseen events undermined the best-laid plans. Thus, even as Henry Kravis grew accustomed to the showers of attention at the close of every KKR acquisition, he remained cautious. He liked to put it this way: *"Don't congratulate me when we buy it. Congratulate me when we sell it."*[70]

3 | Redefining Value in Owner-Managed Corporations

"When the deal is closed, the work begins."
– Paul Raether, KKR partner

A s THE BUYOUT MOVEMENT gained momentum, the public response was anything but friendly. "The perception," said Robert Kidder, the CEO of Duracell, "is that buyout specialists are robber barons, that they come into a company, cut it to the bone, and then strip it of its vitality just to make money in the short term."[1] How else could it be? Leverage a company up to the hilt, and one had little choice but to sell off assets, cut jobs, and then run the remains into the ground. This kind of criticism reached a crescendo in the press and the halls of Congress toward the end of the 1980s, and KKR found itself right in the middle of the controversy. Stung by charges that they were plundering assets, KKR partners wondered how their intentions and track record could be so misconstrued.

To Michael Tokarz, the criticism defied common sense. Imagine, he said employing an analogy favored by KKR partners,

that like any other American, we go driving down the street looking at all the pretty houses. We see a house and we like it, so we pay the owner a premium price. *Like every other American, we borrow money to do it.* The average American puts down maybe 10–20 percent to buy a house – a highly leveraged transaction. We do the same thing. So now that we own this house, what do we do? We don't fix leaks? We don't paint it? We sell the garage? We let the whole thing go to the dogs? And yet somehow, after a number of years, we sell this house for a compound rate of return of 40 percent to the next guy? *How does that work?*[2]

In 1988, when Tokarz, Henry Kravis, and George Roberts traveled to Washington to meet with congressional leaders and other government officials, they were confronted in one conference by Senator Lloyd Bentsen, who reportedly tossed a prepared KKR study into a trash can. Bentsen was hardly KKR's worst adversary. Some of the lawmakers present simply could not believe that KKR was doing any more than buying up good companies, overburdening them with debt, firing the workers, and then milking what was left. They had read the newspapers, after all. There was fresh news about layoffs at Safeway in Dallas, a 1986 KKR acquisition. Safeway's problems – and there were many – had come to represent the serious disruptions that could befall ordinary citizens as a consequence of corporate restructuring.

Trouble in Dallas

On May 16, 1990, *The Wall Street Journal* ran a searing exposé of events at Safeway Stores, Inc., nearly four years after its KKR-engineered buyout. The Safeway buyout was certainly good news for shareholders. KKR and Safeway's CEO, Peter Magowan, had just launched a successful initial public offering of 10 percent of the company's shares for more than four and a half times the value of their original equity investment (in what had been a more than $4.7 billion, 94-percent-leveraged transaction!). For the employees and other stakeholders in the supermarket chain, however, it was another, sadder story. The article's author, Susan Faludi, painted a vivid story of shareholder greed, corporate betrayal, and human suffering. The story – "The Reckoning"[3] – won a Pulitzer Prize, was reprinted widely, and even became a staple in business school courses as a lesson in what happens when ruthless efficiency overwhelms fairness, when indebtedness forces short-term profit-seeking at the expense of longer-term investment and job security. Focused as it was on the most familiar of industries, Safeway's buyout experience squared perfectly with a widespread public perception of all that was wrong with Wall Street, and came to stand for the real or imagined ill effects of corporate downsizing.

As Faludi told it, Peter Magowan had a fine track record as a good employer. His father had preceded him as head of Safeway, and he had always regarded the business as a kind of family responsibility. He had promised his mother before the KKR buyout that no one would be hurt by it.[4] Yet no sooner had the ink dried on the closing documents than the "downsizing" of Safeway began. Within three years some "63,000 managers and workers were cut loose . . .

through store sales or layoffs." While most of the laid-off workers "were re-employed by their new store owners, this was largely at lower wages," and "many thousands . . . wound up either unemployed or forced into the part-time work force." The human suffering caused by the layoffs ranged from feelings of anguished betrayal to stress-related heart attacks and even suicides. Those who survived the cuts were finding life hard in the "leaner and meaner" Safeway. "[H]ardball labor policies and high pressure quota systems" became a new way of life in a company once "legendary for job security and fairness." The "new esprit de corps trumpeted in the investment suite emphasizing efficiency and productivity" wrought havoc from the stockrooms to the shopping aisles, as the searing pressure of "KKR-inspired quotas" worked its way down the hierarchy of personnel from the district manager's office to the local checkout counter. No longer protected by traditional shop rules, Safeway's workers were shouldering too many jobs, working too many hours, and generally suffering from "burnout." If that were not bad enough, the closure or sale of about 1,000 out of Safeway's 2,400 stores in Texas, California, and other Western states where Safeway did most of its business had even wider ripple effects in local communities. In Dallas, secondary layoffs reverberated through Safeway-dependent food and beverage vendors and construction contractors, and the North Texas Food Bank was reported to have lost its 600,000 pounds of annual food donations.

This vivid tableau of misery was thrown into high relief by the short list of beneficiaries of Safeway's post-buyout restructuring – a Wall Street crowd all too familiar in the business press of the 1980s. The Dart Group's Herbert Haft family, notorious serial greenmailers,* mounted an unfriendly raid in June 1986, just at the time KKR was making overtures of its own to a reluctant Peter Magowan.[5] The Hafts would reap $100 million by selling out their accumulated shares to KKR in its successful bid to re-

* "Greenmail," more politely referred to as "targeted share repurchases," is a form of takeover defense. In order to ward off a hostile bid, or otherwise rid itself of an unwanted large shareholder, a company may agree to buy the shareholder's stock at a premium above the prevailing market price. Because the price paid by the company to the greenmailer is not offered to all shareholders, the technique is controversial, though not illegal.

organize the company, and would later pocket another $59 million for options they had been granted in the buyout. Then there was

Magowan, who with other top executives and directors of Safeway received $28 million for their stakes in Safeway when its buyout transaction was closed. (Those executives who remained received options to buy 10 percent of the reorganized entity at a mere $2 per share.) There were three investment banks, numerous law and accounting firms, and other advisors who pocketed about $90 million in fees for their pains. KKR charged Safeway $60 million in fees for structuring the buyout. Participating in the transaction was an elite group of equity investors comprised of giant institutions, including state pension funds, insurance companies, banks, and nonprofit organizations. The exiting shareholders, institutions, small investors, and arbitrageurs alike, had all benefited handsomely from the 82 percent run-up in Safeway's market value during the three months preceding the buyout; but, as Faludi saw it, the gains to such a small number of players had come at the expense of the many.

Moreover, she concluded, the buyout had been unnecessary. Before the raiders had forced Magowan into the arms of KKR, Safeway had already been attempting

to accomplish many of the things LBO experts advocate. It was remodeling its stores, . . . experimenting with employee productivity teams, phasing out money-losing divisions, and thinning out its workforce with a program that . . . generally relied on less painful methods like attrition.[6]

How could there be any doubt that the huge debt burden the financial engineers had piled onto Safeway had forced its management to slash costs – at all costs – so that their new masters, the KKR investors, could reap further profits? The only way to make the buyout work was to strip Safeway of assets, to defer capital investments, and to savage years of employee good will.[7]

To drive home the point, the article on Safeway was juxtaposed with a sidebar on Kroger, another underperforming supermarket chain. In 1988, Kroger had taken on massive debt in a poison-pill defense against yet another Haft raid and another "KKR-led takeover" attempt. Heavily indebted and badly in need of repair, Kroger appeared to be achieving improved performance by far less drastic means than those employed by Safeway.[8] The contrasting stories were an affecting representation of the "takeover-crazed" 1980s. The ill that could befall a company after a leveraged buyout was very bad business, indeed.

The story, of course, provided the public with a rare view of what could happen to a bought-out company *after* the deal was done. Yet, in the final analysis, it had distorted what was really at stake. Few would doubt the pain caused to people dislocated by a severe corporate restructuring, but the harsh medicine imposed on the ailing company was essential to its longer-term survival. It would have been a tricky matter to generalize from this one case. Was the buyout of Safeway, or of any other company, nothing more than a get-rich-quick scheme to enrich a few shareholders by simply stripping assets and laying off employees? The next set of equity investors did not think so, when Safeway went public in 1990 at a price more than quadruple its original buyout value. Why would the buyers of the equity have rewarded KKR, its limited partners, and Safeway's management with such a premium over their investment unless the company had become stronger, more efficient, more competitive?

KKR's partners argued that there was no virtue in sustaining people or assets in inefficient or underproductive uses.[9] Nor was it a question of simply enriching shareholders at the expense of others. Safeway's managers were obligated to serve shareholder interests; it could be no other way. On the other hand, the notion that had become popular in many financial quarters – that a manager's *only* obligation was to the owners of capital – was an argument that many KKR partners found academic. Again Tokarz:

We don't subscribe to that doctrine. The corporation has obligations to all of its constituencies – suppliers, customers, employees, retirees, existing management, existing labor, the community, and of course, shareholders. Now, who takes priority? Well, you can make arguments for anybody at any given point in time. We simply do the following: we make as many people in the company shareholders as we possibly can. If managers are really thinking of the shareholders' best interests – including their own – they will properly balance the concerns of all the constituencies relevant to the company. If one constituency's interests gets seriously out of balance, the company will suffer; the shareholders will suffer; society will suffer.[10]

Aligning Owner and Management Interests

Making Safeway a better business required painstaking work on the part of both Safeway's managers and KKR's partners. Value creation was not something that just happened. It did not occur from a transfer of title. It was not the result of exotic tax accounting. Nor was it the by-product of some invisible market mechanism. It was the product of good management – good planning, good administrative systems, good operating regimens – often requiring significant reforms over a sustained period of time. Once a deal closed, therefore, both management and the new owners had their work cut out for them.

The nature of the relationship between owners and managers in a highly leveraged firm rested on a basic principle: make managers owners by making them invest a significant share of their personal wealth in the enterprises they manage, thus giving them stronger incentives to act in the best interests of all shareholders.[11] The idea of this management investment scheme was to assure that managers had enough "skin in the game" to care about their company, but not so much that they might be overly conservative. The downside had to hurt, but not too much; the upside had to be sweet. The important thing was not simply to convert managers into shareholders, but to make them *owners* in every sense of the word – "*owners of the results of their decisions*," as KKR partners liked to put it.

Thus the distribution of equity to management was the essential first step. In a typical public corporation managers held an insignificant portion of the outstanding equity of the firm they managed, in the form of stock grants or as options. Overall, in KKR buyouts from 1976 through 1989, managers' equity ownership in buyouts at the time of their closing ranged from nearly 25 percent to less than 2 percent. The size of management's stake varied with the size of the company and with the managers' personal financial circumstances. Generally, senior managers were expected to invest a significant portion of their net worth in the equity of the bought-out company, including especially any proceeds received from the sale of their pre-buyout stock. If this cash investment by the new management team failed to bring them up to a target level of ownership (generally around 5–10 percent for large transactions, as high as 25 percent for smaller ones) KKR supplemented their equity ownership with options. Options typically carried five-year vesting provisions, and managers' stock was subject to "buy-back" provisions if they left the company without what KKR considered good reason.

All this was not as simple as it sounds; managers financially invested in their corporations might still have interests that differed from those of other shareholders. (Or they might simply be incompetent to act effectively in shareholder interests.) The successful buy-out had to accomplish more than simply converting managers into owners. It had to align managers' performance with shareholder interests, not only through stock ownership, but also through such disciplines as high leverage and careful board monitoring.

At the same time, the successful buyout had to bring owners into alignment with important managerial values. In the typical management buyout, investors could expect to *maximize* their profits only over the long term. They had to be patient. The construction of a buyout partnership, both literally and figuratively, bound the interests of outside investors and managers together in a way that compelled everyone to think about the long-term viability of the business. The idea was for everyone involved to equate profitability not simply with the achievement of short-term operating improvements (desirable as they were), but also with long-term strategies for investment, innovation, and maintenance.

The buyout partnership required equity investors to "unlearn" much of the conventional wisdom, which for too long had held simple asset growth and annual earnings per share to be the most important measures of corporate success. Following its buyout, the health of a company was better measured by its efficiencies, by its ability to generate cash flow, control debt, and improve operating ratios. Profits were taken, not quarterly, not annually, but most often in capital gains at the time of the sale of equity, often years down the road. Since patience was required of investors, it was incumbent on the general partners who engineered the buyouts to educate their limited partners on the need to give managers time, while providing credible assurance that managers would be carefully watched. KKR was therefore in a pivotal position, one that required it to keep managers and passive investors alike focused on the creation of long-term value.

Ultimately, the success of a buyout depended on a set of interrelated factors that linked ownership incentives to the financial structure of the buyout, on the one hand, and to monitoring mechanisms on the other. KKR always took care to describe the leverage in the buyout as a "financial technique," but it was more than that. The leverage was inextricably linked to management performance in the post-buyout environment. If the price paid for a company were too high, the demands for debt repayment could undermine the best efforts of management to achieve long-term strategic and operating efficiencies.

At the same time, the debt imposed an ironclad budgetary discipline, compelling management to take the actions necessary to fix short-term problems. The ability of managers to operate under the "discipline of debt" demanded competencies often untested in normal corporate environments. To ensure that everything was working in timely fashion, the buyout firm exercised continuous board oversight. Indeed, as KKR explained to its fund investors, "the ongoing monitoring role [was] equally as important as the initial structuring and consummation of the transaction."[12]

"Partnership with Management"

There were new rules to the game following a management buyout, regarding both control systems (performance measurements and rewards) and the governance structure of the business (that is, the allocation of decision rights). Executive managers, like investors, had to learn to focus on unfamiliar measures, such as return on market value and free cash flow, instead of earnings per share, earnings growth, and price-earnings ratios. Those who had worked as division heads of larger corporations now had to take responsibility for managing corporate reporting, tax and treasury functions, and for internal control systems formerly beyond their purview. They also had to learn to operate more autonomously, and to take direct responsibility for strategic and policy decisions. Those executives who had presided over private companies had to learn to deal with a new set of owners, more sophisticated monitoring, and more rigorous control systems.

Managers in a post-buyout environment had no choice but to relearn their craft; their capital structure bound them to pay close attention to the debtholders whose loans had made the buyout possible. In a typical case, business plans during the first three years after the buyout had to take into account a rapid paydown of debt, especially the shorter-term senior debt, loaded as it was with irresistible regular service requirements overlaid with covenants. This imposed a stringent discipline on management, forcing executives not only to keep costs down, but also to divest any business that might fetch a price higher than the value they had placed on it. Every budget projection – from growth targets to marketing plans, to new capital outlays, to research and development, to staffing and compensation – now had to be more than the kind of loosely enforced intellectual exercise that budgeting had become in most large public corporations. The strict "discipline of debt" allowed for no slack, no surprises, no deviance. If problems lurked, candor was crucial. Under buyout conditions, management became transparent.

Since managers had to focus on the longer-term interests of the shareholders, they had to avoid the temptation to cut costs for the sake of cutting. So long as cash flow from operations and divestitures remained healthy, and stayed within the bounds of what was projected during the structuring of the buyout, there was no conflict between long-term investment and short-term debt reduction. Cut costs where appropriate; invest and build where the prospects for value creation were good. Indeed, the structure of the buyout set conditions that encouraged management to satisfy debtholders in the short run while building equity for the future.

KKR attempted to ensure this through the role its partners played as corporate directors, where owner-manager relationships were cemented. What KKR came to call its "partnership with management" was no idle phrase, no pitch designed merely to woo managers into a state of ownership. Its partnership with management was nurtured in the bidding process – when KKR discussed with the executives of target companies the entire range of issues relating to strategy, operations, and management equity participation – and was made good after the buyout through the mechanism of the buyout board.

The Buyout Board

Board monitoring under buyout conditions involved considerably more effort than what had normally passed for fiduciary oversight. On the one hand, KKR wanted to avoid the pitfalls of meddling in the managerial process; good managers demanded (and deserved) operating autonomy. The first rule for KKR directors was to respect the proposition that managers be left to manage, or, as Henry Kravis put it: "Management and KKR buy companies – they become partners, but ultimately managers make things work."[13] On the other hand, value creation under the stringency of buyout conditions required vigilance and more. The KKR-controlled board would serve as a conduit to those who could provide critical tax and legal advice, function as a critical forum for strategic ideas, take the lead in financial restructurings, and help managers provide information to fund investors and to public investors following an initial public offering. In the process, KKR partners had to labor in their capacity as board members to a degree unprecedented in contemporary corporate America.

The evolution of the KKR board dates from the Bear, Stearns buyouts of the early 1970s, when the three original partners gained experience not only in structuring buyouts but also in postacquisition restructuring, taking companies public, and finding buyers for disposable assets. During that time they became acutely aware of what they did not know. Unlike Clayton, Dubilier, which had considerable operating expertise in its general partnership, KKR partners made no pretense of being able to run companies. On the other hand, as principal owners of a leveraged business, they could not afford to be the kind of aloof "outside" directors that served as window dressing on most company boards. Nor could they rely simply on their skills as financial analysts to understand the companies they owned in any depth. To be truly effective board members – that is, to play effective roles in monitoring and advising managers – it was essential for KKR to become better informed in both industry- and company-specific activities.

That was relatively easy in the early years, when KKR focused mainly on small manufacturing companies in mature industries. In 1982, the three KKR principals defined a distinct role for its company boards, which they described as follows: to "assist each company in its acquisition program, divestiture and capital investment program, as well as advis[e] the companies as to timing and the best alternatives for obtaining additional capital or achieving liquidity for the investors."[14] After 1979 KKR had also acquired, through its association with Deloitte, Haskins & Sells, expertise in innovative tax planning, which was often the key to the effective structuring of acquisitions and divestitures.

Yet within the broader configuration of KKR's holdings, there was no common strategy that would serve all KKR companies. There was certainly no overarching headquarters bureaucracy, and no common corporate culture – all the more reason to leave managing to management. But there were considerable opportunities for transfers of learning through the financial techniques that KKR had mastered, and there was opportunity as well for the transfer of best practices in accounting and control systems. By the mid-1980s, KKR accomplished such transfers in three ways. First, it assumed responsibility for finding and hiring chief financial officers for firms where high-level skills in finance were lacking. Second, it established broad standards for gathering and reporting financial and operating data. As Michael Cook, Deloitte's CEO put it, "KKR developed an expectation of a common level of communication, a common language that could serve a supermarket in California as well as a battery manufacturer in Connecticut."[15] Finally, it provided advice on the organization and management of internal financial controls, particularly to organizations that had been bought out from larger parents.

By the mid-1980s the firm's acquisitions had branched out considerably – into construction, grocery retailing, broadcasting, hotel management, real estate, and publishing. As the KKR partners grew in number, there was opportunity to tap into more specialized expertise. Following the departure of Jerome Kohlberg in 1987, Henry Kravis and George Roberts continued to sit on each KKR-controlled company board (a practice which continues to this day). Each board was normally guided by one or two other KKR partners who either had, or were fast acquiring, specialized knowledge of particular industries. By 1990 it was possible to identify specific KKR-partner acquisition and board competencies that were transferable to newly acquired companies. Ted Ammon, for instance, acquired expertise in broadcasting and cable, Jamie Greene in retailing, Cliff Robbins and Scott Stuart in consumer products. Mike Tokarz brought with him his experience as a banker, and Saul Fox as a tax lawyer.

Ultimately, the most important function of the KKR board was the same as that for any corporate board – to hold managers to account and, when necessary, to make changes in top management. It was these essential responsibilities that most corporate boards would have found daunting, if not impossible to fulfill (that is, until desperation and the example of the buyout board showed them how). It is important to bear in mind that KKR rarely – practically never before 1988 – started out to replace managers of the companies it bought. The initial assumption was almost always that while companies could be improved, existing managers, with the proper incentives in place, should be able to do the job. The prospect of changing managers of companies after a buyout was regarded as a bad omen. With rare exceptions, KKR would not consummate a buyout unless it could at least harbor the hope that the company's current management – if not the CEO, then at least the core of the senior management team –

would stay on to operate the business. At Houdaille, for example, where a very successful longtime CEO planned to retire once the buyout closed, KKR sought to assure itself that a worthy successor was in place before going ahead with the transaction.

That it often proved to be necessary to change managers within five years after a buyout is testimony in part to the naturally high attrition rate for corporate managers, for any of various reasons, including retirement, illness, defection, or incompetence. KKR's boards had little or no control over the first three of these factors (except insofar as stock vesting plans reduced the possibility of defection), but they worked hard to control for the fourth. Still, it was hard to forecast how well managers would adjust to the changes in outlook and behavior required by the stringent discipline of leverage and the pressure to create shareholder value.

For example, PT Components (PTC), a former division of the conglomerate FMC corporation that produced power transmission equipment, was KKR's first case in which managers who had operated well under the old regime could not adapt to the new. Following its buyout in 1981, PTC was slow to adopt the necessary financial, legal, R&D, and other corporate-level staff functions that had been managed by its former parent. More alarming was the early evidence that the company's managers, while unafraid to take short-term cost-cutting measures, were unable to improve the overall efficiency of operations in the timing and flow of production. Even under the additional pressures of the 1981–82 recession, old habits in inventory stockpiling were hard to break, and costs began to spiral. Earnings before interest and taxes declined from more than $25 million in 1981 to less than $17 million for fiscal 1982 (see figure).

A little more than a year after the acquisition, KKR brought in an outsider, Ronald Morris from Tenneco, to take the helm. As Morris took over, the continuing recession led to negative earnings (although still positive EBIT) in 1983. Cost reductions and dramatic productivity improvements allowed PTC to weather the market downturn, and Morris brought the company back to profitability. In 1986, the company was sold to a group of investors led by First Chicago Investment Corporation, one of the buyout's original investors. PTC generated more than 52 percent annual compound return on its investment.

A similar fate befell Lily-Tulip, another 1981 divisional buyout (from Owens-Illinois), where KKR's initial high hopes for the com-

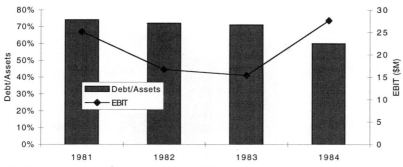

PT Components performance, 1981–1984.

pany's management were again dashed. As Jerry Kohlberg and Michael Michelson explained it, it soon became evident that CEO James Cobb would not sell the corporate airplane, would not remove redundant relatives from the payroll, and would not cut overhead costs required to make the company more profitable. KKR moved quickly to change management, bringing in the turnaround specialist Al Dunlap, who engineered an increase in Lily-Tulip's operating profits by 91 percent in 1983 and another 31 percent a year later, which enabled the company to pay down its bank debt a year ahead of schedule (see figure, p. 104). Lily-Tulip fared well. It, too, was sold in 1986, for an annually compounded return on equity of more than 57 percent.

Interestingly, the large majority of executives who survived the rigors of managing under tight debt discipline did not view KKR as impatient for results. But there inevitably came times when patience ran out, and when it did, the boards moved quickly. CEOs had to be replaced within the first year of operations in five of the thirty-six buyouts KKR made between 1977 and 1990. In addition to PT Components and Lily-Tulip, KKR replaced the top executives at Motel 6, Stop & Shop, and Marley.[16] At Storer Communications, Peter Storer, son of the company's founder and its CEO at the time of the buyout, left unexpectedly for personal reasons within six months of the acquisition.[17] In ten other companies, top management changes were anticipated at the time of the buyout transactions, generally because managers had already decided to move on or retire.

Over time, experience in responding to such (usually unforeseen) shortcomings enabled KKR to consider buying companies in which existing managers would certainly have to go, a circumstance that

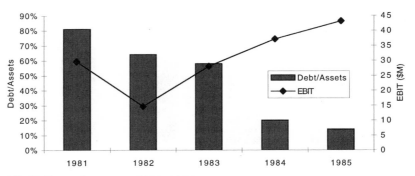

Lily-Tulip performance, 1981–1985.

was present in the firm's largest and most dramatic buyout, RJR Nabisco in 1988. By 1994, KKR had enough accumulated experience, a wide network of talent, and sufficient confidence in its board disciplines that even the prospect of acquiring such an egregiously mismanaged company as Borden, Inc. was no longer unthinkable.

By the end of the 1980s, the firm's partners had developed a seasoned perspective on their duties as board members, on the division of responsibilities between boards and managers, and on how the relationship should best be managed. The mission of the buyout board, from the first day of its control over a company to the last, was to ensure the creation of long-term value. This objective had to be managed carefully, since KKR often found itself acting as a buffer between managers with visionary goals and institutional fund investors with less-than-patient appetites. Managers had to watch their costs, but they also needed support for their business-building strategies – funds for capital investment, for research and development, for marketing. "We are long-term players," KKR partner Perry Golkin explained:

We can't manage quarter to quarter with respect to our fund investors. We often get pressured to issue monthly reports when we don't even want to do quarterly reports, because it misses the point philosophically. We still won't value the privately-held companies more than annually. If the plan is to build value over time you think about things differently; you have to be patient.[18]

KKR saw to it that managers were managing every day to make the major changes, the incremental improvements, and the investments necessary to maximize longer-term shareholder value. How managers accomplished these tasks was left to them to decide; KKR was loath to interpose its views on strategy or operating philosophy. Accordingly, serious tensions in the boardroom were rare. Interviews with KKR partners and company CEOs alike reveal little conflict. Don Boyce explained that while it was natural enough for financiers and managers to see the world differently, KKR never interfered with his management of Idex. And though Charles Perrin at Duracell recalled a couple of boardroom conflicts – one over a stock buy-back proposal (management favored it, KKR did not), another over a plan to construct a new headquarters (KKR acceded after finding a less expensive way to finance it) – such issues rarely came up. According to Scott Stuart, KKR might be more conservative than managers in post-buyout M&A activity, and disagreements might surface over changes in capital structure that could significantly alter managerial stockholdings. Otherwise, Stuart could recall no systematic biases that divided managerial from investor interests in KKR firms. "The fact that managers are so heavily invested financially in their businesses takes care of more than 90 percent of the problems," Stuart said. "The rest, we simply work through."[19]

Board governance in a KKR corporation did not rest on a quarterly or monthly meeting but was a weekly, sometimes daily, series of conversations between KKR and management. This put a heavy burden on KKR partners to become continuously active board members as well as dealmakers. In general, directors were most heavily engaged in governance during the initial three years or so after a buyout, when the debt burdens were most severe and when the opportunities for, and risks of, managerial difficulties were greatest. Afterwards, a lot depended on where a company was in accomplishing its strategic and financial goals and what kinds of problems it had encountered in doing so. Financial strategies commanded the most attention. Merger and acquisition activity would send KKR board members into high gear, as would times of legal or financial exigency. For Bob Mac-Donnell, liquidating EFB Truck Lines to forestall a bankruptcy proceeding became nearly all-consuming for several months in 1985. Mike Tokarz and Perry Golkin became similarly engrossed in the legal problems of Hillsborough Holdings (Walter Industries) following its Chapter 11 filing in 1989. The acquisition of RJR Nabisco required virtually full-time commitment from Cliff Robbins and Scott Stuart over a period of years. More recently, Stuart noted that his commitment to Borden, a relatively new turnaround situation, engaged about 30 percent of his time. He and Robbins held conversations with Borden's management almost daily. At the healthier Duracell, in which KKR owned a minority but still controlling interest, Stuart's involvement as a principal board member was closer to 5 percent of his time, his phone conversations weekly.[20]

Detailed written monthly reports sent to KKR formed the basis for ongoing discussions between CEOs and chief financial officers on the one hand, and KKR on the other. Formal board meetings were less important. (The likelihood of actually assembling all KKR board members and managers was dim at best, and so full-scale board meetings were often deferred or canceled.) There were none of the monthly or quarterly "dog-and-pony shows" that corporate managers typically staged for the benefit of outside board members, whose knowledge of the enterprise was generally superficial, whose awareness of what had gone on between meetings was minimal, and whose personal stake in the business amounted to little more than the annual meeting fees.

In sum, management decisions were to be examined, questioned, and even debated, but rarely overruled. KKR exercised a board's authority to review and help implement strategic financial decisions. It provided advice on accounting and control systems. It insisted on continuous and interactive discussions with management. It did, in short, what corporate board directors are supposed to do; but it did not dictate corporate strategic or operating decisions or meddle with their implementation. And KKR boards proved to be willing investors in management strategies. Capital expenditures, investments in research and development, and employment were generally sustained or increased over pre-buyout levels in KKR companies. Charitable contributions and community involvement were also encouraged.

Ongoing communications – candid, informal, and fluid – better enabled KKR to grasp the changing realities of its holdings while providing managers opportunities to get their ideas heard, their plans critiqued, and their strategies ultimately represented and defended to KKR's limited partners. For Duracell's Kidder, a fiercely independent manager, the KKR board process served not only as a monitoring device but as a useful consultancy. "I like to bounce ideas off of smart people," he said, and "KKR has an extremely dense population of smart people. It doesn't matter who you talk to, you get . . . well thought out answers, almost on any subject, but most certainly on those subjects where their strengths lie." Those strengths, he noted, were precisely in those financial areas that KKR reserved to itself – buying and selling businesses, arranging financial market transactions. "They have a sixth sense about IPOs . . . ; they know when the IPO market is hot. They have substantial deal making experience, and enormous clout with the banks." And yet, at the end of the day, whether the idea for a financial transaction arose from KKR or management, the modus vivendi was for the board and management to come to consensus. "Decisions aren't unilateral," said Kidder. "We're all in the same boat."[21]

Safeway Revisited

We can now reconsider the problems confronting Safeway's management in a somewhat different light. At the time of its acquisition, Safeway's problems were greater than those of most KKR buyouts. The kind of growth Safeway had achieved before its buyout was placing owners, managers, and workers alike in economic peril. The company was in danger of failing, caught in a competitive environment that called for much lower-cost, more efficient service than Safeway was providing its customers. The first order of business was to seek value through shedding assets and cutting labor costs.

It was not that Safeway's management had failed to recognize its problems. In 1981, Safeway initiated what would be a multiyear reorganization of its operations; by 1986, Safeway had reduced non-store personnel by 22 percent, consolidated divisions, and sold off poorly performing operations in the U.S. and Canada. Its earnings from 1981 through 1985 more than doubled, from $108 million to $231 million, and Safeway was first or second in virtually all its markets. Yet the chain was still not performing up to its potential, which is precisely why it was such an attractive takeover candidate. KKR's due diligence had revealed considerable room for improvement in the company's day-to-day operations and management control systems. One glaring problem, Peter Magowan conceded regarding Safeway's accounting practices, was that "we did not know what our return was on a division-by-division basis." It became obvious that even though Safeway had made a large capital investment in modernizing its stores, much of that investment had been misallocated to operations that were simply not viable for the long term.[22]

Moreover, a serious problem arose from Safeway's costly labor agreements. The company's wages had risen from 13 percent above the industry average in 1980, to more than 33 percent above the average in 1985. That was a very bad sign in an industry where profit margins averaged only about one percent, and where labor costs were typically two-thirds of nonmerchandise operating expenses.[23] Following the buyout, therefore, increasing shareholder value would require not only considerable asset sales and better operating and accounting disciplines, but also some layoffs. Once the short-term problems were addressed, Safeway's management would then be in better position to prepare the business for growth – investing in the right places and creating new jobs. How this happened will be evident from a reexamination of Safeway's progress after its acquisition by KKR on August 29, 1986.

The Safeway buyout had been structured by George Roberts and Bob MacDonnell in two steps: a front-end cash tender offer followed by a "clean-up" merger.[24] The end result was a very heavily leveraged financial structure (see table). The high leverage, of course, put pressure on Safeway's management to improve its cash flow. KKR and Safeway's management, in cooperation with the lending banks, had already developed a plan for asset sales intended to effect a rapid paydown of Safeway's bank debt. Safeway committed to the banks to sell about $1.8 billion in underperforming assets. To improve its operating disciplines, KKR determined that Safeway would need some outside help.

To that end Roberts and MacDonnell urged Magowan to bring in Burd & Associates. Steven Burd, a onetime Arthur D. Little consultant, had previously advised the CEOs of two other KKR-controlled companies. He came to Safeway with a tripartite mandate: to help Safeway cut operating costs; to rationalize the company's distribution, pricing, and control systems; and to make the company which had long prided itself on size and growth, leaner and smaller. Burd's job, that of a quasi–chief operating officer, was complicated by Safeway's geographically organized divisions, which appeared to have little internal logic to their organization. Burd wanted to know how each might perform as an independent unit.[25]

Safeway buyout financial structure

Type of Financing	Amount ($ millions)	Percent of Financing
Revolving Bank Loans	2,035	47%
Senior Subordinated Notes	750	17
Subordinated Debentures	250	6
Merger Debentures	1,025	24
Redeemable Preferred Stock	45	1
Cash from Working Capital	84	2
Common Equity	130	3
TOTAL	$4,319	100%

To identify underperforming divisions, Burd and his staff determined the prospects for each division – could it be profitable as a stand-alone business, and what could it be sold for? The questions were answered by measuring the Return on Market Value (ROMV) for each store and division. Determining ROMV – calculated as cash flows from each store divided by the appraised (expected market) value of its assets – required an analysis of thousands of leases and contracts. Diverse accounting procedures were translated into standard GAAP formats in order to get a distinct and comparative picture of each division. After thus reviewing the performance of every division, Safeway and its board of directors came up with several candidates for sale.

The first sale occurred in February 1987 when the 132-store U.K. division was sold for about $920 million to Argyll, Inc. Later that year, the 61-store Salt Lake City division was sold to Borman's for $68 million. Safeway shut down its 144-store Dallas division, selling the stores piecemeal. Other sales included divisions in Oklahoma for $165 million, Kansas City for $143 million, Houston for $180 million, and southern California for $405 million; the Liquor Barn division for $105 million; and a host of smaller sales. Overall, by August 1988 Safeway had divested 11 major operations, including 1,000 stores. Meanwhile the company's workforce had dropped from 185,000 to 107,000 employees. Safeway cut its headquarters staff by 300 people, or 20 percent, which alone saved $15 million annually.[26]

During the asset sales Safeway aggressively renegotiated most of its 1,300 labor contracts. But the union in Dallas – the prime subject of press reports – offered stiff and angry opposition. It was a watershed event, because when approached with a proposal to sell, the union wanted Safeway to sell to a union shop. KKR was willing to do so if the union would agree to concessions that would make the division competitive with nonunion supermarkets. There was some sabotage; customers were treated rudely, "shrinkage" increased dramatically, and the Dallas division started hemorrhaging dollars by the millions. After fruitless discussions between managers and union officials, Safeway shut the division down. Though the conflict with the Dallas union had an unfortunate impact on KKR's public reputation, not to mention the Dallas area workers, the episode served as an example to union locals elsewhere. Faced with the possible sale of entire divisions to nonunion owners, other locals became more willing to make deals, and Safeway was able to get concessions on wages in exchange for a pledge to sell stores to union shops.[27]

Throughout these events, KKR was evaluating the data on operations. By 1987, it became apparent that the vast real estate holdings of the company needed more careful management and closer oversight than the accounting resources of Safeway could provide. Safeway's real estate, both owned and leased, was undervalued on its books. In particular, a number of properties could either be developed or sold to third parties for leasebacks. Safeway was also faced with losing huge tax benefits on some nonoperating properties if they could not be sold by year end. To deal with these issues, KKR turned to the real estate expertise of Peter Bechen of Pac Realty Trust, another company KKR controlled. Bechen organized a joint real estate partnership to handle all of Safeway's real estate development issues. Properties Development Associates (PDA) then borrowed about $400 million and began to unload some properties, to convert others, to lease some, to acquire entire shopping centers in which important company properties stood, and generally to enhance the value of the real estate in the Safeway portfolio.[28]

As the real estate problems were resolved, Safeway's management began shifting its attention to other areas requiring reform: site evaluation, capital spending, and methods for tracking the progress of Safeway's various capital expenditures programs. To accomplish the necessary reforms, Burd would have to overhaul the compensation system for Safeway's divisional management, stimulating managers to strive for more efficient business practices.

There had been a serious problem in the way Safeway's managers thought about their performance. Managers' bonuses, 20 percent of their salaries, were usually paid out on the basis of company growth. Their expanded ownership should have helped managers to appreciate the need to increase shareholder value, but old habits were hard to change. Altering mindsets required not only education but also changes in the structure of incentives. One of Burd's most important reforms was to evaluate divisional managers, not on sales, but on how well their operations earned ROMV.[29] This change encouraged division managers to work harder to keep costs in line and to become more alert for opportunities to sell off underperforming assets. Managers responded by paying closer attention to local store operations, labor efficiencies, and inventory controls, and to selling off stores whose cash flows from operations did not justify their high-priced location. Because targets unmet were bonuses unearned, profitability and efficient asset utilization replaced growth as the key measure of a division manager's success. It worked: by 1990, Safeway was again poised for growth in employment and revenues.

In the meantime, reducing Safeway's debt was of particular concern to KKR. By the end of 1987, the company's asset sales *in toto* had raised more than $4.2 billion, far more than necessary to meet the terms of the bank covenant requiring $1.8 billion in divestitures. KKR directed the proceeds to reduce bank debt from $5.7 billion to $3.1 billion and to redeem other outstanding notes and debentures. In April 1988, KKR helped Safeway redeem the outstanding preferred stock for $57.1 million, and renegotiated the bank credit agreement to reduce the cost of the remaining bank debt by 150 basis points. Such interventions were a normal and vital part of KKR's role in overseeing the financial performance of its companies. Safeway's directors remained alert to any opportunity to adjust the capital structure. Whenever market conditions warranted, it was KKR's practice to restructure debt – even increase it – if a company's ability to generate cash flow could support it.[30]

Equally important for KKR was determining when the time was right to sell a business, or at least a portion of it, by offering shares to the public. For Safeway the moment seemed ripe in April 1990, when the company launched an initial public offering, selling 11.5

million shares at $11.25 per share (the original investment had been $2 per share). The net proceeds from that transaction were plowed back into the business. As the company's operations and stock performance continued to improve, Safeway prepared a second offering in April 1991 with the sale of 17.5 million shares at $20.50. All of this activity – from managing the balance sheet to improving operating disciplines – involved very detailed analyses, a commitment to incremental improvements, and good working cooperation between corporate management and its board.

There was no time to relax, however. In the early 1990s, despite all the restructuring, asset sales, operating improvements, and success with its public offerings, Safeway ran into further difficulties. Between 1989 and 1992, the company had enjoyed 15 percent earnings growth per year; most of the earnings growth had come from Burd's cost-cutting programs, but the evidence of strong longer-term performance was not so good. Operating cash flow had fallen (see figure), and between 1991 and 1992, sales remained virtually flat at about $5.1 billion. As sales stagnated Safeway found itself losing market share to new entrants – giant discount merchandisers like Costco and Price Club. Steven Burd, meanwhile, had gone to work at Fred Meyer.

At that point, KKR determined that it had to make a change in top management. Peter Magowan, who had become the general partner of the San Francisco Giants, was clearly too distracted to take further effective measures at Safeway. In October 1992, Burd was called back to become Safeway's president, and in May 1993 he was made CEO. Placing a career consultant at the head of Safeway was a risk, noted Jamie Greene, KKR's point man on the company's board, but having observed Burd's progress through four KKR companies, Greene considered it a risk worth taking.[31] Systematic and precise by nature, Burd turned out to be the right man for the nuts-and-bolts operating improvements that would be required, division by division, store by store.

"We detected that the problem was more than just a sales loss to the warehouse clubs," Burd explained, "that there were [still] some very fundamental problems that needed fixing." There was some chilling irony in what he found. Operating expenses had risen as a percentage of sales – the result, to some degree, of overzealous cost cutting. In their haste to reduce costs, many store managers, rather

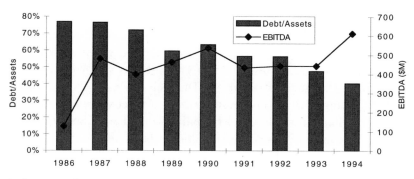

Safeway performance, 1986–1994.

than looking at their operations systematically, had simply eliminated or misdeployed their workers, which had the effect of increasing costs. Burd undertook yet another overhaul of in-store operations, intended to tailor merchandising to local markets and to ensure more optimal staffing. As Green described it, the whole process was hardly glamorous; it was just basic improvement in all aspects of operations. "Steve made the investment in systems, not esoteric kinds of systems, but systems that people could use. He saw that there were things that we could do to save labor in some [back-room] operations, and then reinvest that labor in more service at the front end. There were also opportunities for better pricing, which would enable Safeway to drive its sales higher." As sales grew to $15.2 billion in 1993 and $15.6 billion in 1994, operating cash flow soared. At the end of 1994, Safeway's stock, for which KKR had paid $2 per share, was valued at $31.875.[32]

Efficiency, not asset growth, was the hallmark of Safeway's approach to management. In the five years between 1991 and 1996, the number of Safeway's stores decreased from 1,020 to 881, while the total number of employees declined from about 92,800 to 82,800. Operating profit margins for the same period increased from 2.9 to 4.4 percent, and the average wage by 20 percent.[33] As for KKR, by the end of 1997 it had accumulated total cash value of $4.97 billion on an original $130 million equity investment, for an annually compounded rate of return of 42.7 percent.

Duracell

Duracell was a somewhat different story, a happier case than Safeway from beginning to end. Acquired in 1988, it was sold to Gillette in 1996 in an exchange of stock: one Duracell share for .904 share of Gillette, giving KKR an (as yet unrealized) market value for Duracell of $2.8 billion. An additional $1.3 billion had already been received during the course of Duracell's operations. The sale closed an investment that had met KKR's best hopes for realizing value in undermanaged assets. The contrast with Safeway is instructive. Before its buyout, unlike Safeway (which had grown too large at the expense of efficiency), Duracell had plenty of room to grow. Safeway was more a turnaround from its inception; its CEO had been a reluctant seller. Duracell's buyout was initiated by its executives. As a division of Kraft, the processed food giant, Duracell was a classic "orphan" – too small and too different from its parent company's other businesses to get the kind of senior management attention it deserved. Its managers felt hamstrung by what they regarded as laborious bureaucratic requirements, incessant meetings, and corporate presentations that impeded their ability to implement their own marketing and investment strategies. In short, the problem confronting Duracell at the time of its buyout was not one of *creating* value through a restructuring of its business, but rather one of *unlocking* unrealized value in a basically healthy enterprise.

Fortunately, Kraft, which had acquired Duracell in its buyout of Dart Industries in 1980, was ready to deal. Expected synergies had never materialized, and despite its high margins, Duracell had never been much of a cash generator for Kraft's other operations. Duracell's 1986 earnings had been depressed by some weak operations in secondary lines of business, excess capacity, and problems overseas, particularly in Europe. The division's managers believed that they could bring these problems under control, but they would need more investment in technology, in research and development.

When an inquiry from Kodak about Duracell's availability encouraged Kraft's management to put the division up for sale, the battery maker immediately attracted attention from a bevy of prospective buyers. Kraft anticipated competing offers from such potential strategic bidders as Kodak, Matsushita, and Gillette; but Duracell's thirty-nine-year-old CEO, Bob Kidder – young, ambitious, with an eye on the main chance – had other ideas. He hastened to New York to assess the company's prospects for a management buyout. As he shopped around, he found kindred spirits not among the corporate buyers, but in the financial community, particularly among such buyout firms as Clayton, Dubilier; Forstmann, Little; Gibbons, Green; and KKR. These were potential buyers who might give him not only the freedom he had missed at Kraft, but also an opportunity to own a significant share of his own business.

KKR liked Duracell's potential for growth. Even though the company had an impressive record of sales growth, the untapped potential for international expansion was great – particularly in its sale of alkaline batteries, which constituted only 12 percent of the world market outside the U.S. and Europe. Reviewing Duracell's operations, Henry Kravis concluded that the company's margins could be increased by improving its product mix, expanding advertising, and lowering production costs. But KKR's competitors had also seen the potential, and in order to win the bid the firm would have to overcome a buyout plan proposed by Brian Little of Forstmann, Little.

Little's plan for the buyout, as Duracell's managers explained it, called for using subordinated debt at lower cost than the junk bonds KKR would use in the buyout capital structure. Forstmann, Little would make a proportionally small equity investment, which would enable Duracell's management to get higher leverage on their own portion of the common stock. KKR's plan to put more equity into Duracell – that is, to leverage it less – reflected its belief that Duracell's projected growth plans would dampen cash flows. "We tried," said Kravis, "to show them that in reality our lower debt-to-equity capital structure was going to be more attractive over the long run." Here the discipline of debt was to be sufficiently relaxed to give management more freedom, earlier on, to invest heavily in new capital and marketing projects.

The entire process, from solicitation of bids to Kraft's decision, lasted about five months; and throughout, Forstmann appeared to have the inside track. Before making KKR's best offer, Kravis asked for and received a commitment from Kraft's advisors at Goldman, Sachs that this would be the final opportunity for all concerned. In the end, KKR's bid of $1.8 billion – about $50 million higher than Forstmann, Little's – won the day.

Duracell represented KKR's sixth largest buyout. Its acquisition required in excess of $2.05 billion, of which $1.8 billion covered the purchase price – a full half-million dollars more than Kodak had offered. KKR structured a two-step financing for Duracell. In the first step the bank financing and other debt instruments totaled $1.7 billion. Of this amount, nearly $750 million was provided by a bank term loan. The remaining sources of funding were initially provided by a revolving bank credit facility, a bank bridge loan, and a special KKR Fund subordinated bridge loan. Soon afterward, KKR would undertake the by-now-routine second step in the capitalization process, refinancing short-term loans with long-term junk bonds.

The Duracell buyout showed how important the structuring of the equity in a buyout was in providing incentives to management. Thirty-five of Duracell's managers contributed about $6.3 million for their shares. Bob Kidder invested $1 million in cash for 200,000 shares, a relatively low proportion (about 5 percent) of the total management participation, so that others could enjoy a significant degree of up-front ownership. In addition, he received options for another million shares. Other senior-level managers bought shares, each investing substantial portions of their personal net worth, and each receiving options in addition to their original contributions. Ironically, as Charles Perrin, then a Duracell vice president, recalled, had the option feature been fully explained to them during the bidding for Duracell, KKR would have been able to close the deal sooner.

We had no idea how many options we would be granted per share that we bought. We knew that Clayton, Dubilier would probably be on the low side, maybe two to one. We would have guessed that Forstmann and KKR probably would have offered three to one. With KKR it turned out to be five to one! That could have been a major influencing decision. It would maybe even have swayed Bob Kidder [earlier in the process].[34]

The plan for Duracell was simply to find the best way to increase its business. There was initially no thought of divesting any assets. Operating efficiencies were to be reaped by reorganizing some underperforming operations, and in particular by eliminating small plants and consolidating production, especially in Europe. Otherwise, Duracell would be encouraged to follow the rising trajectory of its sales, to continue its international expansion, to promote its products through aggressive marketing and advertising, and to invest in the research and development necessary to make its batteries longer-lived and more environmentally friendly. In other words, KKR, as Henry Kravis put it, would simply "unshackle" Duracell's management to grow their business in accordance with what Kidder and his staff had projected in a very aggressive five-year plan, a plan that promised annual sales growth of more than 15 percent.

That level of growth was to be achieved largely by taking market share from Eveready in the U.S., and by expanding more aggressively internationally. Called the "exorcist plan" by Duracell's management ("We were going to exorcise Kraft out of our system," said Wade Lewis, Duracell's chief financial officer), the aggressive strategy seemed plausible enough to those who pledged to implement it. "From our perspective," said Lewis, "it wasn't a great change in terms of *how* we would do business. We would simply carry on with fewer constraints." Those constraints would be further alleviated by the tax structure of the buyout, which freed up significant cash to support rapid growth.[35]

But cash flow remained a concern, as did the company's lack of experience with corporate internal control systems. As a division of Kraft, Duracell had no legal, treasury, or tax departments, no audit, no sophisticated financial controls. The new Duracell board devoted considerable time and effort to helping management achieve competencies in these areas. Wade Lewis explained that

Tom Hudson, KKR's accounting expert, and Kevin Bousquette, helped us right from the start in terms of recruiting the individuals, establishing the departments, and providing us with feedback and commentary on our financial systems. We'd have a series of follow up meetings perhaps once a month or more frequently in the early days just to make sure that we were pushing ahead. Hudson would be on the phone to Bob Kidder daily trying to urge us to get things done, to become a self-standing corporation.[36]

Duracell's management also learned how to focus on cash flows and efficient asset utilization, taking into account the opportunity cost of the capital employed in any given operation. They learned to forecast the performance of their investments on the basis of "economic value added" measurements* designed to assess projects and performance in ways that reflected valuations in the capital market. It was measures such as these that helped bring managerial thinking in line with that of investors.

The buyout board mechanism allowed the owners and managers of Duracell to meet on a collegial basis and modulate their different perspectives. The managers were as eager to invest in the expansion of the business as KKR was to generate cash flows to pay down debt; but everyone knew that both were required to make money for shareholders. The managers were initially worried that KKR might dampen their plans for new investment, but that proved not to be the case: "As long as we performed well, as long as they saw us moving down the learning curve, KKR treated us with a good degree of patience and forbearance," said Wade Lewis. KKR increased Kidder's spending authority for capital investments from the pre-buyout level of $250,000 to $5 million, granting him complete authority to administer compensation for his subordinate managers. His desire to develop new technologies in what Kraft had viewed as a mundane business met with KKR's approval. "Not once in the seven or eight years that I was there working with them, did Henry Kravis or George Roberts, or any one of the board members ever ask, 'How can we cut R&D?' In fact, they asked just the opposite, 'Should we be investing more in R&D in order to insure that we have a technological edge for the long haul?' " By the same token, as owner-managers Duracell's executives sensed the limits of their ambitions, and exercised appropriate restraint. "Did we all of a sudden go crazy spending capital?" Kidder asked rhetorically. "No. Did we all of a sudden give crazy increases in compensation? Absolutely not. After all, we also owned the company."[37]

Duracell's cash from operations increased by an annual compounded rate of 17 percent from 1989 to 1995 (see figure). Higher

* Economic value added, or EVA, became a popular technique for evaluating managers and determining bonuses in the 1990s. Developed and popularized by the consulting company Stern Stewart Management Services, EVA purports to align managerial and ownership interests by measuring how well managers make use of the capital under their control. Similar in many ways to the traditional management accounting measure of "residual income," EVA, rather than measuring profits, focuses on how efficiently assets are being used. Accordingly, EVA subtracts a capital charge from net income so that managers are compelled to account for the actual value of the capital that they are using to generate that income.

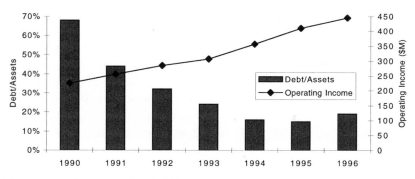

Duracell performance, 1990–1996.

gross margins were achieved through improved manufacturing efficiencies – the results, largely, of new capital investment, as well as from rigorous cost control systems put in place soon after the buyout. In the meantime, Duracell's management tended to the nuts and bolts of the business – upgrading, standardizing, and rationalizing its production facilities around the world. Much of its success depended on its international business, plans for which accelerated after the buyout. Duracell quickly became the leading brand in the new Europe (except for the former Soviet Union), where alkaline batteries came to represent half the market. The company expanded its sales in Latin and South America, Africa, the Middle East, and the Pacific Rim. Duracell formed manufacturing alliances with German and Japanese producers; and its joint ventures in India and China, in which Duracell became the majority partner, supported the construction of in-country manufacturing facilities in those huge and fast-growing consumer markets.

As Duracell grew larger and more competitive, it breathed new life into a sleepy industry. An infusion of R&D expenditures sped the development of a series of new products in almost rapid-fire succession. A mercury-free alkaline battery, which the company had been struggling to develop for some time, was brought to market. In newer departures, the company developed a rechargeable nickel hydride battery, which found a market in laptop computers and other portable consumer products. In collaboration with Intel, Duracell introduced a "smart battery," which substantially prolonged the usage time of unplugged laptops; and it worked to develop an even more sophisticated, high-powered lithium ion battery. Investment in marketing increased as well. The introduction of such consumer product "enhancements" as the package battery tester, the freshness date code, and multipacks improved Duracell's brand image and increased its domestic market share. By increasing the number and strength of its distribution channels, it had expanded into more than 500,000 retail outlets worldwide by 1996.

Along the way, KKR orchestrated a series of timely refinancings and stock offerings. In May 1991, less than three years after the buyout, KKR decided that it was time to float an initial public offering of 34.5 million shares of common stock. The $15 per share offering price netted the company $488 million, which was tapped to pay down $347 million in debt. The proceeds came as a pleasant surprise to Kidder, who recalled, "if you had asked me four months ahead of time were we going to do an IPO, I would not have said, yes." But Duracell had "beat every number in their five-year plan," said Paul Raether, "so we were thus able to take part of the company public before we had originally anticipated."[38] Five months later, in October, Duracell offered 12 million shares at a price of $28.75 per share. At this time the limited partners began to realize some of the company's rising value, as proceeds from the sale were split between equity and debt holders. Subsequent offerings enabled KKR Fund investors to liquidate more of their holdings, as the stock price continued to rise; a March 1995 offering sold at $42.625 per share.

As the stock price moved up, KKR gradually sold off shares, while Duracell's managers increased their personal holdings and broadened employee ownership as well. In 1992, Kidder implemented a companywide stock option plan. By 1995, senior and upper-level middle managers owned approximately 8 percent of the company, and another 300 middle managers were to be compensated in part on the basis of a phantom stock plan, tying their prospects for bonuses to corporate equity returns.

KKR retained its majority control of Duracell's board of directors, and its discussions with Duracell's management included some typical hair-splitting between cautious owners and confident owner-managers. KKR grumbled a bit when Duracell's management decided to build a new headquarters facility, and in 1994, the board engaged Kidder in a debate over his desire to repurchase stock on the open market, thereby increasing the ratio of debt to equity. For their part,

Duracell's managers believed that they could comfortably operate at higher leverage. "We had more than enough cash and a balance sheet that was conservative and attractive by any standards. We, as a management team, believed that we should be buying back shares." But then, asked Paul Raether, "Why buy back stock when it's trading at 22 to 25 times earnings?" – quite high by historical standards. Kidder recalled that "George Roberts asked the same question. 'Trees,' he said, 'don't grow to the sky.' "[39]

We had a very good conversation about that with the board, a very professional conversation. When the arguments were heard, George said, "Look. We're just going to agree that we don't agree. You guys do what you think is right." It turned out we didn't do it. We didn't want to do something when we didn't have unanimity of views. But to KKR's credit, they didn't lumber in with a big mallet, hit us over the head, and say, "This is the way it's going to be done." That's not the way they do business.[40]

The board authorized modest stock repurchases in December 1994 and January 1995.

At the end of 1994, Bob Kidder decided to retire. He was fifty, rich, and well aware that his lieutenants were "waiting for their day in the sun." Just five and a half years after the acquisition, Duracell's stock was valued at more than $45 per share (on an original investment of $5 per share), plus cumulative dividends of $1.68 per share. With his shares Kidder could start yet another career – in the wine business, he hoped – and looked forward to participating in other KKR investments. When he left, Charles Perrin took over as CEO, stepped up the company's investment in human resources, and further advanced management ownership participation. By mid-1996 both those managers and KKR's fund investors had made fortunes by participating in a well-managed buyout. Upon the sale to the Gillette Corporation of their remaining holdings in Duracell, KKR, after nearly eight and a half years, had realized a 39 percent annually compounded total return on its original equity investment. The total return on the original $350 million investment had been nearly $4.22 billion.[41]

Reflection on Contrasting Cases

The occasional buyout perhaps succeeded simply because its purchase price was a bargain or because fortuitous trends in the market made its assets more valuable. But most buyouts required relentless hard work, not good fortune, to succeed. Managers of bought-out firms had to bring costs under control, and had to regard shareholder interests as paramount. Yet the key to success was long-term value creation, not short-term profit taking. How to get there varied with each company's circumstances.

KKR's experience with Safeway showed that successful long-term value creation in a troubled business could be a ceaseless struggle, progressing by fits and starts. Safeway had been subject to some considerable misallocation of resources and lax cost controls before its buyout. Progress was impossible until the company put its assets and employees through a harsh downsizing. The divestiture of assets, overhead cuts, and layoffs were a necessary prelude not only to saving the business, but also to making what remained more productive. The company began to grow until new management determined that it was better, once again, to shrink the business. In time, Safeway's managers showed how an ailing company could not only be restored to health, but also create substantial economic value by rejecting what once had been conventional wisdom about corporate stability and growth.

The Duracell buyout, by contrast, was not undertaken in the expectation of solving problems, but rather to realize the latent potential in assets that had been seriously undermanaged. Once the bureaucratic shackles were removed from its managers – once they were empowered to invest in what they knew to be good products, to manage their operations without undue interference – Duracell grew rapidly and profitably.

The longer-term impact of the buyout discipline on Duracell – now the subsidiary of a parent company once again – remains an open question. Charles Perrin and most of his senior management team took the capital gains earned on their equity and departed. Such a transition raises some important questions for the ultimate fate of companies that have undergone buyouts. How far do the benefits of the buyout governance system flow into a company's future? Are the operating disciplines acquired under the pressures of leverage and rigorous board monitoring merely transitory, or can they still affect corporate performance years down the road? Are the lessons Duracell learned – about management ownership incentives, investment in product research and development, and aggressive marketing – transferable into the future when ownership changes? To a large extent, the answers to these questions depend on the corporate values, management incentives, and monitoring disciplines of those who acquire companies that have completed the buyout cycle.

4 | *When Risk Becomes Real*
Managing Buyouts in Distress

Life . . . looks just a little more mathemati-
cal and regular than it is; its exactitude is
obvious, but its inexactitude is hidden; its
wildness lies in wait.

– G. K. Chesterton

ON THE FACE OF it, the Canadian financier Robert Campeau's
1989 hostile takeover of Federated Department Stores appeared to be just as *Fortune* described it: one of the "looniest
deals" of the 1980s.[1] When Campeau first set his sights on Federated
it was a lumbering retail giant, a bloated corporation suffering from
a gross excess of capacity and ripe for efficiency improvements. Campeau financed a takeover of Federated for $7.67 billion, nearly double
its market value – with 97 percent leverage. Within months, the company was in distress, its cash flows insufficient to meet its debt payments. In 1990, the company filed for bankruptcy. Overpriced and
badly structured, the Federated buyout came to symbolize the folly
of leverage in an overheated market for corporate assets. Perhaps so;
but behind Campeau's failure lurked another, brighter story.

While Federated was struggling to meet its debt payments, the financial economist Steven Kaplan was tracking the company's fortunes
from his office at the University of Chicago. Examining the data, Kaplan spotted something remarkable: when it went into bankruptcy,
Federated appeared to be a better company than it had been before
its acquisition by Campeau. By 1990, asset sales, store closings, and
management reforms had reduced costs enormously. In February
1992, when Kaplan revisited the business after it emerged from Chapter 11 protection, his calculations revealed that Federated's private
market value had increased, by a conservative estimate, some $1.6
billion![2] The Federated buyout could by no stretch of the imagination
be judged a success. It is quite likely that the bankruptcy led to more

disruption and layoffs at the company than would have occurred had the buyout been priced correctly.[3] In bankruptcy, equity holders lose their money; managers their jobs. Yet here was a case where a miserable outcome for many of a corporation's stakeholders could be counted a gain for society.

In other words, financial distress, even bankruptcy, did not necessarily mean that a highly leveraged investment had failed to create value – often far from it. In a more recent study, Kaplan and Gregor Andrade examined 29 highly leveraged companies that had run into financial distress, concluding quite simply "that high leverage, not poor firm performance or poor industry performance" was the primary cause. All their sample firms in fact had "positive operating income at the time of distress."[4] Unlike Campeau-Federated, moreover, most of these companies worked their way out of distress (and many went on to generate good returns to their equity investors). These findings may seem, at first, counterintuitive, but they are not so surprising when we consider more carefully what financial distress means, under what conditions it occurs, and the timing of its occurrence in highly leveraged companies.

Financial distress exists whenever a company is at risk of not meeting its current cash obligations.[5] Financial distress occurs along a continuum, from "technical default," which means that a company has simply violated the terms of a debt covenant, to the final liquidation of assets, the proceeds from which are then apportioned to creditors in accordance with the "seniority" of their claims. Between those extremes a company could run into distress by defaulting on a principal or interest payment; or beyond that, by filing for bankruptcy – a moratorium on meeting all cash obligations during a supervised restructuring of the company's finances. These distinctions are important, if only because financial distress is all-too-commonly associated with the more extreme cases of bankruptcy or liquidation (which are often confused).

In leveraged buyouts, the probability of distress was greater, if only because it would happen sooner in the course of a company's decline. Simple logic dictates that a company would default on a debt payment far more quickly with an 80 percent debt to asset ratio than it would if the ratio were, say, 20 percent. Distress in highly leveraged situations could therefore be an opportunity. The prospect of early default necessarily triggered corrective action sooner in the development of any underlying problems. The leverage in the buyout, in other words, carried within it a kind of early warning mechanism.[6]

Early warning systems were often absent in more conventional U.S. corporations. Imagine, for example, what might have happened if the nation's steel and automotive corporations had been forced to address in the late 1960s and early 1970s what we now know to have been profound managerial and technological deficiencies. Companies in those industries – characterized as they were by dispersed shareholdings, weak boards, and low levels of debt – were bereft of any signaling mechanism to uncover and react to serious deficiencies, until the situation became so desperately obvious that the problems could no longer be fixed. On the other hand, when distress occurred under buyout conditions, latent problems in the business became quickly manifest, alerting investors, mobilizing directors, and prodding owner-managers to action. Assuming that a highly leveraged transaction had been neither overpriced nor badly structured (very important assumptions), the probability that the company would go into default was relatively high, while the probability that it would fail was relatively low. The likelihood of losing money in a leveraged management buyout was thus hedged to some degree by the leverage itself – one more paradox of the genre.

With all that in mind, we can see how Federated was but one dramatic example of how the leverage in a management buyout was a double-edged sword. Born of necessity, high levels of debt financing enabled buyout investors and managers to acquire expensive assets with a small equity investment. The debt was key to achieving the buyout's basic economic objective: to increase value by linking the long-term interests of managers to owners. The risk in the debt then stimulated performance; with their own equity at stake, managers had strong incentives to move aggressively to improve cash flows in the near term and to pursue value-maximizing strategies over the longer term. But, even if the incentives worked, buyouts could still fail, precisely because the leverage also increased the risk of distress.

It behooved buyout specialists, therefore, to weigh very carefully the entire series of risks heightened by the leverage, from the selection of buyout candidates to the possibility that unforeseen contingencies might upset cash flow projections. As little as possible could be left to chance. Though it was impossible to know the future, the already higher probability of distress in a leveraged buyout could be exacerbated on the very day of closing by the acquisition of the wrong kind of company. Buyout specialists thus tended to avoid companies with large capital requirements, overly specialized assets, highly cyclical markets and hence irregular cashflows, or excessive legal or political liabilities. Distress could also arise from paying too much for a given set of assets, from the selection of poor management, or from faulty structuring of the balance sheet, whereby the ratio of cash flow to debt service was dangerously low. Such decisions were generally within the dealmaker's control and, if poorly made, were the hardest to reverse when problems surfaced. After the buyout closed, the prospects for avoiding or working out of distress were modified, for better or worse, by the competence of managers, the vigilance of boards, and the degree to which the buyout firm could maintain harmony among investors.

One would think that, by design, every KKR buyout began its journey tacking close to the winds of financial distress. But KKR partners would disagree. Their approach to every buyout was, by their estimation, conservative. They carefully screened acquisition targets for their ability to manage under highly leveraged conditions. They were far more disciplined than Campeau (and others) had been in paying for acquisitions. They crafted financial structures based on cautious projections of cash flows, and made those structures as flexible as possible. They looked for "margins of safety" in every investment, and anticipated alternative plans for generating cash, should that become necessary.

In most cases, managers were able to pay down acquisition debt quickly, steering their companies through surprises, crises, or simply routine difficulties that might otherwise have led to a shortfall in their cash positions. Whenever that became difficult, KKR was poised to intervene. Still, none of KKR's buyouts were exempt from laws of probability, and some of them ran into distress. The industrywide data are imprecise, but Kaplan and Stein, using a sample of 124 of the largest leveraged buyouts in the 1980s, find a default rate on LBO debt of about 2 percent on buyouts organized before 1985, and a default rate of about 27 percent on buyouts organized between 1985 and 1989. Of these later defaults, slightly more than a third went into formal bankruptcy.[7] By comparison, during the slightly longer period from 1976 through 1990, KKR experienced problems in many of its investments, but the vast majority of those were remediable. During that time, just three of KKR's thirty-seven fund buyouts entered default (either technical default or actual missed payments). The three – Eaton Leonard, Seaman Furniture and Walter Industries – all filed for bankruptcy.[8] KKR's shortcomings are most often associated with its largest investment, RJR Nabisco, *which actually never went into default*, although it failed to generate meaningful returns to its equity investors.

We have already examined some instances in which operating problems called for intervention by KKR boards, resulting in changes in management or financial restructurings. This chapter looks more closely at companies that ran into severe financial distress – or, in the case of RJR Nabisco, came perilously close to it. When that happened, how did KKR respond? To what extent was distress simply a matter of fortune? To what extent might it have been prevented? What actions did KKR take to minimize the damage of distress, to protect its investors, to minimize conflicts, and ultimately to preserve its reputation? Even when financial distress per se was not at issue, how did KKR cope with serious threats to its investments?

Conflict and Reputation

KKR's long-term survival depended on its reputation, which in turn depended not only on the success of its good deals, but on how it dealt with its bad ones.[9] Managing buyouts in crisis also meant managing conflicts among the buyout's key participants. At the moment a buyout closed, its leveraged capital structure bound managers, owners, and lenders alike into a community of interests to which the buyout firm was responsible. Financial distress would inevitably cause friction among these constituencies. Bankers would weigh in with their covenants, bondholders with their claims, and equity owners with their pleas for patience. It was in KKR's interest not simply to seek to honor its debt obligations, but to work hard to resolve the tensions between different classes of lenders, and between lenders and owners.

This basic reality was not always well understood. Well into the 1980s, the prevailing idea was that lenders, under conditions of high leverage, were particularly disadvantaged, because shareholding managers would care little for their risk. Jensen and Meckling in 1976 and Myers in 1977 pointed to the potential adverse consequences of a leveraged capital structure: high leverage would create equity incentives for managers systematically to undertake risky investments, *even if they could anticipate a high probability of negative returns*. That would happen, they argued, because managers (and, by extension, directors) who had paid relatively little for their up-front equity holdings could afford to treat their equity positions as a kind of option. Since managers could always expect to capture the upside, debtholders would be left to bear most of the downside risk, with their fixed claims on the assets.

It was a perfectly sensible hypothesis; but it failed to anticipate how the then-emerging buyout firms were solving the problem of managerial opportunism under conditions of high leverage.[10] In what was generally a conservative market for debt, cultivating relationships with lenders for highly leveraged transactions was a slow and painstaking process. If a buyout came a cropper, creditors were unlikely to lend again to the same dealmakers. Buyout firms – the successful ones, in any case – had to make it clear that they were playing a long-term game in which one bad experience, badly handled, could sour their reputations beyond repair. Consider how KKR confronted this issue the first time one of its buyouts failed.

The EFB trucking company had been created in a 1979 merger following a $12.7 million leveraged buyout of the F-B Truck Line Company, a regional carrier based in Utah. The merger combined this specialty carrier of heavy industrial goods with Eagle Motor Lines, a company that KKR's founders had owned since their days at Bear, Stearns. Thus combined, the entities comprised a business with national scope, one of the top three specialized carriers in the country with authority to operate in thirty-three states. On the face of it, the strategy made good sense. But there were complicating factors. When the executives of both constituent companies decided to step down, KKR, contrary to its normal preference, had to appoint new managers at the outset. On the political horizon was a bill to deregulate the trucking industry, which was almost certain to become law. In time, the juncture of these internal and external developments would prove deadly.

In its first year of operations, EFB increased its revenues from $60 million in 1980 to $103 million in 1981, while substantially cutting costs and paying down its buyout debt on schedule. But in 1982, volume declined, and the company posted an operating loss. The prevailing economic recession was a factor, but the company's problems ran much deeper. Industrywide deregulation severely punished less-than-efficient firms long accustomed to operating in a stable market environment. The release of competition in the wake of the Motor Carrier Act of 1980 had thrown the mass of independent owner/operator truck lines into desperate straits. The entire industry became caught up in a frenzy of price cutting. Squeezed on the one hand by high interest rates and rising fuel and capital equipment costs, and by cutthroat competition on the other, EFB's managers could hardly cope. They could not cut costs enough to offset shrinking margins, and chronic accounting problems and delinquencies in receiveables made matters worse.

When EFB could no longer keep pace with its debt service, KKR was faced with a classic problem in the management of distress. When a company reached the point of distress, no one could be certain whether the condition was temporary or likely to be permanent. Equity holders would tend to believe the former; debtholders the latter. To some extent these views could be brought into closer alignment by the buyout's capital structure at the time of the acquisition. The acquisition of F-B Truck Lines, which cost $12.7 million, had been financed with 9 percent equity, 24 percent bank debt, 39 percent "senior" ten-year bonds, 4 percent subordinated debt, and 24 percent preferred stock. KKR had sold most of the debt in "strips," so that principal bondholders held a mix of senior and subordinated debt along with some warrants for common stock. Strip financing helped to mitigate potential conflict among classes of lenders, and in this case, the buyout's capital structure bought EFB some time to make a clearer assessment of its chances for success. With that in mind, KKR's Robert MacDonnell, who had worked with George Roberts on structuring the buyout, rolled up his sleeves and began "doing whatever I could to salvage this business."[11]

EFB sputtered along until 1984, when it finally became clear that there was little hope for survival. Although many of its competitors had fallen by the wayside, it was simply too late for the company to recover. Its volumes were up slightly, and revenues along with it, but EFB finished the year with a negative $2.3 million in operating income – along with an overhang of debt that was still more than 40 percent of its total assets. With little prospect that its fund partners would ever receive any return on their equity investment, KKR could have resorted to placing EFB in bankruptcy, but decided instead to close the business. In 1985, MacDonnell began the tedious work of liquidating EFB's assets. "The question," he said, recalling the sense of urgency he felt at the time, "was how do we get out and make our lenders as whole as we can?"[12]

MacDonnell disposed of real estate, truck stops, distribution centers, and long-term trucking contracts. He renegotiated terms for outstanding bills. He pursued aging receivables from customers who perhaps thought they might get away with withholding payment under the circumstances. He held "solitary board meetings" in his office in San Francisco, while dealing with lawyers from Salt Lake City and company creditors. Slowly but surely, he wound the company down from the top of the balance sheet – "asset by asset, liability by liability, just grinding it out." Four years later, all the company's senior debt had been repaid, and the insurance companies who had bought the strips got far more of the subordinated debt back than they would likely have realized had the business filed for bankruptcy.[13]

It was a miserable experience, recalled MacDonnell, lamenting the fact that a buyout gone bad always absorbed more time and energy than a good one. There was no longer any equity to salvage, and it was costly for KKR to devote one of its handful of West Coast principals to the task of satisfying a small group of creditors. So the question arises: why bother? Why did KKR not simply rid itself of EFB? Why did it not turn to a bankruptcy court to work out a settlement of claims? Why did it devote so much of a partner's time to salvaging what was a tiny piece of its burgeoning holdings?

The answer was simple enough. Bankruptcy was sometimes useful, but only after other alternatives were exhausted. It was in KKR's interest to try everything feasible to make its lenders whole short of bankruptcy. As George Roberts explained it, maintaining faith with lenders was essential to KKR's long-term survival: "We didn't have a perpetual capital source like General Motors." The more trust that lenders could place in the owners of the business, the more likely they were to provide financing for new acquisitions and to cooperate when problems threatened their particular interests. As shareholders and fiduciaries for their equity partners, KKR was primarily in business to create equity value; but at the end of the day, Roberts said,

We were accountable to all our investors – lenders, fund partners, managers – all. It was their money. I didn't like losing my own money, but I hated losing someone else's worse than I did my own. We had to take *all* those relationships seriously.[14]

The Demise of Eaton Leonard

When interests came into conflict, KKR would not invariably prevail. Consider the case of Eaton Leonard, a small West Coast machine tool company, which KKR acquired in 1980 at a cost of $13.5 million. Still a young fast-growing business, Eaton Leonard had increased its revenues 50 percent annually from its start-up in 1973 through the year before its buyout. Its main asset was an ingenious automated computer-controlled technology for bending tubes (such as those found in automotive mufflers) on a mass production basis. It had an apparently predictable, stable income stream, derived from geographically diverse customers, no one of whom accounted for more than 12 percent of revenues. The company simply needed more capital to continue growing. It was developing "exciting new products" and might have been, said Bob MacDonnell in retrospect, a more appropriate candidate for a venture capital fund.[15]

The Eaton Leonard acquisition occurred at a time when highly leveraged transactions were hard to finance amid high inflation and stringent credit. KKR envisioned a new strategy, which, if successful, would mark a significant departure for the firm. Normally, KKR would acquire a business, leverage it, pay down bank debt and senior notes (often from the proceeds of asset sales), and then sell the business within a few years. But in this case, Eaton Leonard might form the basis of a larger growth strategy, in which the company would first be combined with other manufacturing concerns, much in the way the highly successful Dover and Carlisle Corporations had been assembled from small companies in the 1950s. In this way, the combination of small companies could reap the benefits of increased scale – improved stock multiples, lower costs of capital, and better overall management.[16] This, then, might become a platform for more acquisitions. Though it sounded a bit like a conventional conglomerate strategy, it anticipated the kind of "leveraged build-up" that KKR would pioneer later in the decade when it created K-III Communications.[17]

Eaton Leonard, as it turned out, would not serve the purpose. In the short run, KKR had to worry that the company's existing team of managers might be unable to run the business after the buyout without substantial help. Ray Harmon, a former executive at Sargent Industries, another recent KKR acquisition, was brought in to oversee Eaton Leonard as its board chairman. He was to monitor the business for KKR and groom an executive capable of managing the larger, more complex business Eaton Leonard was expected to become.

From the beginning, Eaton Leonard had difficulty paying down debt; and over time, its debt load increased. Oversight was minimal, allowing weak management and poor accounting practices to get the company into trouble. Perplexed by a stream of financial statements that showed positive operating profits but negative cash flows, KKR discovered that Eaton Leonard had been seriously overstating inventories and understating the cost of goods sold. In an attempt to set things right, KKR became more directly involved. KKR's principals infused about $1 million into the company's capital structure, and brought in Gene Clayton (later cofounder of Clayton, Dubilier and a long-time ally of Jerry Kohlberg) to manage the business. Clayton moved quickly to cut costs and fix the accounting problems; but after a few months he departed, his patience taxed by the pincer-like pressures of management complaints and lender anxiety. KKR then brought in another specialist, but again to no avail. KKR considered, then rejected, pressure from its largest lender, Teachers Insurance and Annuity Association (TIAA), to combine Eaton Leonard with the cash-rich Rotor Tool, another of its machine-tool companies. KKR's equity partners asked, why saddle a good company with poorly performing assets?[18]

The fact that TIAA held all Eaton Leonard's notes in a strip, which included senior and subordinated debt *and 30 percent of the company's equity* should have mitigated conflicts between KKR and TIAA. Yet, the relationship soured as Eaton Leonard's problems became more apparent. KKR's proposal to sell the faltering business to another of its companies, USNR, a small industrial conglomerate, was met with what TIAA regarded as an unacceptably low bid. Convinced that KKR was not showing good faith, TIAA accused the firm of having structured the acquisition badly and demanded an infusion of cash. KKR demurred, and the conflict resulted in a standoff. The matter was ultimately resolved in Chapter 11. When Eaton Leonard filed for bankruptcy in April 1986, it became another tortuous headache for Bob MacDonnell. In one particularly acrid meeting, the interested parties "screamed at each other for hours and hours and hours," he recalled.

When tempers finally cooled, the business was allowed to fail. Eaton Leonard's lenders recovered most of their principal, and its equity holders came away empty-handed. In retrospect, according to MacDonnell, Eaton Leonard might not have met such a bad end had KKR paid closer attention to it from the beginning. "There was a really good potential market, a lot of up-side, and terrible management," he said. "What was missing, was good day-to-day leadership, effective monitoring, and better financial guidance. It was a lesson that we were fortunate to learn in a small business."[19]

In each of these cases, KKR learned hard lessons it would endeavor not to repeat. But other problem buyouts with new wrinkles would follow. In 1991, just after the leveraged buyout wave had subsided, three other KKR companies suffered serious financial problems: Seaman Furniture Company was spiraling into bankruptcy; Walter Industries was mired in asbestos litigation; and a third, RJR Nabisco, KKR's largest investment, was scrambling to avert a looming crisis.

The Bankruptcy of Seaman Furniture

On the face of it, Seaman was a jewel of a company. Morton Seaman was a second generation co-owner of the business when, in 1979, he framed the low-cost merchandising and marketing concepts that would make him famous in retailing circles. Almost single-handedly, he propelled what had been a small and sleepy company into a high-growth, chain-store merchandiser.

Seaman's merchandising concepts were as simple as they were well executed. Offering a limited selection of standardized products, and taking no special orders, Seaman could charge lower prices while promising faster delivery than its competitors. Its extensive promotions paid off handsomely and more than justified the expenditure of ten percent of its revenues on advertising. A state-of-the-art control system enabled the company to turn inventory six times a year, nearly twice the industry average. By requiring large cash deposits from customers, and by deferring payments to suppliers until customers had paid in full, Seaman had, according to a KKR financing document, enhanced its ability to sustain "excellent cash flow from operations, even in periods of economic uncertainty."[20] Between 1983 and 1987, sales grew from $72.1 million to $224.8 million, while pretax income increased from $8.4 million to $31.6 million.

Morton Seaman wanted to expand his retail operation well beyond its base in Long Island. He had floated an initial public offering of common stock in 1985; and within two years, he had created a chain of twenty-nine high-volume furniture stores and two warehouse clearance centers, primarily in the New York/New Jersey metropolitan area. With 1,200 employees, Seaman was Long Island's fastest growing business, ranking second in a November 1987 *Forbes* list of the 200 best small companies in the country. Though publicly traded, Seaman remained family-controlled; the four employed family members looked forward to liquidating their assets.

In late June 1987, KKR's Clifton Robbins contacted Seaman to discuss a leveraged buyout. There had been a marked slowdown in the Long Island economy, and the prospects for a sale were further dampened by a strike at Seaman's New Jersey warehouse. These appeared to be short-term problems. After a brief hesitation, KKR made an offer to buy Seaman on the condition that Morton Seaman continue to manage the business. At age fifty-five, Seaman had several good years left, and seemed willing enough.

As is often the case with family-led firms, there was little depth in executive management at Seaman Furniture. Its success had been utterly dependent upon the vision, skill, and leadership of a singular character. Not only had he conceived and implemented the company's merchandising and marketing strategy, Morton Seaman had also been responsible for developing a management and sales team that was personally loyal to him. His twenty-seven-year-old son, Jeffrey, who had joined the business after graduating from Wharton with an MBA degree, showed some longer-term promise of following in his father's footsteps. What the buyout offered, in Paul Raether's words, was "an avenue for Morty to liquidate the entire family's position and allow him and his son to come back in by making an investment in the company."[21]

On October 19, when the Seaman buyout was about to close, the stock market crashed. The company's stock lost more than half its value. On November 9, KKR delivered a formal tender offer to Seaman to acquire 77 percent of its common stock at $26 per share, a substantial premium above its current $14.25 market price. Furniture industry analysts deemed the offer excessive, but KKR saw it differently, considering the uniqueness of the company and its stock multiple relative to that of a broader group of specialty retailers.

In the debt-inured climate of the late 1980s, the financial structure of the Seaman's buyout was remarkably simple. KKR raised $265 million of the total $387.1 million acquisition cost in bank financing, and issued junk bonds for another $73.6 million. Sales of common stock to KKR partnerships and to Morton Seaman accounted for another $48.5 million, or 12.5 percent of the capital structure. Morton subscribed to 17 percent equity interest in the company at a cost to himself of approximately $8 million, once the tender offer had been completed. The level of his investment would become a problem. Hefty in absolute terms, $8 million did not represent a large portion of Morton Seaman's net worth, and paled by comparison to his and his family's gains from selling the business.[22] For most managers, an investment of that scale would have been out of reach; in this case it would prove insufficient.

KKR's plan for Seaman was to support the expansion of its retail outlets into the Philadelphia market, the erection of a new warehouse, and heavy investments in advertising and promotion. Despite these commitments, the projections for Seaman's growth were cautious. Morton Seaman did not expect the business to sustain the pace it had during the early 1980s; the buyout financing anticipated revenue growth of just 5 percent over five years. In the worst-case scenario, in which revenue growth fell to zero, the debt service "would still have been manageable," Paul Raether said. Seaman's projected cash flows should have covered what KKR believed to be a conservatively structured buyout based on conservative projections.[23]

Why did the Seaman buyout, which seemed so attractive (and straightforward) at the time it closed, go wrong? It certainly went awry in a hurry, as Seaman's growth strategy ran up against unexpectedly hard times. In hindsight, said Henry Kravis, "We made a bad deal. We just overpaid for it."[24] It is a simple – and no doubt correct – conclusion, but as it bridges a big gap between expectation and performance, it begs for more detailed explanation. The 1987 stock market crash hurt retailing in general, and the entire New York metropolitan region, especially Long Island, skidded into what would be a prolonged economic recession. Real estate sales and housing

starts suffered disproportionately. Exacerbating Long Island's problems were rising taxes, the closing of the Shoreham nuclear power
plant, which forced energy prices up, and massive layoffs at Grum-
man Aircraft, one of the region's largest employers.

After its buyout, Seaman's sales, which had grown by more than
20 percent annually between 1979 and 1987, failed to meet KKR's
nominal growth expectations. In August 1988, Seaman Furniture
came up short on a $3.1 million interest payment, and the rating
agencies responded by downgrading the company's credit rating on
its junk bonds. Seaman's auditor warned that the company might not
survive, and industry observers grew pessimistic as well.

There was little room to maneuver. Cost cutting would be possible
only by laying off sales personnel and reducing advertising, the life-
blood of Seaman's business. Constrained in its options, Seaman
pressed ahead, hoping for a turnaround in the New York regional
economy. One thing that KKR could do was to restructure Seaman's
balance sheet, which it did in October 1989, when the company
missed a $10 million debt payment. The portion of bank debt that
required cash interest payments was cut from approximately $275
million to $125 million, and lenders were persuaded to convert debt
into equity. Banks and debenture holders collectively received 47.5
percent of Seaman's equity. So concerned were they to shore up this
investment, KKR's principals dipped into their own pockets. They
contributed $7 million, a signal to both their limited partners and the
larger financial community that they were taking responsibility for
Seaman's woes. "It clearly has not been a good investment for any of
us," Raether explained to all parties, "and we are prepared to put up
a disproportionate share of the new money going forward. We've
worked hard to solve this problem, and hopefully we've got it
solved."[25] The Seaman family sold back much of its stock for a nominal dollar, which represented another $7 million contribution. This
meant that as KKR's stake in the outcome increased, Morton Seaman's diminished.

The refinancing increased Seaman's cash reserves by more than $40
million, while sparing it some $34 million a year in interest pay-
ments.[26] Still, the solution Raether had hoped for was not at hand.
There was no longer enough flexibility in Seaman's financial structure
to cope with the problems, which were only growing worse. The regional economy remained flat. As its sales declined, so did Seaman's

margins and cash flows.[27] Nervous about the company's ability to cover its short-term obligations, suppliers now demanded immediate payment. Raether spent weekends visiting stores and countless hours talking to customers, but Morton Seaman was fast losing his enthusiasm for the struggle. A merchant at heart, he had grown tired of the financial struggles and of constantly answering to Wall Street. One industry-watcher observed that the worst thing that could happen to the company would be for Morton Seaman to be "hit by a bus."[28] The bus came – but it was driven by Morton's son, Jeffrey, who had been urging his father to join with him in starting a new business. In 1990, with little financial incentive left to hold him, the elder Seaman packed up and went with his son to Florida, where they established what would become a highly successful venture called Rooms-To-Go.

Aware of Morton's restiveness, KKR had been searching for a potential successor for several months. He would be hard to replace. KKR went outside the industry to recruit Matthew Serra, formerly the head of G. Fox. His plan was to open new stores beyond the New York metropolitan area, then to expand Seaman's product line into bedding. "It might have worked," Raether asserted, "except business got worse under him, too."[29] Unremittingly bad economic conditions crushed KKR's hopes for salvaging the business. In March 1990, Seaman wrote off approximately $200 million of goodwill, which reflected the value of the company's brand name. Sales continued to stagnate. By late 1991, the company had finally worn down the patience of its vendors, and was no longer able to obtain the trade credit necessary to continue full-scale operations. Seaman was less than a year away from having to make a major principal payment on its debt, and although it had reached an agreement in principle with its lenders for lower interest and principal payments, the lenders could not settle on the precise conditions for yet another refinancing. After looking at the economic and business forecasts for 1992, Seaman no longer anticipated any substantial improvement in its markets. It filed for reorganization under Chapter 11 at the turn of the new year.[30]

Seaman Furniture would survive, but before it emerged from bankruptcy fifteen of its thirty-eight stores would close, and KKR would lose most of its equity in the business.[31] In the postmortem, KKR's principals searched for the meaning of this miserable outcome. Seaman's problems, they concluded, had arisen from a combination of factors, no one of which was decisive, but which together proved fatal to KKR's investment. In the first place, Seaman was a rare case of poor selection. KKR leveraged up a cyclical consumer business that was overly dependent on a local economy. In an economy increasingly prone to "rolling recessions," a transregional chain (Levitz, for example), even if not particularly well run, had a far better chance of offsetting poor sales in one area with higher sales in another. Seaman also suffered from a lack of depth in potential executive management, a problem made worse by the weak financial incentives the transaction provided for a uniquely qualified CEO. Had the economy been better, these mistakes might have been overcome; but they were mistakes nonetheless.

The Trials of Jim Walter

Economic activity teems with legal liabilities; lawsuits are a cost of doing business. But a lawsuit can occasionally be fatal to a corporation, especially in the arena of product liability. Like a cancer, even a remote liability can erupt and spread, ultimately savaging its host. In the case of Walter Industries, the cancer was rooted in a historical – and what would prove fateful – connection to asbestos. Legally, this connection was weak, if not altogether spurious; and it was ultimately survivable. But considerable damage was done to the company's value.

Had Walter Industries not suffered its exposure to asbestos, its $3.3 billion leveraged buyout financing would be better remembered for its innovative structure. *Institutional Investor* acclaimed it as one of the most important transactions of 1988, a year which by any benchmark was one of the most remarkable in the annals of finance.[32] Instead, Walter Industries[33] is now remembered by Wall Street as one of KKR's mishaps. It is a complicated story, the final chapter of which has yet to unfold. For Henry Kravis, Walter Industries stood out as "one of the best deals we've ever done." Once it became clear that legal liabilities would impair its ability to generate returns to the partnership, "it would have been easy to forget the $143 million we had invested in Walter," he said. Instead, the partners in charge of this ill-starred venture did "everything humanly possible to make it work."[34]

When KKR bought the company in January 1988, Jim Walter, Inc., ranked among the nation's 100 largest industrial concerns. The company had been run conservatively by its eponymous founder since 1946, becoming a diversified construction business serving markets in construction, home building, remodeling/renovation, and water and waste water transmission. When KKR examined it, Walter's strengths appeared to be in its low-cost, shell home construction business and its very high-quality mortgage portfolio, which had a yield of 17 percent to maturity. A large amount of unreported value lay hidden in the mortgage portfolio of the Walter's Homebuilding Group, which constructed and financed shell homes. The company's outmoded straight-line accounting method had grossly underestimated the value of its stated $1.1 billion portfolio. KKR partner Michael Tokarz recalculated it using more favorable amortization methods, and uncovered another $600 million in book value.

During its negotiations with Walter's management in the spring of 1987, KKR became aware of pending asbestos claims against Celotex, a home construction products division that had not sold asbestos in more than a generation. Although the punitive and compensatory damages sought by the numerous plaintiffs were substantial, there was ample insurance to cover all the existing claims. Walter thus appeared to be a good buyout opportunity with considerable flexibility; its divisions appeared to have potential sales prices that in the aggregate were well above the company's $2.4 billion stock purchase value. KKR overcame competitive bids for the company from Paine Webber and Drummond/Citicorp Financial Partners, paying nearly $3.3 billion for Walter's equity and assumed debt. KKR's 1986 Fund invested $143 million.

Financing the buyout was a particularly creative exercise, which would involve three distinct steps from September 1987 through April 1988. It began with a tender offer, which enabled KKR to take control of the assets in one of its now-familiar "mirror financings." (This was the last time KKR would use the technique, which was subsequently disallowed by the IRS.) Not all went smoothly, however. The tender offer included a short-term bank bridge loan, and the normal course of refinancing was derailed by the October stock market crash. This shock called Walter's value into question and changed all assumptions about the buyout's financial structure. The pressure on the bond market raised the cost of both the variable rate senior debt and the junk bonds, the latter from around 13 percent to 17 percent. The steep increase in debt service threatened to eat up much of Walter

Industries' projected returns. KKR floated 10 percent of Walter's second-round financing in the form of variable rate junk bonds that carried an interest "reset" provision, hoping that the company would get a lower interest rate when the markets calmed down.* Under these more stringent conditions, KKR revised its strategy for Walter. The company would now sell off more divisions, sooner than originally anticipated, and use the proceeds to pay down some of the higher-cost debt.

In April 1988, KKR completed the third step in the buyout, a mortgage financing designed in part to capture what KKR had earlier identified as the true value of Walter's mortgage portfolio. This enabled KKR to substitute long-term debt for much of the high-interest, shorter-term instruments used in the buyout transaction. By using the higher valuation they had calculated for Jim Walter's mortgage portfolio, KKR was able to collateralize new notes issued by Mid-State Homes with a financial guarantee from Financial Security Assurance. These collateralized mortgage obligations (CMOs), Tokarz explained, "allowed us to refinance what had been A rated notes with $1.45 billion of AAA rated notes." The CMOs had interest rates averaging just over 9 percent – virtually all fixed-rate – at a time when the rates on Jim Walter's other debt averaged 16.625 percent. This was followed by an array of other refinancings to reduce debt-service exposure.[35]

* In principle, a reset worked as follows. Buyers might purchase bonds with a face value of $100 with interest coupons paying 12 percent per annum, along with a promise that the principal will be repaid after a specified period of years. Buyers typically might wish to sell their bonds in the "secondary market." The question, then, was what the bonds would sell for, once they began to trade. Over time, depending on market conditions, they could trade above or below face value. To protect the owners of the bonds, the issuer might agree to adjust the interest payments to render the trading value closer to face value. Much of the risk of the bond was thus transferred from the bondholders to the issuer. The risk remained, however, that if the reset were fixed at too high a level, the issuer's cash flows might no longer support repayment.

By May 1988, Jim Walter had about $800 million in bank debt, $400 million in senior notes, and another $700 million in subordinated debt to go along with its $1.45 billion in CMOs. Later in the year, KKR had an opportunity to replace high-cost senior notes with a bank facility, but chose to defer that option for a more propitious time. It also allowed the reset notes to rise one-eighth of a point. Still, Walter's debt costs remained too high for comfort; it would have to rely on the fortunes of the securities markets to restructure its balance sheet on more favorable terms.

In the meantime, the divestiture program was proceeding. Four companies had been sold off in 1988. Four more would be divested in 1989. KKR anticipated reducing Walter's debt substantially through the proceeds, after which there would be an opportunity to return to the banks for refinancing on more favorable terms. In all, Walter disposed of eight businesses, which enabled the company to cut its $800 million remaining in bank debt down to $240 million, while reducing the principal on its senior notes from $400 million to $180 million.[36]

Among the companies divested in 1988 was Celotex, which was sold for $125 million to Gary Drummond, one of the original bidders for Walter. When KKR bought Walter Industries, it had assumed no value for Celotex and had burdened it with no debt. The sale, though modest, was an unexpected boon. The assumption on both sides was that Celotex, well insured and throwing off between $25 and $40 million in cash, would easily pay off its claims. That the sale would come back to haunt Walter Industries was the farthest thing from KKR's mind.

In the summer of 1989, a group of plaintiffs' lawyers brought suit against Celotex and, in a surprising move, against Walter as well. There was nothing in the law that imputed any liability from Celotex to Walter, except the asserted claims of plaintiffs' lawyers in search of deep pockets. What made the suit so threatening was the venue in which it was filed: Beaumont, Texas, a notoriously friendly venue for plaintiffs' suits. In the wake of the highly publicized massive RJR Nabisco buyout, KKR's visibility made Walter all the more vulnerable to attack. "It was as if someone had painted a big target on us," Tokarz complained – and sure enough, lawyers for asbestos victims relished the prospect of pursuing such a high-profile adversary. The plaintiffs turned up the heat when "they took the extraordinary step of suing Henry and George and me and, for that matter, everybody," said Tokarz. "That was intimidation!"[37]

It was also a force majeure. The filing of the asbestos claims occurred just as the securities markets turned sour. In the fall of 1989, the high-yield bond markets fell into disarray following the indictment of Michael Milken, the collapse of the UAL buyout, and new government restrictions on savings and loan investments. The concatenation of these events completely destabilized Walter's financial structure. Because of the litigation, the company could no longer divest assets to improve cash flows. KKR, in the meantime, was unsuccessful in persuading bondholders to accept a restructuring of Walter's debt obligations that would have relieved the company of what had suddenly become an onerous requirement to reset interest payments. Faced with these constraints, the company filed for Chapter 11 protection in December 1989. The bankruptcy proceeding – the first for any KKR company – was held in Walter Industries' headquarters city, Tampa, Florida, where, in 1991, the company's attorneys temporarily warded off plaintiffs' attempts to "pierce the corporate veil" between Celotex and its former parent company. Adjudication of the issue, as it turned out, did not take place until 1993.

Notwithstanding the delay, Walter's management continued to operate the business in bankruptcy, and ran it well. They exceeded their business plans in four of the five years from 1987 through 1991. CEO Jim Walter was consumed by the litigation. KKR attracted G. Robert Durham, former head of Phelps Dodge, to head up the company's operations in 1990, and he managed to steer Walter effectively through the economic downturn of the early 1990s. Through it all, KKR partners Tokarz and Perry Golkin labored to keep the company's finances in good order. They substantially deleveraged the company (see figure), and helped refinance mortgage debt to staunch bleeding from the company's cash balance. With the improved liquidity, they approved increases in capital expenditures aimed at growing the company's core businesses.

The overhang of asbestos litigation continued to depress the market for Walter's bonds, which attracted the interest of a new breed of "vulture capitalists" – specialists in the purchase of distressed securities. In 1993, when Apollo Advisors, a firm led by Leon Black, a former Drexel Burnham partner, purchased the failed California insurer Executive Life (one of Drexel's more reliable buyers of high-yield securities), they also acquired that company's holdings in Walter Industries junk bonds, paying 15 to 20 cents on the dollar. Shearson Lehman was buying up an even larger position in the distressed bonds. Other vultures joined the fray, igniting a conflict of interests that KKR could not control.

The rise of the vulture funds signified a change in the way the

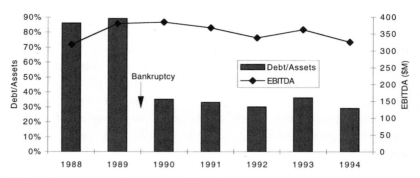

Walter Industries performance, 1988–1994.

holders of subordinated debt were responding to distressed buyouts. Recall that buyout firms had always to worry about the inherently conflicting interests among lenders and owners, and among various classes of lenders. More often than not, bankers holding the senior debt could afford to be patient when companies ran into distress, so long as they could be assured that whatever happened they had a good chance of recouping their principal. At the other extreme, the interests of private equity holders in a buyout were satisfied only in the event of a strong recovery, so they had little choice but to be patient. Between the extremes were various classes of senior bondholders and subordinated debtholders. In the early years, when distress occurred, the common use of strip financing techniques helped to mitigate the conflicts among debtholder classes, just as the issuance of convertible securities helped to forge some links between the interests of lenders and owners.

After 1984, the increasing application of junk-bond financing introduced a new element of potential conflict into the mix. The holders of junk bonds received extraordinary yields precisely because they had such low seniority, and thus could expect to receive little should the underlying assets be liquidated. In distress, therefore, junk bondholders could grow impatient and could threaten, as an interested class in bankruptcy proceedings, to hold up a negotiated reorganization if they did not receive an acceptable payout. So long as Michael Milken wielded his extraordinary power to control the placement of what the markets regarded as particularly desirable junk bonds, his influence could help keep anxious bondholders in line, but after 1990, with Drexel out of the picture, such controls were off.

The descent of the vulture funds on Walter Industries' bonds de-railed the company from what seemed to be a good track. From KKR's perspective, Walter was likely to emerge as the winner in its asbestos case. Apollo and Lehman would lead the bondholders into revolt. To move out of bankruptcy, Walter would have to pay off its nonsubordinated bonds at par plus interest. Willing to forgo their interest, Lehman and Apollo were willing to take a flat 90 cents for each dollar's worth of bonds, and pledged funds for a settlement with the litigants from the interest owed to them by Walter. The plaintiffs appeared willing to settle on that basis.

This arrangement would effectively take the legal proceedings out of KKR hands, which was profoundly disturbing to the ethical sensibilities of KKR's partners. "Our principle," said Perry Golkin, "was that we would pay everybody what they deserved. We thought that the asbestos bar was entitled to nothing." Particularly appalling to KKR was Leon Black's involvement in the proceedings. Black had represented Walter Industries when it had first issued its junk bonds. He thus came away with an insider's information on the company's financial structure, its management, and KKR's approach to the buy-out. KKR sued him over what it considered a breach of duty to his former client. Lehman's position was also troubling. KKR had thought, based on their conversations when Lehman began buying up Walter's bonds, that it could rely on the investment banking house as an ally. Instead, that firm joined Apollo in a move to resell the junk bonds as quickly as possible. That could happen only if Walter would hasten to settle its legal claims and make a speedy exit from bankruptcy.[38]

KKR was pinched tightly between the demands of the bondholders and the ongoing realities of the litigation. Even though Walter had prevailed in bankruptcy court in 1993, even though it had won an appeal in the U.S. District Court in 1994, and even though its position was likely to be affirmed in the Eleventh Circuit Court of Appeals, the possibility that the plaintiffs' lawyers would persist in other venues remained very much alive. The bankruptcy court judge, Alexander Paskay, explained to Henry Kravis that Walter might continue to win on the facts, but he held out little hope that the litigants would give up and urged a negotiated settlement. Faced with that advice, Kravis said: "We had to achieve finality."[39] KKR would reverse its course. It would not only accede to the proposed settlement, it would participate vigorously in the restructuring required to bring Walter Industries out of bankruptcy.

In November 1994, KKR joined with the bondholders in filing a consensual bankruptcy reorganization plan. All the bondholders traded their interest claims for a payout that more than satisfied the vulture investors among them. The banks at the top of the pyramid pressed successfully for their principal, interest, penalties, and equity shares. Unsecured bondholders received $48.4 million in cash, $365.2 million in new five-year senior notes, and $684.3 million in new common stock, or about 60 percent of the equity. The asbestos litigants received $375 million – $16.6 million in cash, $124.7 million in new senior notes, and $233.2 million in new common stock, or about 18 percent of the equity.

KKR saw to it that its investors received shares of a new issue of common stock upon reorganization, along with rights to receive additional shares. By the end of 1995, KKR investors owned about 20 percent of the common stock; its 1993 Fund had put $58 million more into the company. And though return on the KKR investment was poor, Walter Industries was a far stronger business on an operating basis than it had been prior to the buyout.[40] Though it had been a bitter experience, the aging Jim Walter, who had stayed on as chairman of his company throughout the entire ordeal, could finally retire with some satisfaction that matters had been set right.

The Perils of Tobacco

In time, most markets trend to excess. Wall Street is no exception. By the mid-1980s, history's fourth great wave of corporate mergers and acquisitions had become something of a craze. As the availability of credit increased, more deal-hungry buyers entered the fray, driving asset prices ever higher. In a more competitive market for assets, exiting shareholders grew more demanding, and were able to extract more of the anticipated post-acquisition value of their assets.

Greasing the wheels for leveraged buyouts were the public junk bonds that had replaced more conventional private subordinated debt financing. This made debt financing easier, increasing the potential for bad deals. Banks providing lower-cost senior debt were ending up with smaller portions of leveraged transactions, and demanding accelerated payments and stiffer covenants. The higher proportion of subordinated debt, combined with more stringent senior debt terms, further increased the risk of distress. (The ratio of cash flow to acquisition price decreased at the front end and the more common use of junk bonds without interest-bearing coupons increased the costs of restructuring later.)[41] In general terms, the lower-grade, higher-yield securities had made acquisitions easier, but in the long run more expensive and more risky. Michael Milken began talking about the growing risk.[42] It was time to deleverage, he said; but few listened. To Drexel's emerging and would-be competitors, Milken's comments sounded self-serving – and in part, no doubt, they were. Drexel kept selling junk bonds, and buyers kept buying.

As buyout financings were accomplished with more costly subordinated debt, the banks that provided the senior debt were taking relatively smaller positions. At the same time, banks were tightening their covenants and demanding accelerated payments of principal. The Tax Reform Act of 1986 had eliminated some of the more creative devices for enhancing post-buyout cash flows, putting even more pressure on buyers to ensure that post-acquisition cash flows from anticipated operating improvements, divestitures, and so forth would service the debt. In general, there was a decline in the "coverage ratios" (ratios of net cash flow and EBITDA to total debt obligations), which fell sharply after 1985, implying "a sharp deterioration in the ability of buyout firms to meet their total debt related obligations."[43]

Like everyone else, KKR was paying higher multiples for assets. Still, there were plenty of undermanaged assets in the economy, for which the discipline of debt could work wonders. The problem, as always, was not in the technique but in the particular application. With leverageable assets growing more expensive, and with fewer tax benefits to exploit, there was less margin for error. Flexibility in balance-sheet structures (and in the credit arrangements that lie behind them) was more important than ever. As more dealmakers entered the market, and as its own acquisitions increased in scale and volume, KKR had to tread more carefully.

When KKR made its final bid for the mammoth RJR Nabisco, the buzz on Wall Street was that the firm had thrown caution to the winds. Public accounts of the bidding contest depicted KKR in the unaccustomed throes of a bidding frenzy, contending for history's largest acquisition against a host of formidable competition. Had the firm lost its usual cool, its classic discipline? Had ego triumphed over reason in a titanic struggle among ego-driven financiers? The evidence seemed manifest, especially in *Barbarians at the Gate*, which provided vivid detail of a firm as much in confusion as in command. KKR had become involved in its only hostile acquisition, which greatly decreased its ability to project cash flows based on complete information. The RJR board's directive to management that they cooperate with all bidders was being honored in the breach. Conducting its analysis in an unaccustomed veil of ignorance, KKR's best information of the company came from John Greeniaus, an odd man out in CEO Ross Johnson's plans to buy out the company. In a round-the-clock marathon of number crunching, Scott Stuart discovered at a critical juncture in the bidding that he had seriously underestimated (by some $1.3 billion) the cash available for post-buyout debt reduction, casting into question all of KKR's information. In mid-November, just two weeks before they tendered their final bid of $109 per share, the KKR partners were debating whether $98 was too high a price.[44] When the final moment arrived, KKR was still not entirely comfortable with its data.

There is no question that RJR Nabisco was a unique transaction for KKR, and that in the end it failed its equity partners. The snap judgment would be that the firm had simply overpaid; but once again, this is not a very useful explanation of what went wrong. Unbroken debt coverage and marked improvements in the company's operating performance tend to belie it; poor equity returns tend to confirm it. The post-buyout history is far more complex. At different times, under KKR's aegis, RJR Nabisco confronted different kinds of problems, each of which had profound negative impact on its equity performance, yet none of which was a direct consequence of the acquisition's original cost.

On the other hand, the *financial structure* of RJR Nabisco at the time of the buyout posed serious problems early on. It is more than a semantic difference to distinguish between the cost of the buyout and its financial structure. When the frenetic contest for control of the company was over, KKR and its allied investors had put only $1.5 billion in equity into the transaction, leaving nearly $30 billion to be financed with debt. In this case, the high leverage sharply narrowed the range between projected cash flows and debt service, leaving the company little to buffer itself against adverse circumstances. As it turned out, the deal's capital structure could not absorb the shocks soon to come.

The first eighteen months following its buyout went very well for RJR Nabisco. Projections for the buyout had required some $5 billion in asset sales, which were exceeded with dispatch. In 1989, KKR orchestrated the sale of the European food business of Nabisco to the French food conglomerate BSN for $2.5 billion. Holdings in Del Monte were sold in two separate transactions. The tropical fruit division of Del Monte fetched $875 million, and the processed food business netted another $1.3 billion. Assorted odd assets – including most of the company's eleven infamous corporate jets and its 20 percent interest in ESPN – were sold for an aggregate $500 million. The prices fetched and earned in the divestitures were "fair by any measure," industry analysts said.[45] As the asset sales proceeded, the company's new management, headed by Louis Gerstner, settled in quickly. They slashed costs by cutting staff and workforce in tobacco manufacturing and by promoting productive efficiencies through investment in technology. The result was an increase in operating income from $2.367 billion in 1988 to $2.8 billion in 1990.

Then, just a year and a half after the acquisition, almost everything that could go wrong, went wrong. The nearly simultaneous collapse of the UAL buyout negotiations along with news of other problem buyouts, touched off a panic in the markets for high-yield securities. Drexel Burnham, the major market maker for high-yield securities, began its descent into oblivion. Meanwhile, public and corporate antipathy to takeovers had been working its way through the political system, resulting in congressional and regulatory actions that further dampened the market for acquisition debt. Even in this hostile environment, RJR Nabisco's junk bonds were relatively strong. KKR's Scott Stuart noted ruefully that they were "of better quality than other issues and more liquid, cursed with being the best of a bad lot in the junk bond market." When Moody's lowered RJR Nabisco's debt rating, on Friday, January 26, 1990, the company's bonds were worth just sixty-six cents on the dollar. On Monday they slipped another dime. Looming on the not-too-distant horizon was a 1991 deadline for a "reset" of interest rates on the company's junk bonds.[46]

Why had KKR originally structured the buyout transaction with a reset provision on the junk bonds? The reset provision had been an almost accidental inclusion in KKR's bid, the result of a now-famous gaffe in communications between KKR and Drexel in the heat of the bidding process. KKR had discussed it with Drexel and Lazard Frères, an advisor to RJR Nabisco's board, who had warned that the board was not likely to look favorably upon ordinary fixed-rate junk bonds, because they were unlikely to trade at par value. The reset provision was offered orally by Drexel to RJR Nabisco's law firm in a telephone conference, without KKR's final approval.

As it turned out, KKR decided that the reset was crucial to getting the deal done. Without it, the firm would have looked forward to financing the transaction with 19 or 20 percent fixed-rate high-yield bonds, which would have rendered the deal infeasible. In any case, said George Roberts, "we thought we were going to do pretty well, and that we could reset the bonds at lower rates."[47] The credit-worthiness of RJR Nabisco, combined with its improving performance, should have made it so. Instead, with the collapse of the junk bond market, KKR came face to face with a looming crisis.

Although it was not technically obligated to reset the bonds until April 1991, KKR had to move quickly to stave off fears that RJR Nabisco might default. The junk bonds carried a nominal interest rate just under 14 percent; at the current trading price, resetting them might involve up to a 50 percent hike in rates, which would be a serious drain on cash or, if paid in kind, would generate new bonds at an intolerable pace. RJR Nabisco was not generating enough cash to redeem the bonds, and proceeds from asset sales were committed to paying down bank debt. And there was no way to restore confidence in the bonds in the existing climate. It would be difficult to overstate the seriousness of the threat, not to mention the embarrassment. Hailed for its financial wizardry in 1989, KKR was now subjected to incessant flack from the business press and cold shoulders on Wall Street. Junk bondholders hectored Henry Kravis at a conference; institutional investors and banks, so eager to do business with KKR months before, turned openly hostile. A few of KKR's advisors, including Marty Lipton, the prominent takeover lawyer, suggested that RJR Nabisco file for bankruptcy. It was a chilling thought – about a quarter of the 1987 Fund was invested in the company. The deal was still fresh, and though the potential for distress existed, the problems were far from insurmountable. Still, the multitude of parties with different interests presented an extraordinary challenge. Working out a problem of this magnitude, without causing irreparable conflict among various investors, would require KKR's best mediating skills.

Another potential source of conflict was internal. This was exactly the kind of crisis that was causing many of Wall Street's buyout and takeover teams to fall apart in the early 1990s, now that the good times had subsided. "We're going to solve this together," Kravis told his partners. There would be no recriminations. In George Anders's description, KKR's professionals regrouped and searched for an answer, feverishly cranking out "more than 200 scenarios aimed at rescuing RJR from its financial plight. Associates . . . filled entire offices with stacks of gray and blue binders, analyzing every possible scenario."[48] It was almost as intensive an experience as the original pre-buyout analysis. When complete, their efforts led to a radical restructuring of the right-hand side of RJR Nabisco's balance sheet.

In July 1990, KKR undertook a complex $7.6 billion recapitalization of RJR Nabisco. It arranged for $2.25 billion in new bank loans, and for the sale of another $1.8 billion in convertible preferred RJR Nabisco stock. KKR then exchanged $547 million cash and 129.4 million shares for $1.2 billion in exchange debentures. The key to unlocking all these transactions was the injection of $1.7 billion in equity into the company, more than doubling the $1.4 billion KKR and its fund investors had put into the original transaction. The proceeds were used to pay down nearly $4.4 billion in junk debt, to retire the remaining short-term tender offer debt, and to repay the remainder of a $500 million bridge loan. The combined effect of these actions was to restore calm to the debt markets. RJR Nabisco's bond prices rose steadily, and on July 15, Lazard Frères and Dillon Read, acting on behalf of the bondholders, determined that new interest rates of 17 and 17 3/8 percent on the remaining reset bonds would be fair – a far better assessment than generally expected.

KKR had acted well ahead of schedule; but in hindsight, they had moved just in the nick of time. "Just one month later, Iraq invaded Kuwait, and the financial world stood still until January 1991," George Roberts recalled, with just a hitch of remembered relief in his normally measured voice. "Had we not gotten the bonds reset when we did, we would have had an even more significant crisis."[49] The bondholders were satisfied; and KKR, with its reputation for complex problem-solving somewhat refurbished, could breathe easier.

From the vantage point of the business press, everything had turned rosy for RJR Nabisco. From his vantage point in federal prison, Michael Milken applauded the moves, observing to *Forbes* that by infusing more equity into the capital structure, KKR had restored RJR Nabisco's bond prices to a premium and hoisted its capitalization from $24 billion to $28 billion. If nothing else, he said, both the problem and the solution should persuade anyone not hopelessly mired in conventional financial theory that "capital structure matters."[50] Thus far, RJR Nabisco had added a staggering $17 billion to the wealth of the shareholders who had sold and bought it. (The pre-buyout shareholders had already reaped capital gains estimated at $13 billion.) By repairing the flaws in the original capital structure – most notably, too much leverage and not enough flexibility – the 1990 recapitalization put RJR Nabisco back on course. KKR's expectations for the now diluted equity investment remained optimistic.[51]

Dramatic as it was, the 1990 RJR Nabisco restructuring was not complete. There were two more steps to take in the following year: a new $1.5 billion senior note offering, whose proceeds were used to pay down bank debt and exchange debentures; and an initial public offering, in which RJR Nabisco sold 115 million shares of common stock at $11.25 per share, which represented a doubling in value of the $5.61 blended cost of KKR's investment.[52] Refinancing activities continued; a series of transactions in late 1991 and 1992 reduced the effective interest rate on RJR Nabisco's long-term debt from 10.4 percent to 8.7 percent. (Interest expenses fell from $3 billion in 1990 to $1.4 billion in 1992.) Rating services restored the company's bond ratings to "investment grade," and its shares traded on New Year's Eve at $8.625. At that price, the company's stock was trading down from the enthusiastic premium it had commanded at the public offering; but as a whole, the business appeared to be on track. Pretax earnings were up, and capital expenditures were down, both of which greatly improved the company's cash flows. After three years of losses net income was back in the black. The top line, at $15.7 billion in sales, was equivalent to 1987 levels, and was being generated by only half the number of pre-buyout employees. The aggregate operating ratio had improved from 16.8 percent to 18.5 percent.[53]

Much of the credit for RJR Nabisco's success was due to John Greeniaus, the young, dynamic leader of the Nabisco division. Greeniaus was one of only three senior managers retained by KKR after it swept the executive suites nearly clean in the takeover. He proved his mettle, steadily exceeding the high expectations he had established for Nabisco's revenues and profitability. The tobacco business, on the other hand, was lagging KKR's initial five-year projections. Although KKR had taken into account the growing public concern over smoking's health risks, domestic cigarette sales had fallen off more sharply than anticipated, and premium package prices were coming under sustained attack from discount and generic brands. The division's managers, moreover, had been less zealous than their counterparts in the Nabisco division in trimming the fat in their operations. Nonetheless, RJR's domestic market share was holding steady at an aggregate 30 percent, and international sales were growing rapidly.

The next year brought with it yet another crisis, one far more deleterious to KKR's equity returns than the diluting effects of the 1991 restructuring. Price skirmishes had become frequent in the cigarette industry, as discount and generic brands made inroads into the markets of premium brands. On April 2, 1993, a day that became known in tobacco annals as "Marlboro Friday," industry leader Philip Morris slashed the price of its flagship brand by 20 percent, a full 40 cents a pack. Though aimed at discount-price cigarettes, it seemed like a desperate move, one that would hurt the profitability of cigarettes across the board. (Later, when Philip Morris's CEO stepped down, this decision was widely thought to be the reason.)*

* Although Philip Morris actually gained market share as the result of the Marlboro price cut (at the expense of both RJR Nabisco's premium and generic brands), the wisdom of this move was widely questioned at the time. An alternative strategy, one that RJR Nabisco had been pursuing, would have been to raise prices on corporate-owned competitors to generic brands, while keeping premium brand prices steady. Still, there is no doubt that the move had the longer-term effect of increasing Philip Morris's market, largely at the expense of RJR.

"Marlboro Friday just absolutely knocked the wind out of us," said Henry Kravis.[54] Exquisitely timed for peak annoyance, it was the day of RJR Nabisco's annual meeting, heaping insult upon injury. The damage registered immediately on Wall Street – Philip Morris's equity market value plunged by $13 billion by the end of the day. RJR Nabisco's stock price fell from $8 per share at the opening of business to $6.75, and then continued to fall; one week later it was down by 26 percent. Philip Morris's stock price stabilized, but RJR Nabisco's decline continued; by early May 1993 its stock was trading at around

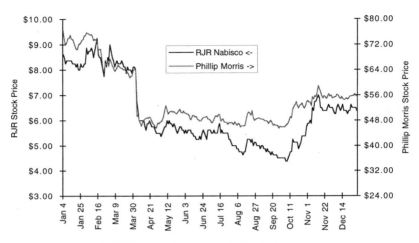

RJR Nabisco and Phillip Morris stock prices, 1993.

$5.50 per share, a 32 percent drop (see figure). RJR Nabisco's equity languished in this low territory for much of the next two years.

Underlying this severe judgment of the market was the stark reality of RJR Nabisco's tobacco business. The company's tobacco earnings fell by 43 percent in 1993, adversely affecting overall corporate operating income, which plummeted from $2.89 billion to $1.378 billion. Even though the company had cut its total debt load nearly half since the buyout, Standard & Poor's put the company on a credit watch in the fall of 1993; in December, the company laid off about ten percent of its workforce. All these difficulties had been aggravated by a transition in top management following the unexpected departure of Lou Gerstner, who had been wooed away by IBM in April, just as the aftershocks were reverberating through the marketplace. It was, to say the least, an awkward time to have to replace a CEO. But KKR was able to find a successor quickly, in the person of Charles M. "Mike" Harper. The former head of ConAgra, Harper was a well-regarded manager whom KKR had come to know when he had bought KKR's holdings in Beatrice.

"An incredible thing then happened," Cliff Robbins related. "Jim Johnson, who ran the tobacco division, and Mike Harper sat down, mapped out a new strategy, and over the next eighteen months took another billion dollars in cost out of their business."[55] At last, the tobacco division's operating performance was coming into line with that of its food division. When some measure of price discipline was restored in the domestic tobacco market, RJR's tobacco profits began to climb until they reached 75 percent of pre-Marlboro Friday levels by the end of 1994.

Yet once again, renewed prospects for smooth sailing were roiled by crosscurrents in the environment. Mounting social opposition to tobacco was working its way through the political system as never before. Legislative and regulatory responses were far more serious threats to cigarette sales than all the industry's lawsuits, which had long been accepted as a routine cost of doing business. And though plaintiffs had consistently lost in the courts, new evidence regarding the ill effects of secondary smoke and nicotine addiction were causing anxiety on that front, as well. The entire industry, and RJR Nabisco along with it, was under siege. Domestic tobacco sales had stagnated, and package prices continued to remain below their pre-Marlboro Friday levels. The prospects for international growth aside, the clouds hanging over the tobacco division were beginning to look permanent.

The Nabisco division's far greater potential value was locked into tobacco's fortunes. Unlocking that value was now the order of the day; but finding a way to do so was a tricky business. KKR had actually considered spinning off Nabisco at the time of the buyout, as one of several long-term exit strategies. But the tax code would have severely penalized the move, had it occurred within an IRS-mandated five-year waiting period. Now that the five-year point had been reached and the time was ripe, KKR's hopes for spinning off the Nabisco division were thwarted by legal risks. Plaintiff's lawyers, seeking a new strategy for attacking the seemingly impregnable courtroom defenses of the industry, had launched a novel attack via class-action suits. With the resulting proliferation of "contingent liabilities," KKR's attorneys warned that the firm's principals, in their capacities as corporate board members, could be sued for the "fraudulent conveyance" of any assets that might be held subject to legal claims. "Neither we at KKR, nor the outside directors, nor the managers who served on the [RJR Nabisco] board were willing to take that risk," Henry Kravis said.[56]

The best alternative now was to issue "lettered stock," a device well tested in the equity markets by such large corporations as General Motors and USX. As Kravis explained,

We would have kept the two companies together, food and tobacco, under the umbrella of a holding company. Shareholders would have then received certificates – A and B stock – that gave them the rights, in effect, to separate streams of earnings in food and tobacco. There would be separate dividends, but no need for separate boards. It was a way to try to get value of the food part of the business, which was in effect tied to the lower multiples of depressed tobacco stocks.[57]

But placing the lettered stock posed a forbidding host of arcane tax, financial, and legal complexities. KKR had to think of something else. It finally decided simply to offer 19.9 percent of the Nabisco division to the public. On January 26, 1995, 51.75 million shares were sold at $24.50 per share, and the entire proceeds of $1.2 billion were used to pay down bank debt. By keeping the offer below 20 percent, KKR preserved its option, under the tax code, of doing a tax-free spin-off later, should such a move become less risky in terms of the legal liabilities.

For more than five years, a relentless series of inopportune events – the crash in the junk-bond market, Marlboro Friday, the tide of social pressure against smoking – had rendered KKR's biggest deal its biggest headache. Yet despite the litany of woes, KKR had toiled ceaselessly to extract the equity value in RJR Nabisco, while making good on its debt. By selling off a variety of subsidiaries, by encouraging a variety of operating reforms, and by careful stewardship of the company's balance sheet, KKR had managed to reduce the company's debt from about $29 billion to under $9 billion. It had overseen a major turnaround in the operating efficiency of RJR Nabisco's business. The firm's partners had done almost everything they could to position the company to generate even more cash flow and better earnings. But the stock price would not budge – the legal and political clouds were too foreboding.

KKR's RJR Nabisco team included Cliff Robbins, who along with Scott Stuart was most responsible for KKR's intensive, day-to-day monitoring of the business. George Roberts, in the meantime, had been putting constant pressure on everyone to come up with some way to extricate KKR from its dilemma. KKR was running out of options. It had tried simply to provide for better management, to run the company better. It had considered splitting the company in two, spinning off divisions, merging with other con-

sumer goods companies, making acquisitions in complementary industries. It had tried share repurchases, special dividends, and
targeted or letter stock.[58] None of those options was availing, however; it seemed little could be done to enhance the company's stock
price. It was time to exit.

The means to exit surfaced serendipitously, in the form of a new
acquisition prospect. Borden, Inc., a once-great name in perishable
consumer goods, had degenerated into a poorly managed company,
and KKR had been following its misfortunes since 1992 as a potential
buyout opportunity. Henry Kravis and Cliff Robbins approached the
company a year later. Borden, they knew, was in trouble. Its marquee
brand names and market position had seriously eroded. Its sales and
earnings were plummeting; its short-term debt was piling up rapidly;
the market value of its stock was steadily declining. (Borden had suffered losses to the tune of $364 million in 1992 and would lose an-
other $631 million in 1993. Its stock price was in a free fall: in 1991
it had been $36 per share; it would be $11 by late 1994.) The company was investing little in R&D or in marketing, the life-blood of a
consumer goods concern.

Despite their company's woes, neither Borden's executives nor its
board showed any interest in KKR's overtures. Traditionally shy of
turnarounds, KKR persisted, in the belief that it could muster a management team to fix Borden's problems. As the stock price careered
downward, KKR waited for another chance to make a pitch to Borden's directors, who in the meantime had been churning CEO's in the
hope of restoring the company's profitability. KKR kept in touch with
the takeover defense lawyer Martin Lipton, who was close to Borden's board; and with Louis Perlmutter of Lazard Frères, who had
been retained by Borden to pursue potential strategic buyers for the
company. Lazard brought in KKR toward the end of 1993, by which
time Borden was deep in the throes of a liquidity crisis.[59]

Borden was a great opportunity, with plenty of potential upside;
but it was so burdened with debt (made worse by the company's
deteriorating cash flows) that it could not stand any leverage in an
acquisition financing. This posed a dilemma for KKR: how would it
raise the funds necessary to purchase the equity in timely fashion
without doing its usual buyout? Then, as the KKR partners were
brainstorming their problems with Borden and RJR Nabisco, they

drew a connection. Cliff Robbins explained how the two problems –
RJR Nabisco and Borden – coalesced into a common strategy:

During the time period of 1993 and 1994, I was looking at Borden as
Borden. . . . Somehow in the summer of 1994, we realized that maybe we
could convince the Borden stockholders to take our shares of RJR Nabisco,
just swap them for Borden. The beauty of this transaction was that there
was no need to raise new debt, no need for a new corporate transaction.
And RJR Nabisco was not at all party to it. It was just us, KKR, doing an
exchange offer with our RJR Nabisco shares to acquire Borden.[60]

George Roberts realized that by using such an exchange of stock,
KKR would not have to raise new capital to acquire Borden. It would
also obviate the need for KKR to make a distribution to its 1987
Fund investors on what had essentially been a flat investment in RJR
Nabisco. "They continue to have a lot of money at work," he said,
"and the investment hopefully is going to be okay for them over the
longer term."[61]

When no one else arrived with a bona fide offer, KKR and Borden
jointly announced that they would swap Borden's stock for KKR's
remaining 40 percent of RJR Nabisco, which in fact occurred in a
two-step transaction from December 1994 through mid-March 1995.
In December, KKR exchanged 238 million shares of RJR Nabisco
stock for a 69.5 percent interest in Borden. In March 1995, the remaining shares were purchased with 119 million RJR Nabisco shares.
The total value was approximately $1.9 billion. Borden quickly sold
off 231 million shares of the RJR Nabisco stock, applying the net
proceeds to pay down $1.2 billion of debt, which enhanced its ability
to raise new funds for investment in its flagging operations. KKR also
renegotiated the terms of the remaining debt, reducing both loan margins and restrictive terms in their covenants. This solution had three
benefits: it provided Borden with a debt-free balance sheet; it enabled
KKR to extricate itself quietly and cleanly from the mounting political
and legal problems of the tobacco industry; and it allowed KKR to
move forward without having to close its 1987 Fund's investment in
RJR Nabisco. Not every limited partner liked the outcome; but Jerry
Kohlberg, now with his own firm in Mt. Kisco, New York, watched
approvingly as KKR engineered the transaction. Borden was "very
cleverly maneuvered," he said. "Very clever. I would like to have
thought of that. . . . It was brilliantly done."[62]

Thus the Borden buyout became, in effect, an extension of the RJR Nabisco acquisition, with an estimated market value at the end of 1995 of about $4.7 billion, close to its purchase price.[63] On the eve of the exchange, the RJR Nabisco investment stood more or less at a breakeven point. The impact on the value of KKR's 1987 Fund had been severe. Without RJR Nabisco, its after-carry rate of return to investors would have been nearly 24 percent by mid-1997; with it, the return was closer to 14 percent.[64]

The Residuals of Unsuccessful Buyouts

One would like to believe that the financial rewards for firms like KKR, as rich as they can be, come from doing the right things. This may be generally true, but not even the best efforts at dealmaking can anticipate every adverse contingency. Leverage is especially unforgiving to weak financial structure, poor business judgment, or bad management; yet it was always possible that even good decisions and sound stewardship might be overwhelmed by extraordinary developments. Every buyout is at the mercy of unpredictable market dislocations, management failures, and threats from the larger social and political environment. Seaman Furniture, a victim of a change in market conditions, was even more a victim of faulty strategic assumptions and post-acquisition management problems, the latter stemming from overreliance on a single personality whose ownership incentives were weak. By contrast, Walter Industries demonstrated how a perfectly appropriate candidate for a buyout could be undermined by a risk that exceeded reasonable calculation. In that case, even a small corporate exposure to asbestos proved to be toxic to leverage.

As the cases in this chapter suggest, contingencies abound, but sheer fortune is rarely the culprit. There are always practical lessons to be learned from failure. We have seen in the case of EFB how concerns unaddressed at the front end of an acquisition could come back to haunt a company under high leverage. In hindsight, the trucking company was a poor candidate for leverage. Its basic characteristics did not make it a good buyout candidate even by KKR's standards. It was dependent on highly cyclical revenues. Its success would depend on new management to direct the merger of its two constituent companies. With deregulation, EFB also became subject to unpredictable changes in the motor carrier industry structure. So too, perhaps, was

Eaton Leonard unsuited for high leverage. It was a high-growth specialty machine tool manufacturer. Its failure was a combination of
faulty strategy, poor management, weak monitoring, and sour investor relations. Even so, its problems might have been worked out had
lender resistance not been so intractable. In this instance, KKR signaled to its bondholders that there was a limit beyond which it would
not stretch equityholder resources to meet every lender demand. The
fate of these two small companies demonstrate just how difficult it
was to resolve creditor claims while keeping equityholder interests
in view. Striving to satisfy the claims of all investors was vital to
KKR's long-run success, but conflicting claims were not easy to reconcile.

Walter Industries revealed how antagonistic investors could become
once a company ran into distress. In this case, KKR could not stay
the impatience of subordinated debtholders, and so lost control of the
company. This episode proved far more serious to KKR's equity interests than had its earlier conflict with TIAA over the fate of Eaton
Leonard. When Seaman Furniture became distressed, KKR was able
to bring all its investors through a Morganesque restructuring, converting debtholders into equity holders. The firm's unusual show of
good faith – its principals personally put more equity into the firm's
capital structure – helped bring harmony to the crisis; but it could
not, in the end, stave off bankruptcy when vendors pulled Seaman's
credit. On the other hand, the firm's relatively rare experience with
such conflicts indicates just how well, in skilled hands, investor relations in highly leveraged companies could be managed through distress. In the case of RJR Nabisco, distress was narrowly avoided, and
conflict abated, as KKR warded off a looming crisis by diluting shareholder interests to satisfy bondholder claims.

Our broader finding on RJR Nabisco is that its post-buyout problems had no single cause. Its first big problem, which led to the 1990–
91 financial restructuring, occurred because the balance sheet at the
time of the buyout was insufficiently robust, lacking the flexibility to
cope with what was a transient crisis in the junk-bond market. The
missing ingredient was the measure of flexibility that had enabled
many other highly leveraged KKR investments to weather hard
times.[65] KKR might have reduced the leverage in the deal, or else it
might have hedged the transaction with better protection against the
potential downside risks. As it happened, the reset provision on the

junk bonds became a more severe limitation on flexibility than anticipated. KKR resolved the problem – before it became a crisis – with
the brute-force solution of more than doubling the equity investment.

After the restructuring, RJR Nabisco's balance sheet per se was no
longer the main concern. Until Marlboro Friday swept its gains away,
the company's stock had been trading at a handsome premium over
the $5.61 per share that KKR and its 1987 Fund investors had paid.
It is not clear, in retrospect, that KKR could have coped much better
with the company's subsequent difficulties. The combination of competitive and social pressures on the tobacco markets undercut efforts
to increase equity value by shedding underperforming assets, improving management discipline, and increasing operating efficiency. And,
even though the performance of the Nabisco food division surpassed
all expectations, every attempt to unshackle its value from the restraints of the tobacco business proved unavailing. Scott Stuart's final
verdict on the investment may have been the best one could have
hoped for under the circumstances: "Everything went wrong," he
said, "but we paid our creditors in full, and we at least got our equity
partners their money back."[66] Whether they would get much more
remained to be seen.

Thus it was that with some of KKR's distressed investments, post-
buyout financial difficulties reflected underlying strategic or management problems which became exacerbated under high leverage.
Hence, values were destroyed in two small businesses, EFB and Eaton
Leonard, and the beleaguered Seaman Furniture emerged from bankruptcy a much-diminished company. For KKR's two largest troubled
buyouts, however, the net financial gains to society – if not to equity
investors – were substantial. High leverage combined with strong
ownership incentives and good monitoring to enhance operating performance at Walter Industries. And though it may have been small
comfort to KKR's limited partners, there is no question that RJR
Nabisco was better run and more efficient during every phase of its
rocky tenure with KKR than it had been prior to its buyout.

And finally, it is worth highlighting the intensity of KKR's efforts
to find remedies for its distressed companies' problems. Sustained
commitment to solving financial problems was built into the incentive
structure of the buyout business: the big money was earned only when
assets were sold. KKR's concern for creditor interests was also tied
to longer-term motives; its success in raising money for future trans-

actions depended on its reputation, not simply for making money, but for dealing fairly with all its investors. In some of its distressed buyouts, as with EFB and Walter, individual KKR professionals expended great effort to work through problems, even as the prospects for equity returns grew dim. This, too, was evidence of long-term thinking.

And yet, even when a company's difficulties seemed manageable, would long-term incentives always prevail? People were prone to respond to short-term stimuli, and even the most sophisticated buyout specialists were hardly immune from the normal tendencies of human behavior. In the final analysis, reinforcing long-term commitments and subordinating individual efforts to KKR's larger community of interests was an ethical and organizational problem. It was a problem that KKR's senior partners strove to address in the unusual way they ran their firm.

5 | KKR as an Institutional Form
Structure, Function, and Character

> To business that we love we rise betime,
> And go to 't with delight.
>
> – *Antony and Cleopatra*, IV, iv

DAVID CHUNG WILL NEVER forget the moment he got the call, on June 25, 1995. He was sitting in his office at McKinsey & Co. in New York when the phone rang. George Roberts and Todd Fisher, one of KKR's younger associates, were on the line. Fisher had called him twenty minutes earlier to see if he was ready to talk, and now Chung was nervous. "David," Roberts said, "there are still a few things we're not convinced about. Would you mind answering a few questions?" Chung, one of 100 candidates for a position at KKR, had been through countless interviews with the firm's associates and partners. He steeled himself as Roberts began: "Can you give me the square root of one million sixty-four?"

And I said "Well, okay . . . ah, um." My heart was racing. I had to grab my calculator. I couldn't find it. What a time not to have my calculator! I began fumbling around, and then I realized "Wait a minute, a million sixty-four must be 1,008," but that wasn't the right answer. I fell into the trap. George let me off the hook and said "Okay, that's fine. Now, can you tell me how many gas stations there are in California that are owned by Chevron?" – a classic, consulting-type interview question. I slogged through it, "Well, let's see. There are X number of blocks and X number of gas stations per block." George had numbers in his head and he kept throwing them out at me. . . . It was painful![1]

At some point, Chung heard Fisher "snickering in the background," and Roberts said, "That was a little better. Let me ask you my third question. Would you like to come work for us at KKR?"

Chung, elated, should have known. These were not the kinds of drills KKR put its candidates through. Having been through the interviewing mill at McKinsey, he had been surprised at the difference in KKR's lengthy interviewing process. All the members of the 1990s generation of KKR associates – including Fisher, Nils Brous, Alexander Navab, and Mark Lipschultz – had encountered much the same thing. As they were passed along from KKR's younger associates to the more senior partners, none of the interviews resembled the case-oriented drills in business problem-solving they had been subjected to before. These were not oral exams. The interviewers seemed more interested in understanding how one ticked than in what one knew. "Tell me about certain investment ideas that you've had; tell me about things you've worked on recently; tell me about why you think it might've been a good business or not." Each interview, beginning with the most junior associate until the candidate finally reached the senior partners, was designed to find out who the candidate was, why he wanted to work for KKR, and what had motivated his choices in life.

Chung recalled that he had not encountered any of the aggressiveness or smugness he had expected. "I was pleasantly surprised at how nice everyone was," he said. The firm's other new hire for that year, Mark Lipschultz, who had worked as an analyst at Goldman, Sachs, was equally surprised. "I had envisioned the 'Barbarians,' " he said. "I came in for my first interview thinking that I was going to be dealing with people who are as tough and perhaps as arrogant as any Wall Street person would be." Instead, "I met people who were tough-minded, but very down to earth and very likable." Alex Navab, who had come into the firm with Todd Fisher in 1993, had a similar experience. "The strong sense I got when I went through the process was that these guys were obviously very accomplished, but really likable. They made me feel welcome, at home."[2]

KKR, they agreed, was anything but business as usual. The 1990s class of KKR associates were attracted to KKR by the opportunity it afforded them to become active principal investors in sizable companies, rather than intermediaries or advisors. They also felt that they were becoming part of the unfolding history of an unusual and important venture. Still a small firm in 1995 – the number of KKR's principal investors was just fifteen, plus a support staff of some eighty-five people in New York and Menlo Park, California – KKR had become one of Wall Street's more formidable entities and one of its most prestigious venues. If its holdings had constituted a corporation,

KKR would have ranked among the largest diversified firms in the world. Nor was KKR a typical Wall Street firm. It functioned as a financial intermediary, to be sure, but also as a merchant bank, an equity fund general partner, and a corporate directorate. As general partner and corporate directorate, KKR performed its most important economic function: long-term value creation.

Corporations, Conglomerates, and the LBO Association

Value creation was managed within what has come to be called the "LBO association," a logical structural response to the strategy of buyout investing. The LBO association looked a bit like a conglomerate, and there was some irony, at least on the surface, in the apparent similarity.

While leveraged buyouts occurred as individual events [wrote George Baker and Cynthia Montgomery], many were carried out by the same firms, the same partners, and housed in the same portfolios. After a number of years, these partnerships found themselves at the centers of industrial or retail empires, often with controlling interests in a widely diverse and highly decentralized group of companies. The LBO associations had come to resemble the very conglomerates they were supposed to be disassembling.[3]

Yet the likeness was less real than apparent. What was the LBO association precisely? Was it an improvement over the traditional corporate form? To understand better how it did what it did, we can compare the LBO association to the more conventional corporate headquarters.[4]

In the 1980s, large companies engaged in multiple businesses were typically organized as "multidivisional" organizations. In this so-called "M-form" structure, a corporate headquarters could administer a large number of diverse businesses, each of which might be organized either as a subsidiary company or as an unincorporated division or "unit." The various businesses were usually *related* in some fashion, say, in their technology or markets, but remained distinct in their day-to-day operations. By delegating executive responsibility for running the various businesses, the top managers of such corporations were free to concentrate on the big picture – to assess the environment and how it would impact on their mix of products and services and to formulate long-term strategies for investment.

In their administrative responsibilities, corporate managers acted as agents of their boards: monitoring divisional financial performance, consolidating their accounts for reporting to shareholders, raising new capital, allocating resources, and investing in new business opportunities. The corporate headquarters also contained financial and accounting staffs to control operations and a range of services deemed common to the enterprise as a whole. Such types of service might include real estate, legal, insurance, public relations, research, engineering, resource allocation, regulatory compliance, and other functions, insofar as it seemed economically efficient to consolidate these functions and centralize their staffs.

Conglomerates were a subset of the M-form corporation. What distinguished them was their higher degrees of diversification and decentralization. They had smaller headquarters offices and fewer staff functions. In its purest form, a conglomerate headquarters looked much like a holding company with highly circumscribed acquisition, oversight, and financial functions – undertaking acquisitions of unrelated businesses, monitoring and reporting on the performance of its operating units, and providing those units with such services as financing assistance and cash management. The more a conglomerate attempted to realize financial or operating "synergies" among its constituent companies, the more its headquarters might take on executive and support-staff functions like those of the more conventional multidivisional corporation.

The LBO association was of another breed altogether. Not merely a portfolio of investments, it was not a conglomerate, either. The firms that developed the LBO association as a means for controlling assets did not take the time to explain what they had conceived. The management literature tried to keep pace, but it was no easy task to analyze and interpret what was clearly a new organizational form.

Reaching for a useful analogue, scholars drew comparisons between the LBO association and the large conglomerate enterprises of the Japanese business system. Michael Jensen wrote in 1991 that "LBO partnerships play a dual role that is similar in many ways to that of the main banks in the Japanese *keiretsu*, which held equity stakes in the companies they financed, controlled access to their capital, and monitored their performance."[5] (A more apt comparison might have been the earlier *zaibatsu*, typically a conglomeration of enterprises controlled by a closely held partnership.) Jensen was careful not to stretch the comparison any further; but the idea was picked up and elaborated in an influential, though somewhat misleading, article by the historians Allen Kaufman and Ernest Englander, published in 1993.[6]

KKR's LBO Association

Kaufman and Englander argued that while KKR had begun its life buying and selling assets, its holdings had evolved into a system of interrelated investments amenable to strategic coordination. KKR had "signaled its intention," they wrote, "to create among its holdings a group of interrelated firms, which may do business with one another and may jointly seek new business opportunities." They envisioned KKR's investments as a set of "industry blocs" that were ripe for some degree of financial and market coordination. KKR's recent investments in banking institutions – the firm had acquired minority stakes in the First Interstate and Fleet-BNE – were seen as deliberate steps toward acquiring more direct control over "capital resources that can be used to finance future acquisitions and internal projects."[7] This inference, while imaginative,[8] misconceived KKR's intentions and overlooked the limits on its legal and organizational ability to create anything like a business empire. Regulatory constraints would have made it impossible for KKR to exploit its investments in banks in such a fashion, even had the firm been inclined to do so.

KKR was decidedly not a *keiretsu*-like system, nor was it conglomerate. Like a conglomerate, the LBO association was both acquisitive and diversified, but it was fundamentally different in other key respects. For one thing, it was not a holding company, either in its legal form, capital structure, or function.

While a conglomerate was typically organized as a perpetual corporation, the LBO association was a set of limited partnerships organized as equity funds. Limited partnerships had limited lives, and the life of a KKR limited partnership was typically twelve years, at the end of which it had to sell its investment and then return the capital to its fund investors.[9] And though the closing of any one limited partnership did not mean the close of the LBO association (at any one time, an LBO association might consist of investments from as many as three or four equity funds),[10] the requirement to do so constrained it to behave quite differently from a conglomerate corporation.

For example, while conglomerates and LBO associations were both acquisitive, conglomerates were typically slow to divest, unless exigency forced them to do so. The documented behavior of successful conglomerates shows that they tended to be opportunistic buyers but reluctant sellers of companies. So long as constituent business units continued to meet minimal corporate performance criteria, they were unlikely to be sold.[11] KKR, on the other hand, not only had to put the equity capital from its funds to work as soon as feasible (the capital had to be fully invested within six years), it also had to realize gains for its limited partners from the sale of the stock of its businesses. The effect of this mandate meant that KKR had to be both a systematic buyer and seller – opportunistic as to timing, but purposeful in each of its actions, from pricing the acquisition to the final disposition of the assets, driving the businesses to create as much equity value as possible.

Only occasionally, when good fortune allowed for it, was KKR able successfully to divest a business very quickly. Four of its 1980s buyouts – Golden West, Amstar, Cole National, and Storer Communications – were sold within three years of their acquisition for very high returns, in each case to take advantage of rapidly rising markets for their assets. The main asset of Golden West, for instance, was television station KTLA in Los Angeles, which experienced a huge increase in value amidst a boom market for television properties. KKR seized the moment and generated a 76.7 percent return upon selling Golden West in 1985, after a holding period of just 32 months. Amstar, an unlikely amalgamation of sugar and industrial companies, was sold in 1986, within three years of its acquisition, for an even higher return of 80.5 percent, even before KKR could implement its plans to divide the business into more sensible core components. Apart from those unusual cases, KKR held most of its companies for more than five years, ample time to implement structural and operating reforms. KKR maintained an interest in ten of its pre-1988 acquisitions for more than ten years, usually retaining effective control over their governance while liquidating portions of its fund investment along the way[12] (see figure).

It was in the way it functioned that the LBO association was so

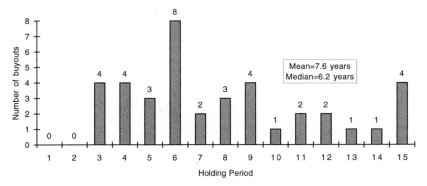

Holding periods for KKR buyouts done between 1977 and 1990, as of 12/31/97. The holding periods reflect the entire time that the KKR funds retain some equity interest in a company.

remarkably different from the typical large corporation, conglomerate or otherwise. The LBO association that KKR ran could only be loosely interpreted as having any kind of corporate headquarters. Since each investment within KKR's ambit stood alone as a legally independent corporation, with a separate capital structure and different equity investors, each investment was monitored by its own distinct board of directors (see figure).

KKR monitored the companies it controlled, but it did not attempt to exercise managerial authority over them. Among the major LBO firms, only Clayton, Dubilier, with its cadre of experienced operating managers, could effectively play that role.[13] Lacking that kind of expertise, KKR's primary responsibilities were to watch over its companies on a close and continuous basis, to help structure executive compensation, to intervene in timely fashion when management ran into serious problems, and to engineer corporate financings and refinancings, acquisitions and divestitures.[14] It was in financing where KKR was especially qualified to act. The firm's standing in the capital markets helped to lower the costs of capital to its constituent companies, and its intimate knowledge of their ongoing financial needs enabled it to restructure debt, issue stock, and otherwise make timely and efficient changes in capital structures.

Thus KKR had neither the luxury nor the temptation to engineer the kinds of financial or managerial synergies that were commonly sought by corporate conglomerate managers. Since each KKR acqui-

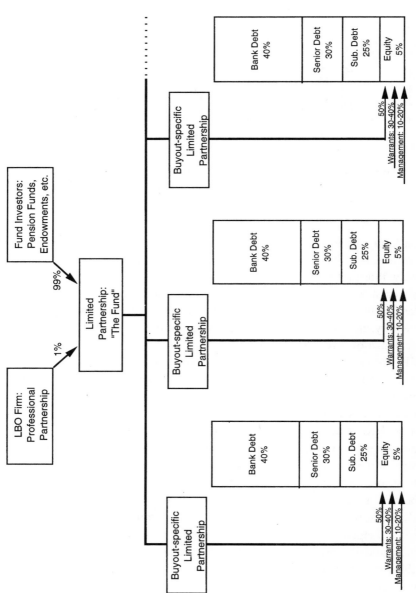

Structure of a typical LBO association.

sition was organized as a separate and distinct entity with its own equity structure and its own board of directors, there would be no consolidation of accounts. Nor could KKR transfer cash from one company to another, so that one operation might support another's operations or investments. Since each investment had separate equity holders, any attempt to intermingle activities in the separate companies was fraught with difficulties. There would be no cross subsidies, no forced interfirm sales, nor anything that might distort the market realities in which the constituent companies operated. Any quest for synergy might also impede the flexibility KKR and its constituent company managers needed to sell assets on an opportunistic basis. For example, when Donald Kelley took the helm at Beatrice, after KKR had acquired the company in 1986, he reviewed a plan by his predecessor to integrate the Tropicana juice business with the packaged cheese operations. Realizing that such integration would hamper his ability to sell either division for its maximum value, Kelley killed the initiative.[15]

Budgets and performance incentives were also unique to each company, embedded as they were in the debt and equity structure of the original buyout investments. During the critical years following a buyout, when a company was under great pressure to restructure its assets and reform its management systems, debt covenants determined and controlled budgets to a degree uncommon in the typical corporation. And just as the terms of the debt were specific to each buyout transaction, each company's management compensation was harnessed to the market for its assets. KKR helped all its constituent companies to devise incentive plans for its managers in order to achieve an alignment of managerial and shareholder interests; but the forms, details, and amounts were tailored case-by-case.

Nor did KKR impose on its companies the kinds of common controls that were typical of a corporate parent. "We had no black book," said Henry Kravis, referring to the standard systems conglomerate corporations impose on their acquisitions. "We try to work with whatever structures and systems a company has used historically and go from there."[16] The firm did offer guidance and help in the development of controls systems in cases where they were not already in place. Through its long-standing relationships with law firms, accountants, and consultants, KKR could bring a wide range of legal, financial, and management expertise to meet specific organizational needs. Thus, while there was no "one best practice" for all companies, KKR's principals looked for optimal solutions to particular problems. Serving as a criss-crossing network of board directors, they facilitated the transfer of ideas across company boundaries.

By the mid-1980s, KKR had developed relationships with a group of executives whose specific skills in managing buyouts it could effectively redeploy among its assets. In 1983, when KKR acquired PacTrust, a small real estate investment trust, its CEO Peter Bechen and his associates became virtual in-house advisors on complex real estate restructurings. They helped make possible, and profitable, several of KKR's subsequent investments, particularly in retail chains. David Johnson, who participated in the Dillingham buyout in 1983 as that company's chief operating officer, later became CEO of Red Lion and, later, KinderCare, both of which had required help following problems with its existing management. Bob Kidder was urged out of retirement following his successful stint at Duracell to take the helm at Borden. Steven Burd, who had originally been hired as a consultant for Dillingham Corporation and Safeway, Inc., was asked to troubleshoot problems at Fred Meyer before becoming CEO of Safeway. The accumulation of such managerial and advisory expertise enhanced KKR's competitive position in the increasingly crowded market for both assets and investment capital.

Shaping the Firm

The regimes KKR developed for acquiring and overseeing companies would not have been so effective had KKR not also been developing its professional partnership in ways appropriate to the tasks. Everything about the firm's structure and incentives were geared to increasing the long-term financial value of assets. With that in mind, Kravis and Roberts, as the senior members of the firm, attempted to foster social values like teamwork, collegiality, loyalty, and integrity. It was a matter not just of private morality but of business survival that they do so. Since it relied heavily on external sources for finding and minding companies, and since it had to bring investors back to the table time and again, KKR also encouraged the kinds of personal behavior that would promote trust in the markets for information and capital.

None of this was easy to achieve. Dealmakers that they were, KKR's founders had little time to spare for organization building.

Theirs was also a very personal business. They had intended to create a firm, but Paul Raether observed that when the three original partners left Bear, Stearns in 1976, they did so with the knowledge that it was they, not the institution, that mattered more. "Not even Bear, Stearns," he said, "had been much of a calling card. The calling card was really Jerry Kohlberg, Henry Kravis or George Roberts, [each one] trying to establish personal relationships with people, and really living by their wits."[17]

And so they continued through the first five years, with Kravis and Kohlberg in New York and George Roberts in San Francisco. They had help from Robert MacDonnell, Roberts's brother-in-law, who had left his own investment business to join KKR in 1976; and Donald Herdrich, who had joined Kohlberg and Kravis in New York in 1978, having been recruited from First Chicago Investment Corporation, an early investor in the three partners' deals. (Nicholas Forstmann was also with them for a brief stint in 1977, before leaving to found one of KKR's better-known competitors along with his more famous brother, Ted.) This small group worked feverishly, devoting their waking hours to financing acquisitions, overseeing the companies they had already acquired, and constantly searching for more opportunities.

The firm in the early years was owned entirely by its three founders. Kohlberg, the senior member, held 40 percent of the shares (he had put up the lion's share of the $120,000 capital to start KKR); Kravis and Roberts held 30 percent each. By the time they left Bear, Stearns, Kohlberg's mentoring job was essentially completed; his younger partners had matured and were fully equipped to undertake the kinds of sophisticated financings that even small leveraged buyouts required. In addition to helping to find business and advise on transactions, his distinctive role was to contribute a senior presence within the firm, "the gray hair."[18] Among the firm's early deals, George Roberts took the lead in structuring and closing AJ and USNR, Kravis in L.B. Foster and Houdaille. Kohlberg played the role of somewhat detached senior partner, helping to sell, exercising oversight, and staying in communication with the firm's other members. In 1981, Kohlberg's persistent, more-than-decade-long pursuit of Fred Meyer resulted in a successful deal; but afterward, the senior partner's direct involvement in KKR's buyouts waned.

A balding, distinguished-looking man with good contacts on Wall Street (Joseph Flom, the head of Skadden Arps, was a particularly close friend), Kohlberg had a flair for putting prospective sellers and investors at ease. "We were constantly dealing with psychology – the managers, the sellers, the lenders, the equity investors," Kohlberg said. "We were basically psychiatrists!"[19] He was especially adept at calming prospective investors, educating them in an unfamiliar and risky idea. Kravis and Roberts, still in their early thirties, had to work harder to inspire the same level of confidence. Ray O'Keefe, the CEO of KKR's first transaction, A.J. Industries, recalled how he had at first been drawn to Kohlberg's gray hair and his quiet, unassuming style. It took him a little longer, he said, to appreciate the analytical acumen that the youthful George Roberts brought to the table.[20]

Yet, Roberts and Kravis, young as they were, were cultivating relationships that would matter for years to come. They combed the countryside, hoping for the occasional personal contact that might get them in the door of a prospective buyout candidate or help provide the financing for an investment. In the process, they developed a growing network of investment bankers, deal finders, investors, lenders, and CEOs. It worked: within five years of KKR's founding the firm closed fourteen buyouts, all but one (Fred Meyer) the fruits of their intensive prospecting.

Finding appropriate companies for buyouts was difficult and extremely time consuming. In the heat of the 1979 Houdaille buyout, Kravis became keenly aware of the problem besetting all small firms: how coping with the business one had in hand always got in the way of finding more business. "I've got to hire somebody else in New York, because if I spend all my time working on financing and monitoring, I can't be out looking for the next deal," he told Raether, then a 34-year-old investment banker at Blyth Eastman Dillon & Company. Raether, who had been interviewed at the suggestion of a mutual friend, joined the firm on April 1, 1980.

In KKR's small headquarters on Fifth Avenue, Raether's first office was the conference room. "I had a box," he said, "and every time somebody had to use the conference room, I'd clear all my papers into my box and I'd go into the office of whoever had gone into the meeting." In his first weekend with the firm, Raether flew to Los Angeles to meet with the five other KKR principals for a two-day encounter at the Beverly Hills Hotel, "talking about the firm, what we were trying to do, and how the companies in the portfolio were doing." More important was the question of "where were we going in terms of looking for new business. Each person had a list of companies he was calling on, including a list of subsidiaries that Jerry called 'orphans.' " It was one of those orphans, discovered by George Roberts as he foraged for opportunities in the natural resources industries, that would become Raether's first project: the forest products division of Bendix corporation.[21]

The next year proved an extremely busy one, as KKR's six professionals completed seven new buyouts, while helping Houdaille with a major acquisition. The buyouts were varied in their financing and industry characteristics: American Forest Products and Fred Meyer, a retail company, were departures from the kinds of industrial companies on which KKR had previously focused and required novel financing techniques. George Roberts found the time to recruit Michael Michelson from Latham & Watkins, the law firm that helped KKR with its West Coast business. The firm's professionals would team up in pairs for every new transaction; when transactions were completed, they would continue to monitor them. By 1981 all that activity – stretched as it was among only seven professionals – made for extremely long days and nights, even by Wall Street standards.

That year, when the twenty-nine-year-old Michelson joined the San Francisco office in August, he was struck as much by the firm's utter lack of formality as by the intensity of its transactions. "There was no hierarchy, no management structure," he said. Nor was there "any articulated strategic plan as to what we were going to do over the next five years. We were just trying to do transactions and make investments." In New York, Raether was concerned that KKR's limited capabilities were being outstripped by the accelerating pace of its business. There was but a lone bookkeeper, who managed the accounts for both East and West Coast operations. Nor were there enough secretaries to go around. With some fourteen distinct companies to oversee, and an equity fund (raised in 1980) to manage, KKR had reached the point where it would need to put its affairs in more efficient order.

We had to keep track of people's commitments and how much they'd invested. We had to start to generate reports for these people about the status of the companies we had acquired, and we started coming under pressure to meet on a regular basis. None of those things were done when I got here. The partners wanted to do deals and look after their investments. They didn't want to do administration.[22]

KKR in the meantime had moved from its original New York locale on Fifth Avenue to larger offices on Madison Avenue, and the administrative demands grew as the deals grew. In 1982, with the economy squeezed by high interest rates and recession, the firm completed no buyouts, but it took advantage of the hiatus to raise a new equity fund, positioning itself for a new round of investments. At the same time, refinancings and divestitures were becoming as much a part of the firm's dealmaking activities as the buyouts themselves. Three modest-sized deals came in 1983, followed by five more in 1984, when KKR raised a billion-dollar equity fund.

Expanding the Partnership

The year 1984 was a signal one for KKR. It began badly when Jerry Kohlberg underwent an operation for an acoustic neuroma, a benign brain tumor that had caused debilitating headaches. He would be incapacitated for months, while the firm's investing activities increased at a frenetic pace. In February, KKR acquired Amstar, a half-billion-dollar transaction referred to the firm by Kohlberg's friend and longtime business ally Joseph Flom of Skadden Arps. Wometco Industries, the first billion-dollar buyout, closed soon afterward, and was followed by Malone & Hyde and Cole National Corporation, which greatly extended the boundaries of financing techniques to include tender offers and junk bonds. Pace Industries was then acquired for more than $1.6 billion, and after that "the curve was straight up," Raether said. "That's really when we had to change the way we were doing business. Finding deals was no longer the problem; we now had to prioritize what deals we really wanted to do."

To help with the increasing volume of work, KKR recruited eight new professionals between 1984 and 1987. They were all male (reflecting the prevailing culture of Wall Street, especially in the M&A arena) and young, ranging from 26 to 35 years old. Each had some seasoning in the buyout markets, albeit from different perspectives; three had legal backgrounds. Saul Fox, like Michelson, had cut his teeth at Latham & Watkins; he was a tax specialist. Theodore Ammon came from the Chicago law firm of Mayer, Brown & Platt and had worked with KKR on the Wometco buyout. Kevin Bousquette, who had been a lawyer at Latham &Watkins, had worked on KKR deals in the M&A department at Morgan Stanley. Michael Tokarz and Jamie Greene were commercial bankers – the former from Continental Illinois, the latter from Banker's Trust. They too had worked on KKR deals and could provide considerable expertise on bank financing and loan structures. (See figure.)

In 1986, Perry Golkin was one of three new hires. He was a lawyer with Simpson Thacher & Bartlett, KKR's East Coast advisors, and had also been a certified public accountant with Price Waterhouse and an accounting instructor at Wharton. Golkin was hired to oversee KKR's equity funds, with the expectation that once he had settled into that role he would go to work on buyout transactions as well. The hiring profile then began to shift; KKR began searching for candidates with more formal education in financial techniques. Edward Gilhuly, only twenty-six years old, had worked at Merrill Lynch and had just completed Stanford Business School. Scott Stuart had experience with Lehman Brothers, McKinsey & Co. and with General Atlantic, a private venture capital firm. Clifton Robbins arrived in 1987 from Morgan Stanley & Co., where he had been working on mergers and acquisitions. Michael Chu rounded out KKR's new 1980s dealmakers in 1989, having come from Pace Industries, where he had served as chief financial officer following a stint with City Investing Corporation.[23] Gilhuly, Stuart, Robbins, and Chu represented a new generation of professional investment bankers with not just breadth of experience but also depth of knowledge in the new computer-age analytical techniques for financial modeling.

The firm's deal flow and intensifying fund-raising efforts now called for more specialized administration. In 1985, John Gerson came aboard as the firm's chief financial officer, Salvatore Badalamenti as controller, and Jerry Sullivan as risk insurance manager. Annette Guarnaccio, who had joined the firm as a secretary in 1981, assumed staff responsibility for Fund administration. In 1986, Raether and Michelson began to meet with Kravis and Roberts to discuss annual adjustments in partnership shares and compensation. Other partners would assume responsibility for East and West Coast office administration.

Doubling the number of dealmakers between 1984 and 1986 increased the pressure on the firm to formalize its understandings with

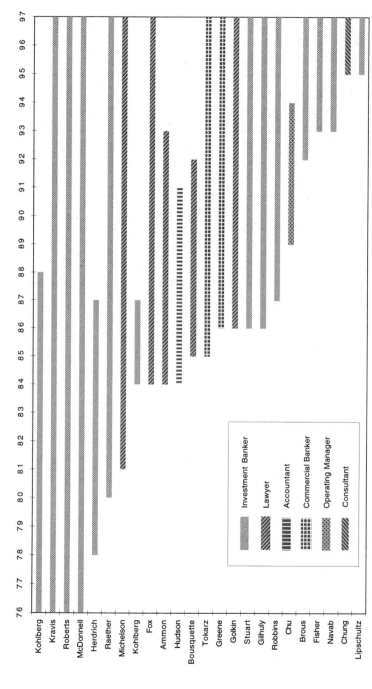

KKR partners' and associates' tenure and backgrounds, 1976–1997. The placement of each bar represents the person's starting and ending year with the firm.

its professionals. The partnership had been slow to open up. Before 1981, there had been no formal compensation structure; MacDonnell and Herdrich had been granted stakes in the firm's investments on an ad hoc basis. In December 1980, the partners made what was one of the most important policy decisions they would ever make. They granted the associates a more predictable "economic interest" in all the firm's new investments, based on percentages that would be readjusted annually. There remained no predictable path to the general partnership, however, until Bob MacDonnell – after some urging on his part – was admitted in January 1982. It then became obvious to Herdrich, Raether, and Michelson that they, too, had an opportunity to become partners. Four years would pass until Raether was made a partner in 1986. By then, Don Herdrich had more than satisfied his financial and career ambitions; in the middle of his partnership negotiations, he decided to retire to a life of relative leisure. Michelson was elevated the following year. It seemed inevitable that KKR would further broaden its partnership and elaborate its administrative structure with the continuing expansion of its business. But before that could happen, the founding partners had to resolve a serious disagreement among themselves over the future of the firm, a disagreement that would end in Jerry Kohlberg's departure.[24]

During Kohlberg's absence in the spring and summer of 1984, Henry Kravis had taken charge of the day-to-day business of the New York office, and along with George Roberts had begun to ratchet up KKR's capabilities in the buyouts of large corporations. When Kohlberg returned, what had been an ongoing discussion about their partnership shares resumed. Kravis and Roberts had anticipated that Kohlberg might retire, or at least significantly scale back his participation, which would make it easier to offer shares to the other professionals. (By then the three senior partners each controlled about twenty percent in the firm.) In early 1985, however, Kohlberg proposed to Kravis and Roberts a new partnership agreement that kept their shares equal until Kohlberg's seventieth birthday, ten years hence, and asked for a veto power over all firm matters.[25] Kravis and Roberts were confronted with a dilemma. Differences of opinion about how to reallocate the senior partners' shares might have been resolved, Roberts thought; but Kohlberg's request for a veto power, which would have altered the terms of authority among the partners, was unacceptable.[26]

A parallel issue had already surfaced when Kohlberg brought his son, James, into the firm in the summer of 1984. The younger Kohlberg had delayed his college education in order to play on the professional tennis circuit. Though he had worked for a while as a commodities broker, he lacked the experience that other new professionals brought into the firm. He went to work in San Francisco, where George Roberts, a close friend to Kohlberg's family, took him under his wing for on-the-job training. Jim Kohlberg finished his degree and worked on KKR projects, but his performance proved to be another source of conflict. In late 1985, when the elder Kohlberg offered to allocate to his son shares of his own participation in the deal for Red Lion Hotels,[27] Kravis and Roberts refused. The question was simple: was KKR to operate as a quasi-family business or a more formally professional firm? To grant anyone profit participation outside the established protocols would have triggered an exodus, Paul Raether was convinced.[28]

It took a long time for the three senior partners to come to a resolution, so personally painful was their dispute. Kohlberg brought the matter to a conclusion when he resigned on March 13, 1987. The entire matter had been kept so confidential that when he announced the event two months later, at a gathering of KKR's equity investors, it caught both Wall Street and the business press by surprise.[29]

Jerry Kohlberg left KKR with a generous agreement that provided for a gradual reduction in his share of future KKR buyouts – from just over twenty percent in 1987 to one percent by 1998. He would continue to participate in KKR deals on that basis.[30] Kohlberg went into business with his son, and Kohlberg & Company conducted a series of successful smaller-scale buyouts. Their firm became the nucleus of a cluster of family-run and financed enterprises, including a nonprofit charitable foundation and an organization dedicated to campaign finance reform. For their part, Kravis and Roberts redoubled their efforts at firm building, as KKR entered into a more intensive period of buyout activity than even they had anticipated.

The Kravis-Roberts Nexus

Even as late as 1988, it was not clear that KKR would outlive its two remaining founding partners. The firm possessed a stable, close-knit, loyal, and seasoned corps of professionals. It had a number of companies under its wing, and a well-established reputation – a brand name, so to speak. But as an entity it was almost completely identified with the personae of Henry Kravis and George Roberts. Had they both been run over by the proverbial bus, the firm would have had trouble surviving. They were involved in every one of the firm's deals and held seats on all constituent company boards. They also exercised a unique leadership role in the firm, guiding its strategies and setting the standards and tone for the firm's ethical culture. Externally, they had established powerful personal reputations and had forged invaluable relationships in the investment community. Fortunately, they were just forty-five years old; slowing down was the farthest thing from their minds. "They don't want to be . . . flashes in the pan," Saul Fox said. "They want to build something that will last beyond them."[31]

They would attempt to institutionalize the firm, in part, through sheer example. "We hoped that how Henry and I treated each other would be a lesson to our younger professionals," Roberts said.[32] From the composite portrait painted by their colleagues, Henry Kravis and George Roberts, friends since childhood, had managed to weave a seamless relationship that remained a source of wonder even to those who worked with them. The two men were cousins. They had been fast friends since their days at Claremont College, where George had graduated a year before Henry. Both were small in physical stature, yet decidedly charismatic; they each could command attention through force of presence and sustain it through force of intellect. Both were gentlemen in a crude era – articulate, polite, formally correct in social intercourse. Both were entrepreneurial, energetic, extraordinarily enthusiastic about their business, and unflagging salesmen for their ideas.

They were cousins, but not twins, Kravis noted. He was the firm's more public face. His private life and charitable activities filled the newspaper columns. Gregarious by nature, he was aggressive in making contacts, swimming the social mainstream of New York City. New York was anathema to George Roberts, who shunned the limelight as if it would give him skin cancer. He had always preferred the West Coast and the quieter climes of California, where he enjoyed spending time at home with his family and occasionally teaching at Stanford Law School. More reserved than his cousin, he was laconic and intense in demeanor, though no less skilled in making business contacts. His approach was to seek out people on a one-on-one basis, while his cousin Henry enjoyed working the crowd.

The intellectual differences were subtle, though noteworthy, if only because both men were highly regarded for their strategic sense and their acuity in deal making. Their partners regarded Roberts as more analytical and Kravis as more intuitive. Roberts explained things succinctly, sometimes tersely, with pinpoint precision. Kravis was more likely to surround his subjects with vivid verbal imagery. In the process of deal making, Roberts excelled in designing complex financial structures, while Kravis was more geared to working with managers and financial institutions. Yet both men were masters at assessing deals, picking balance sheets apart, sizing up managers. And both were good with people, a quality which Kravis liked to claim was important to their success.[33]

According to their partners, what set Kravis and Roberts apart was a surpassing ability to cut through masses of detail, to conceptualize the two or three decisive questions in any prospective deal. KKR associate Nils Brous recalled the impression George Roberts made on him shortly after he joined the firm.

We were meeting at Menlo Park, studying an industry to see if it made sense to invest in it, and had identified a potential target. A team of ten investment bankers, some pretty senior, had been working with us in our analysis for weeks. George Roberts, who hadn't been involved to that point, dropped in, and listened to all the reasons why the target company's circumstances made a deal unworkable. Almost immediately, he suggested an alternative way of structuring the transaction that would make the deal feasible. No one else had seen it. The investment bankers were astonished. So was I.[34]

That capacity, Brous soon learned, was shared by Henry Kravis – an attribute of experience, perhaps, but more likely a unique capability, uniquely shared. Brous found it hard to explain.

It was also hard to explain why two senior partners almost never appeared to have serious conflicts. "One office in New York and one in California," said Roberts, "both full of ambitious and aggressive people, was a prescription for a dogfight. But we've worked hard to make it work." The cousins respected each other's turfs. Raether observed that "George never tried to tell Henry how to run the office in New York, and vice versa." This accommodation showed up in superficial ways. Kravis wanted his staff formally attired at all times; female employees wore skirts. Roberts, on the other hand, might arrive to work in shirtsleeves, Menlo Park's secretaries in blue jeans. While such external differences never ran deep, they reflected the modus vivendi the senior partners had developed.

On more basic issues of strategy and policy, agreement was essential. Within the firm's wider councils, differences of opinion between the senior partners would flash on occasion, but then quickly evaporate. There had always been, said Kravis, an agreement between the two to treat each other with abiding respect. Neither was to do anything important without the other's consent; any disagreement on a substantive matter would result in no action taken. KKR refrained from investing in several deals, good and bad, on that basis alone. "We wanted the mutual respect we accorded each other to percolate through the firm," Roberts said. "We wanted our other partners to learn to treat each other the same way."[35]

What Kravis and Roberts agreed on completely was the kind of business they wanted to do, what values they wished their firm to live by, and what they wanted for the future of their firm. They had always wanted KKR to become more than an organizational convenience for their deals; but the organizational manifestations of that desire evolved slowly. By the late 1980s they were working more deliberately toward building a business that would be capable of surviving them, a durable partnership that reflected their values.

Central to those values was teamwork. This was easy to achieve among three or four people, much harder among ten or twenty. Most professional firms purported to believe in it; the problem was how to ensure it. In the highly individualistic culture that Wall Street had become in the almost purely transaction-oriented markets of the 1970s and 1980s, teamwork had become little more than a polite catchword. It was, however, far from a trivial concern to firms engaged in long-term value creation. A successful buyout demanded continuing attention over a period of years. No one person could do all the things necessary to make a deal profitable. The very nature of the LBO association demanded a high degree of cooperation among the general partners and KKR associates.

Financial Incentives

Deal finding, negotiating, financing, and monitoring worked better when intra-firm information was fluid and mutual assistance forthcoming. When deals went bad, the partners responsible for their oversight had to do everything they could to make lenders, if not equity investors, whole. They could not cut and run to the next seemingly more profitable venue. The demands for creative thinking at every critical stage in the life of a buyout were intense, and such thinking was only enhanced when dealmakers were cooperating. There was little if any room for freelancing, from the first glimmerings of an opportunity to the final day of disposition. Collaboration was of the essence. Every time they hired new personnel, therefore, KKR's partners looked for people who seemed collegial in temperament. Once hired, new KKR professionals were then tied to a financial incentive system that would encourage their cooperative instincts to flourish.

In its basic outline, the system was simple. The firm provided two ways for professionals to earn compensation beyond their salaries. One was through ownership of stock in the firm's portfolio companies. From the time of joining the firm, an associate was offered the right to buy stock in each of the deals that the firm closed during the year. The amount offered would increase as the associate gained seniority. In addition, after twelve to eighteen months, the associate would be granted a fixed percentage in the firm's bonus pool. The bonus pool roughly equaled the firm's profits for the year: it included all the firm's fee income (deal fees, management fees, and retainers), plus twenty percent of the capital gains on each investment (the "override"), net of operating expenses for the year. Each professional's percentage of the bonus pool was fixed *at the beginning of the year,* precisely to avoid having to reconcile competing claims over end-of-year bonuses. George Roberts recalled the way he had been forced to rely on Jerry Kohlberg to fight for his annual bonus with the Bear, Stearns executive committee. "I hated that," he told Raether, who explained:

We didn't conform to the usual investment banking procedure, whereby at the end of the year you went in with your list and you said: "I worked on this and that deal, and I generated this or that amount in fees, and so if my bonus isn't what I think it should be, I'm going to quit."[36]

At the beginning of each year, the most senior members of the firm (in the early years, Kohlberg, Kravis, and Roberts; in later years, Kravis, Roberts, Michelson, and Raether) would determine each professional's percentage of the bonus pool. The policy made it possible to reward behavior that aimed for long-term success. It was possible under KKR's system to get an increase in percentage without working on a new deal, just as it would be possible to become a partner in the firm without finding a deal. Solving problems for companies that were not doing well, raising equity funds, devoting time to administrative obligations – all those things mattered, so long as the senior partners could see that such activities supported the efforts of the group and the long-term value of KKR's investments.[37] Percentages were adjusted slowly, as associates gained seniority and as the contributions to the firm of the various professionals changed.[38]

The firm's profit sharing did not end with the investment professionals. All support personnel, including the firm's secretaries, receptionists, kitchen and mail room staff – indeed everyone employed by the firm – were given "phantom shares" in the firm's deals. (The partners and associates put up their own funds for their participation in the investments.) This wider participation helped to generate a strong professional tone throughout the organization, one in which courtesies were unflagging, responses timely, secrets closely guarded, and clocks not too closely watched.

KKR's compensation philosophy helped to reinforce the kind of long-term thinking and loyalty that were important to the success of KKR's investments. Loyalty depended, too, on the perception and the reality of meritocratic advancement; and in a collegial firm, with little hierarchy, merit was signaled chiefly in financial terms. Accordingly, when Kohlberg left, his schedule of declining participation became an important source of shares for the younger professionals. Kravis and Roberts also continued to reduce their own shares in the business, making it less likely that younger partners would leave the firm out of concern that they had no room for advancement.

One might think that profit-sharing schemes of this sort were bound to fail in highly competitive markets. Star performers, after all, could be wooed away with the promise that they would get to keep larger shares of their individual contributions, based on such criteria as the amount of business they could generate or the number of transactions they could complete. Many traditional law firms with collegial compensation schemes, for example, came unglued in the 1980s, as rainmakers became hot commodities in the market for that kind of talent. Traditional Wall Street investment banks, with strong collegial cultures, came under similar pressure.[39] During the 1980s, the buyout business became more competitive, as dozens of boutique firms sprang up alongside buyout departments in the more established investment banks. Talent was at a premium. Yet, between 1976 and 1996, when Saul Fox resigned to set up his own buyout firm, no professional left KKR voluntarily to enter a competing business. At least three factors help explain why.

First of all, KKR did not hire on a star-system basis. "No one was hired over the heads of our younger professionals," Kravis noted. "We were determined to grow our own expertise." The firm attempted to bring in people whose temperaments were thought to be particularly suited to teamwork and whose potential could best be nurtured in a collegial setting. Second, KKR's own "stars," specifically Kravis and Roberts, believed that it was to their own long-term advantage not to press for what could be argued were their full claims on the firm's year-to-year earnings. The split with Kohlberg had also had the effect of making more room, financially, for the younger members of the firm. Finally, even if one could imagine doing better financially elsewhere, KKR provided a working environment that was highly appealing in its collegial ambiance to the kinds of people it had recruited in the first place.

Non-Financial Controls

KKR's compensation system was designed to keep meritocracy and teamwork in equipoise. Yet there was more to ensuring cooperative behavior than financial incentives alone. Promoting collegial behavior and values in an individual member of the firm began in the recruiting process. A prospective recruit was hired only after the entire partnership was convinced that he possessed more than the intellectual capabilities and analytical skills required for creative dealmaking. Would he or she "fit" the firm's culture, be a team player, stay in it for the long haul? The problem, explained Mike Michelson, one of KKR's senior partners, was how to find candidates who did not fit the usual Wall Street profile. How could the firm assess the ineffable qualities of business judgment, intellectual honesty, personal integrity, and – a departure from what most investment banking firms expected – an ability to subordinate one's desire for recognition and economic interests to the welfare of the group?[40] Was it possible to find people with strong enough egos to function as both team players and nonconformists? Was this a contradiction in terms? Michelson thought not:

There is a fundamental "buy in" to the way of doing things here, but once people buy in, we don't want them to be yes men. We want people who are independent thinkers, with different perspectives, different slants on things. . . . We encourage that. We need that. It is necessary for the creative process. In a sense, what I'm saying might appear somewhat contradictory, but it's not. The whole problem is thought through, and we believe we've found an intelligent approach to it.[41]

Thus while the partnership was not created equal, and while economic outcomes varied among the principals, ideas from whatever source were always given equal consideration. Mike Tokarz recalled the first KKR meeting he attended in California, on his first day of work in 1985. "We played tennis and talked about our individual deals. We shared all of the issues with one another. We talked about where we're going, made suggestions, asked questions." He remembered sitting in a room with all the professionals assembled, and how the conversation went.

It didn't matter if you were a partner or not. You could say whatever you wanted. Obviously, the more junior you were, the less knowledge you had of what has already happened, so you listen more, speak less. But George and Henry in particular always asked our opinions. It was a very warm environment in which to discuss things, to be able to contribute and feel included in the process.[42]

The spirit of intellectual equality translated well into the heat of battle. One of the more affecting passages in *Barbarians at the Gate* depicts a meeting in Henry Kravis's office of every KKR professional available on the day KKR pondered one final increase in its bid for RJR Nabisco. Though the younger associates often grew weary of these constant iterations, Kravis and Roberts began their discussion in typical fashion, beginning with Scott Stuart, the youngest member present. This ensured that junior members of the firm would not feel bound to conform to opinions already voiced by their seniors. When

Roberts expressed his misgivings, and Kravis then declared that nothing could happen unless Roberts agreed, it was Jamie Greene, a not-yet-three-year associate in the San Francisco office, who made the persuasive argument for going ahead.[43]

A persistent question was how to prevent the firm from maturing too much, from losing its entrepreneurial spirit, its creativity. Encouraging the younger associates to speak their minds was one way in which the senior partners tried to keep themselves open to new ideas. Other habits reinforced fluid communications. KKR's principals, unless traveling or otherwise engaged in the firm's business, were expected to eat lunch together in the office. It became common practice for KKR principals to invite colleagues to attend meetings with invited guests, often for nothing more specific than the prospect of learning something new about some aspect of an industry.

On a more formal basis, KKR held closed meetings for its professionals at least three times a year – often in conjunction with some athletic event – with neither spouses nor guests in tow. The meetings focused in large part on big-picture, strategic and structural issues. They were also occasions for promoting smaller group and bilateral discussions among the professionals, bringing them up to date on prospects, ongoing transactions, and governance matters. Weekly gatherings of professionals in the East Coast and West Coast offices were also routine (in the 1990s the two coasts would be linked in a Monday morning conference call). All these meetings were to some extent free-form. Agendas were set, but not tightly controlled.

More tightly controlled were the firm's ethical standards, which by all accounts were constantly discussed. The substance and appearance of propriety was especially important to KKR, which operated in a suspicious, when not outright hostile, environment. "We were always trying to find the middle of the table," said Jamie Greene. Mike Michelson remembered the warning from his first days on the job. "We're going to be scrutinized in everything that we do," he was told.

There was a real sense that we have responsibility to our partners, to ourselves, and to our families. We're not going to do anything that's wrong. We're going to toe the straight and narrow, . . . do things only after thinking them through. If there's ever a question of ethics, or a question of appearance, we're going to be so far to the right, that we can't be questioned.[44]

KKR's transactions survived a continuous battery of tax audits; and none of its members was implicated, even by innuendo, in any of the scandals that sometimes erupted around the firm's deals. Its critics might complain about its fees, berate it for its use of debt, or condemn it for being part of an upsetting economic process; but as individuals, KKR's principals were determined to be exemplary in their professional conduct. As a matter of course, professionals had their tax returns prepared by the firm's accountants. They were expected to forego investing outside the bounds of the firm's own deals, and to be as forthright in dealings as possible, not only within the firm but with external parties as well. This point was hammered home time and again by the firm's senior partners, who took pride in the trust KKR shared with its investors. Reputation was everything, according to George Roberts, who worried about both real and perceived conflicts of interest. Roberts could certainly point to the evidence that integrity mattered – like the testimonial sent to him by Daniel Grimm, a member of the Washington State Investment Board, one of the earliest of KKR's institutional investors.

[T]hrough all the years and all the detailed reviews, I don't remember a single instance when anyone ever asserted that anything you ever said was untrue, that any information you ever presented was incorrect, or that anything you ever did was unethical . . . [and] there's no doubt in my mind that your success is . . . attributable to the personal and professional trust you have established over and over again.[45]

More subtle controls were at work in the way KKR's professionals related to each other and to third parties. "There is a tremendous amount of respect for people," said Jamie Greene. "It permeates the entire organization." Kravis and Roberts were always watching how well KKR's professionals treated people in subordinate positions, "those they don't *have to* treat well," as Roberts put it. Anyone who kept a visitor waiting too long for a meeting might be dressed down for it. Job candidates who condescended to the clerical staff were removed from consideration.

Peer respect was deemed absolutely crucial to the firm's success. It reinforced collegiality. Backbiting was anathema: people who joined the firm would find little in the way of petty politics or personal rumor. "I want no gossip in this place," Kravis would say, as animatedly as he could. "There is no room for playing politics, and no time for anyone to engage in backbiting. We won't tolerate any of that under any circumstance."[46] Cliques, office alliances, and interest groups were as inimical to the firm's values as rampant individualism. One associate expressed amazement at how even informal discussions at KKR tended to steer away from "internal issues," personal or otherwise. "We're always focusing outside," he noted, "How do we compete? How do we get this next deal? That's really how we expend our energy, 99 percent of it."[47]

Just as it was important to channel individual energies productively, it was important to sustain individual enthusiasm for what was constantly taxing labor. KKR partners claimed they were mutually vigilant in discouraging obsessive work – exhausted professionals were encouraged to take time off, to spend more time with their families, "to tend to what was really important," as George Roberts put it. But hard work is a relative concept, and buyout specialists could be subjected to brutal schedules for protracted periods – twelve- to sixteen-hour days were common, especially when deals were being fashioned or when postdeal problems demanded close attention. For young men at the start of their careers, hard work could be an exciting elixir; for veterans, it could pale. Attrition resulted mainly from the psychic toll exacted by the firm's frenetic pace or from some change in personal interests. Don Herdrich retired early. Ted Ammon and Kevin Bousquette left in the early 1990s to become head of a printing company and the chief financial officer of an auction house, respectively.[48] Michael Chu remembered those late nights in the conference room, "when you're banging your head against lawyers and investment bankers, and you look out the window and say: "Someday. . . ."" He left in 1993 to become head of Accion, a nonprofit agency for promoting micro-business development in Latin America.

How, then, Paul Raether asked, "do we keep the Scott Stuarts and the Cliff Robbins, the Ned Gilhulys, and the Perry Golkins of the world energized? How do you keep them involved in the place so that they don't want to go off and start their own firm, and do their own thing?" The answer was to involve them in more decisions, increase their percentages, and give them more authority. As Alex Navab noted: "They give us a generous stake in the firm, and the authority and the opportunity to go out there and find the next deal, and the responsibility to convince the firm that it is a good investment. I think that kind of thing makes it a great, fulfilling job."[49]

Most KKR professionals stayed on long after the personal drive to achieve wealth and status had diminished. The veteran Mike Michelson explained his own reason for remaining in the business for more than fifteen years. The money had ceased to enthrall him, he said. "It's just a pleasure to work here."[50]

What Michelson liked most about KKR was its ethical culture. The culture, which stressed collegial cooperation among professionals, a respect for persons, and moral integrity, was hard to institutionalize in the financial world. So were durable partnerships. Firms like Lazard Frères and Goldman, Sachs were categorical exceptions, not the rule, and their services covered a broader array of markets than those of KKR, which remained a small and highly specialized business. Even though KKR's culture and operating systems were well defined by the end of the 1980s, the boom in leveraged management buyouts had begun to subside. The signs were clear that the market for KKR's services was changing.

The simple fact is that most firms in any business fail to survive their founders. And since most firms on Wall Street are especially fragile, as institutions go – dominated by transient personalities highly vulnerable to changes in the environment – it was not a foregone conclusion that a small partnership like KKR would be more than a short-lived phenomenon. On the other hand, its reputation was great; its partners were still young and loyal and showed no signs, yet, of losing their nimbleness, their knack for creativity. The question remained, though: how well would they adapt to the changing realities of the 1990s?

6 | Into the Mainstream
KKR in the 1990s

> Indeed, some of the most fundamental ideas
> consistently deployed through twenty years
> of KKR transactions are today so well ac-
> cepted in modern corporate America that it
> may be hard to remember how radical these
> principles seemed when practiced by KKR
> in the 1970s and 1980s.
>
> – Joseph Grundfest, Stanford Law School

ONCE KKR HAD SUCCESSFULLY laid the groundwork for the
large-scale management buyout, it discovered what happens
to all entrepreneurial ventures: markets mature, profits attract
competition, and innovations become commonplace. In 1997, there
were an estimated 800 "LBO equity" partnerships. Most were small
boutiques, but the high end of the market had also become crowded
with proficient practitioners. The management buyout was so widely
practiced that one has to pause to remember just how far KKR had
come from its obscure beginnings in just two decades.

KKR's founders had a track record, but little inkling of what they
would accomplish, when they set up shop in 1976 to practice their
unusual method of acquiring small companies. What had been known
as "bootstrap" financings had been practiced successfully for at least
twenty years in obscure pockets of U.S. finance, but to most of Wall
Street, the art of highly leveraged buyouts remained a mystery.

To the small group of individual and institutional investors who
helped to finance KKR's early investments, buyouts appeared to be a
highly particular form of wealth creation, suited to privately held,
cash-rich businesses in slow-growth industries. KKR's first limited
partnership equity fund amounted to what then seemed like a boun-
tiful $35 million. Not content to remain small-company investors,
KKR kept honing its skills in prospecting, financing, and monitoring.

In 1979, the firm startled the financial community (and the Securities and Exchange Commission) by borrowing $380 million to buy out a public company, Houdaille Industries, "taking it private" with the expectation of improving the company's cash flow through financial and operating reforms. More than any single transaction, the Houdaille buyout set the stage for the rapid growth of leveraged transactions during the 1980s.

The relationships KKR formed with a widening circle of lenders and equity investors opened up new and greater opportunities. Year after year, as KKR's investments increased in scale they also increased in scope. The firm's original practice of leveraging basic manufacturing concerns widened by the mid-1980s to include companies across a wide spectrum of American industry: perishable consumer products, broadcast and cable television, food and specialty retailing, packaging, printing, publishing, real estate, forest products, and natural resources. With rare exceptions, its management buyouts yielded extraordinary returns to equity holders while repaying lenders promptly, if not ahead of schedule (see Appendix).

After 1984, the growing market for high-yield or "junk" securities made ever larger buyouts possible to finance with layers of unsecured debt. With its unrivaled skills in mobilizing buyout financing, KKR moved to the epicenter of the market for corporate control. The 1986 acquisition of Beatrice proved that even the most complex of ailing corporations could be restored to health by means of the value-creating techniques of the management buyout. Four years later, as the 1980s merger wave began to ebb, KKR controlled more assets than but a handful of giant industrial corporations.

So long as the buyout market remained small, KKR seldom had to face serious competition from rival bidders. That circumstance, as we have seen, changed dramatically after the mid-1980s. Buyout techniques became more widely appreciated, both by worthy and less competent new practitioners of the art. As competition increased, the market for corporate control overheated. The prices of *all* corporate assets rose to levels that made leveraged deals more risky and returns less lofty than they had been in the mid-1980s (see figure). Then, in 1990, the merger wave on which the expanding LBO market had been riding came to an abrupt end. The collapse of the junk-bond market and new political and regulatory pressures made highly leveraged transactions more difficult to finance. Squeezed on all sides by grow-

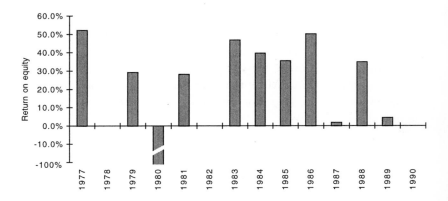

Return on equity for KKR buyouts by year of original investment, 1977–1990.
Each yearly return is the weighted average return on equity (weighted by the equity investment in each deal) for each year that KKR did buyouts.

ing competition, poor market conditions, political pressures, and public hostility, the buyout seemed permanently crippled, if not doomed.
Yet contrary to predictions, the management buyout found new life
as the 1990s progressed.

A fifth merger wave (or perhaps "merger wave 4–B," as George
Roberts called it)[1] would begin to swell in 1992, involving even more
corporate restructuring than ever before. U.S. merger and acquisition
deals swelled to a staggering $1 trillion in aggregate annual value in
1997, with no end in sight. High levels of corporate restructuring
activity, management buyouts included, had become an abiding feature of the nation's economic life. By the mid-1990s, buyouts were
standard components of institutional equity portfolios, which made
ample room for what they now called "private equity" – a category
of higher risk, higher return finance that also embraced venture capital and distressed securities investing (see table).

Thus, a once-exotic financing technique moved from the peripheries
of corporate finance into the mainstream. The typical leverage in a
1990s management buyout was lower than it had been in the 1980s,
when it was regarded with a mixture of respect, fear, and suspicion,
both within and outside the financial community. The buyout's underlying principles – aligning managerial and ownership interests, in-
sisting on more accountability to investors, imposing more rigorous

board oversight – had penetrated the executive suites and boardrooms of the nation's major corporations.[2] KKR's Mike Michelson put it this way: "Buyouts have become more accepted in the corporate world. What we did in the 1980s now gets done by the Business Roundtable."[3]

Completed U.S. mergers and acquisitions, leveraged buyouts, and KKR Fund leveraged buyouts, 1991–96 (continued)

	M&As	LBOs	LBOs as Percent of M&A	KKR Fund Buyouts*
1991	3,126	166	5.3%	2
1992	3,512	207	5.9	3
1993	3,890	158	4.1	1
1994	4,588	155	3.4	0
1995	5,513	163	3.0	6#
1996	6,145	148	2.4	2

* Excluding build-up investments. Note, too, that not all KKR buyouts were highly leveraged in this period.
\# Including Borden, Inc.
Sources: Securities Data Co.; KKR files.

From Buyouts to Build-ups and Beyond

The problem for KKR, as the new decade commenced, was how to sustain the vitality of its business. In a more competitive market for management buyouts, good deals would be harder to find, and the robust returns typical of the early 1980s harder to achieve. Even after the subordinated debt markets recovered from the junk-bond debacle of the early 1990s, the debt available for buyouts would be shallower relative to the demand. The demand came not only from the proliferating specialty houses, but also from the newly formed LBO departments of the large commercial and investment banks. And as the stock market climbed to record levels after the recession of 1990–91, it was the strategic buyers of assets who were best positioned to deploy stock and cash to dominate the merger and acquisition markets.

It was a more difficult environment for all the LBO houses, not just for KKR. Yet clever entrepreneurs keep finding new ways to survive and grow. The more creative LBO houses found niches in which they could more easily exploit their firm-specific strengths. Those with turnaround management skills, like Clayton, Dubilier & Rice, looked for opportunities among troubled divisions of large corporations. Others focused on particular industries to which they could bring concentrated managerial and financing expertise. Some chose to remain small and concentrate on a few select transactions. (Kohlberg & Co. fits this description.) Still others – like Blackstone Group and Carlyle Group – teamed up with strategic buyers in joint acquisitions, adding equity capital and sophisticated financial expertise to the corporation's managerial acumen and industry-specific knowledge. Welsh, Carson, Anderson & Stowe, a specialist in the health care and information industries, provided most of the subordinate debt financing in addition to the equity for its deals, enabling it to compete more directly with strategic buyers in its industry niches.[4] KKR's competitive advantage rested on a combination of experience and sustained expertise. It could capitalize, as virtually no other buyout specialist could, on what economists refer to as strong "first mover advantages." KKR enjoyed a long-standing reputation for meeting its obligations. It had accumulated experience in financing buyouts across a wide range of industries under a variety of investing conditions. Perhaps most important, it had shown an ability to attract, train, acculturate, and retain talented practitioners. The stability of its organization reinforced its institutional reputation and experience. KKR would continue to exploit these advantages at the high end of the buyout market.

To succeed, however, KKR would have to continue to innovate. As the 1980s merger wave subsided, the firm had already begun to deviate from what had been the general pattern of its buyout financings. In two untried industries, banking and publishing, the firm demonstrated an ability to deal with unexpected turns of events by crafting innovative investments. In 1988 and later in 1991, KKR pursued desirable targets in the banking industry despite political barriers to buyouts that were forbiddingly high. First, it made an investment in First Interstate to test the waters; then, after one false start, it subsequently engineered a buyout of the Bank of New England as a fifty-fifty joint venture with Fleet Financial Corporation – the first time since its acquisition of Union Texas Petroleum with Allied Signal Corporation that KKR would enter into a transaction with a strategic partner. When it created K-III Holdings, L.P. (now Primedia, Inc.) in 1989, KKR stood the buyout on its head with its first "leveraged build-up," an acquisitions partnership between KKR and a group of managers with no initial assets. The partnership's mission was to seek out and acquire companies in specialized information media. In setting up K-III, KKR was effectively "outsourcing" LBO functions to trusted experts in a defined set of related businesses.

The K-III story began as a buyout attempt and ended in the creation of a new corporate acquisition vehicle. In 1988, the Macmillan Group, a publicly held publishing company, was put into play after investor Robert Bass made an unsolicited bid for the company. When the British publishing magnate Robert Maxwell entered the fray, KKR made a white-knight offer for the company, but could not overcome Maxwell's rather reckless penchant for spending. His bid for more than $2.6 billion won the day. Nonetheless, during its due-diligence efforts, KKR learned a great deal about Macmillan. It got to know several of its top managers, including President William Reilly, Vice President-General Counsel Beverly Chell, and Chief Financial Officer Charles McCurdy, none of whom were excited by the prospect of working for Macmillan's new owner. In January 1989, KKR offered to back these executives in a newly formed company, K-III, winning them away from Maxwell with an offer to split the ownership of the new business – the company's executives would own 25 percent of the equity. Perhaps even more enticing to K-III's prospective management team, they would be empowered to build their own business from scratch.

K-III's strategy was rooted in the observation that those who could provide substantive content would be well positioned to capitalize on rapidly changing distribution methods in telecommunications and media. K-III's managers were authorized to identify and pursue acquisition targets, after discussing the prospects with KKR. Acquisition targets were divided between "mother ships" – large businesses that could stand on their own – and "minnows" – smaller companies or individual publications or product lines that could be integrated into existing K-III business units.

KKR rarely got involved with the smaller units, but helped to finance those that became the anchors of the enterprise. Between 1989 and 1994, K-III identified 745 companies as possible acquisition targets in a wide range of communications, publication, and media businesses. By 1997, K-III owned such well-known magazine brands as *Seventeen, Weekly Reader,* and *Ward's Automotive* along with more exotic names like *Shotgun News* and *National Hog Farmer.* It had acquired Channel One, the satellite television station, which beamed specialized educational programming into classrooms. Some sixty-three businesses had been acquired for a total of $2.8 billion, creating a company with revenues comparable to those of Macmillan, at less than half the cost.[5]

The financing of K-III's transactions typically employed a much higher percentage of equity – often up to 40 percent – than had KKR's 1980s deals; but in other respects, the tried and true principles of the KKR buyout were at work. As with all KKR buyouts, desirable acquisitions were those that occupied the top or second position in niche markets, and that had strong editorial staffs willing to stay on under new ownership and then take equity positions in the parent company. KKR funded K-III's expenses; plowed back proceeds from equity issues and exploited tax code provisions to pay down debt as rapidly as possible;[6] negotiated new credit facilities and provided ongoing analytical and financing help for the company's acquisitions program. It also monitored the company's operations and saw to it that K-III's managers – some 250 of them by 1997 – became substantial investors in the company's stock. The build-up model would subsequently be applied to KKR's investment in Granum Holdings (1991), a limited partnership designed to acquire properties in broadcast radio; KC Cable Associates (1992), designed to acquire cable television systems; and KSL Recreation Corporation (1992), which focused on destination resorts and golf courses.

The banking ventures were part of a long-term plan by KKR to cultivate value from undermanaged assets in that complex but fertile industry. Always looking to expand its holdings in attractive new venues, KKR for years had been quietly surveying the banking industry, which was rife with excess capacity. There had been a gradual loosening of the regulatory constraints that had kept the U.S. banking system in a fragmented state for nearly two centuries. That, along with the more recent widespread failure of savings and loan institutions and some large regional commercial banks, presented ample possibilities for mergers, acquisitions, and restructurings. On October 12, 1988, KKR made a straight equity investment of $105.8 million to acquire about

6 percent of First Interstate Bank in California. It did so only after concluding that a leveraged buyout would not likely pass muster with regulatory agencies. KKR's minority position in First Interstate would never exceed 9.9 percent,[7] but with this investment, the firm's partners became more familiar with banking regulations and were able to get hearings with the Federal Reserve Board, the Federal Deposit Insurance Corporation, and the Comptroller of the Currency. Not incidentally, KKR became a financial advisor to First Interstate's management on strategic and financial issues, from which relationship it learned a great deal more about the economics of the industry.[8]

It would be difficult to go any further, as regulatory authorities remained indifferent, if not hostile, to KKR's desire to apply the full weight of its buyout regime to banking. KKR was checked in its next attempt, this time to acquire the failed Texas bank M-Corp, because of opposition from the Federal Deposit Insurance Corporation. (The FDIC accepted a lower bid for M-Corp's assets from Banc One.) In 1991, KKR became intrigued by the possibility of financing a buyout of the struggling Bank of New England (BNE) and tried to allay regulatory concerns by teaming up with Fleet Banking Group, which under the leadership of its CEO, Terence Murray, had become one of the nation's fastest growing and better managed regional banks. The acquisition of BNE was to be financed almost wholly with equity, including $283 million from KKR for a half stake in the equity of BNE, the other half of which would be held by Fleet,[9] which would then assume full responsibility for managing BNE's assets. KKR would not put any of its partners on Fleet's board of directors. KKR expected (it turned out to be true) that this arrangement would shield its investments in BNE from regulatory opposition.

Yet how, under these circumstances, could KKR exercise any effective monitoring function? KKR had a great deal of faith in Terence Murray, but it was not about to become a merely passive investor. To ensure that Fleet would continue to act in KKR's interests, the firm structured its Fund's equity holdings in the form of a "dual convertible preferred stock," a novel security that gave KKR the option ultimately to convert its holdings either into shares of the parent (Fleet) or of the subsidiary (BNE). Fleet's management would thus have a clear incentive to focus its efforts on improving BNE, while KKR would benefit from its right to transparent, unconsolidated financial reports on the subsidiary's progress.[10]

With the BNE acquisition, KKR showed just how far it was prepared to go to expand its investment horizons. In this instance, the firm proved willing not only to forgo leverage to effect a buyout, but also to pursue an opportunity under terms that were extremely unorthodox by its own standards, yet only so long as it could substantially influence what happened after the deal was closed. As matters moved ahead, KKR helped Fleet acquire additional banking properties in Massachusetts, New York, and New Jersey; by 1997, it had recorded a nearly 35 percent annually compounded return on its investment.

While KKR retained its investments in the First Interstate and Fleet, it continued to survey the financial services industry. The industry was ripe, and KKR found good pickings in two insurance companies in the property and casualty field: the American Re Corporation, purchased at a cost of $1.5 billion in 1992, and the much smaller Canadian General Insurance Group, Limited, purchased in 1995 for $164 million. The opportunity to realize value in this sleepy branch of financial services came from its concentrated industry structure. Barriers to entry were high, a KKR report noted, but opportunities for "significant restructuring" abounded, since insurance companies were both protected and harmed by an "arcane [industry standard] accounting system" and other tight regulatory controls. Confirmation of that observation came when American Re was sold in 1996 for more than a 57 percent annualized net return.

As competition for assets quickened, the scope of KKR's activities broadened. The firm's experience in financing and monitoring gave it the flexibility to expand its holdings in familiar markets or to explore new ones. Companies like Neway Anchorlock Corporation (1995), Bruno's, Inc. (1995), and Amphenol Corporation (1997) tapped KKR's long experience with manufacturers and supermarket chains. Merit Behavioral Care Corporation (1995) and Kinder Care Learning Center, Inc. (1997) took the firm into newly flourishing markets for human services – health care and education – where companies were typically desperate for financial and managerial discipline. KKR was now well prepared to cope with situations in which management teams had to be replaced at the outset – as was the case with Borden Inc., Bruno's, and Kinder Care.

Canadian General marked KKR's first foray outside the U.S.; its next would be the 1996 acquisition of the British newspaper publisher

Newsquest Media Group, in a divestiture from its parent company, Reed Elsevier, plc. This acquisition resulted from KKR's relationship with Glenisla Group, Ltd., which had been reviewing hundreds of acquisition prospects for KKR in Europe since 1994. The management buyout was still very much an American phenomenon, but the British were beginning to follow suit, though the market for subordinated debt in the U.K. was still underdeveloped. KKR's ability to tap its familiar U.S. lenders for that crucial tier of financing at relatively low cost was decisive in the bidding for Newsquest. Other long-standing efforts to apply KKR's buyout techniques in Europe and Eastern Europe were far slower to develop. Political and cultural resistance to the principles that underlay the management buyout were formidable, particularly fears of the potential consequences for employment stability in countries where there was relatively little regard in any case for the interests of shareholders. KKR persisted, however, through the relentlessly enthusiastic (some would say quixotic) efforts of Mike Tokarz to finance a large trucking business in Russia.

Changing Terms of Leverage and Equity

Early in the 1990s, when the merger and acquisition markets were in the doldrums, highly leveraged transactions all but disappeared. "Debt was out," Henry Kravis was quoted as saying in 1991, around the time of the Fleet buyout. "Equity was in." The observation turns out to have had little predictive value.[11] Equity and cash were then the preferred currency, to be sure, in corporate-financed acquisitions; but opportunities for leveraged transactions soon resurfaced, even if not at the levels they had reached in the mid-1980s. Banks were more likely to demand higher coverage of senior debt with cash flow, and LBOs employing very high levels of leverage became far less common. Leverage ratios generally were closer to 60–75 percent, rather than 80–95 percent, even for smaller deals. Of KKR's eleven buyouts (excluding those of the build-up companies) from 1992 through 1997, only one of the acquisition financings, Flagstar's, was more than 80 percent leveraged. (The 1992 Flagstar transaction was in effect a restructuring of a 90 percent leveraged buyout that had been engineered by another firm.) While the lower leverage ratios might dampen equity returns somewhat, 60 percent leverage was still severe enough to keep managers on point during the critical early stages of post-buyout operations.

*Leverage ratios of KKR buyout
acquisition financing, 1991–97*

Fleet, 1991	0%
American Re, 1992	78
Flagstar, 1992	84
Canadian General, 1995	27
Neway Anchorlock, 1995	51
Reltec, 1995	65
Bruno's, 1995	75
Merit Behavioral Care, 1995	63
Newsquest, 1996	72
Evenflow & Spalding, 1997	63
Kinder Care, 1997	72
Amphenol, 1997	69

Source: KKR active files.

Competitive forces also altered the relationship between KKR and its limited partners. Equity funds for what were now commonly called "private equity investments" were more abundant than ever in the 1990s. In 1996 alone, sixty-six LBO equity fund-raising efforts closed, most exceeding their targets, and forty-four more were launched. Of the reported closings, seven exceeded $1 billion, including KKR with $5.7 billion and second-ranking DLJ Merchant Banking Partners II with $3 billion.[12] But KKR continued to invest even these vast sums. Five of its 1990 buyouts had exceeded $1 billion in acquisition financing. (Of those, Borden, at a value of more than $4.6 billion, was the largest – though not leveraged – buyout investment of the 1990s.)[13] KKR's flow of potential deals was also increasing; but KKR's limited partners, new and old alike, had grown restive; they were demanding that KKR restructure the way in which it managed its funds.

The backbone of KKR's 1996 Fund consisted of state pension fund investors, sixteen in all. They would be joined by sixty-nine other institutional investors: banks, corporate and other private pension funds, university endowments, financial service companies, insurance companies, and such foreign government entities as the state of Singapore and the Canadian Caisse de Depot. With more competition for pieces of their "alternative investment" portfolios, the pension funds were flexing their muscles, leading the demands for altered buy-out fund terms. The key point at issue was whether every deal would rest on its own bottom, or whether losses from bad deals would offset gains from good deals in the accounting for KKR's 20 percent carried interest. When KKR launched its campaign for the 1996 Fund, it was met with demands for "netting" – that is, the aggregation of profits and losses across the deals – in order to achieve what institutional investors were calling for: a better "alignment of interests" between general and limited partners.

The logic behind this demand was simple enough: with investments pooled for their returns, the temptation to jettison bad deals would be reduced. KKR had never done that. No matter how small its equity participation, it had gone the extra mile with its poor investments, principally out of a strongly felt need to keep its reputation among investors intact. But now, it was being held to a new LBO industry standard. Henceforth, KKR would derive its "carry" – its profits on deals – from the net of total Fund profits and losses. Under the terms of its 1996 Fund agreement, KKR also adjusted its traditional trans-action and management fee percentage to decrease as investments grew larger.[14]

KKR Enters Its Third Decade

With the closing of its 1996 fund, KKR was in position to retain its leadership in a highly competitive market, and to do so at the high end. In 1997, with more than $6 billion to invest, the firm's activity increased dramatically. As unprecedented amounts of cash poured into LBO equity funds, and as worries resurfaced about the tendency of markets to run to extremes,[15] KKR worked feverishly to find and negotiate for reasonably priced acquisitions and to structure them as flexibly as possible. The risks inherent in buyout restructuring had not diminished, as the bankruptcies of Bruno's and Flagstar attested. KKR's senior partners could not recall a time when they had been so busy.

Yet the firm remained small. Its partners numbered just eleven, its associates and analysts ten. In 1995, the partners expanded their ca-pabilities for studying economic trends and industries and analyzing companies. They launched a program for recruiting young analysts, usually between college and graduate school, for limited periods of employment. Otherwise, KKR continued to outsource most of its support functions, never augmenting its internal professional capabilities beyond what sheer necessity dictated. It continued to rely on outside agents for deal finding, lawyering, accounting, consulting, and specialized troubleshooting. It continued to meet with outside experts to educate itself on specific industry, market, and financing trends. In doing so, KKR was able to preserve the entrepreneurial integrity of its operations, and avoided the conflicts over status and economic rewards that almost inevitably arise among different professional cultures housed under the same organizational roof. Its business objectives remained tightly focused, its organization uncluttered.

In other words, KKR practiced what it preached. The often-forgotten advantages of specialization were reinforced in the firm's structure. The sheer simplicity of its organization and reward systems had served KKR well through more than $10.9 billion in equity investments in some 58 companies valued at more than $40 billion. KKR assiduously avoided the temptation to diversify its business or to expand its internal professional capabilities beyond absolute necessity. What concessions it did make to an increasingly complex business environment had more to do with upgrading its internal computing systems and communications capabilities. Sometimes small changes in behavior sufficed. In 1995, KKR's professionals initiated a weekly Monday morning teleconference call. These sessions, linking together all the firm's professionals, reinforced the company's teamwork ethic and improved its ability to share timely information, critical thinking, and advice.

The lessons embedded in KKR's firm structure are not widely appreciated at a time when financial firms are engaged in a frenzy of "synergistic" mergers – scrambling to diversify, much like the industrial conglomerates of a bygone era. Better understood are the legacies of KKR's buyout philosophy and its impact on the larger corporate world.

Impacts: Lessons and Legacies

The meliorating effects KKR had on so many industries moved Harvard Business School Professor Malcolm Salter to refer to the firm as "the repair shop of capitalism." That humble epithet only hints at the magnitude of the management buyout's impact on American corporations and their shareholders.

Large investors have gained much from the experience of the buyout movement. While anti-takeover legislation in many key states and more sophisticated poison-pill defenses have given incumbent managers some breathing room, institutional investors have become more assertive than ever, pressing board directors for timely information and justification of corporate policies. Institutional investor activism has increased for a number of reasons, among them experience gained through participation in buyout funds. Investors have learned they have the ability, as well as the right, to use the power of equity to reform underperforming corporations. Though their members do not sit on corporate boards, they can always get a hearing; investors have more authority now than ever before to coordinate collective actions against poorly performing managers. They have become more vocal in their reactions to managerial problems and increasingly influential in pressuring board directors to link executive pay to performance as reflected in equity values.[16] Within the boardrooms, nonexecutive directors have increasingly acquired significant equity holdings in the companies they oversee. While there can be little doubt that most boards remain creatures of their corporations' CEOs, and are not very effective in their monitoring, they are now less supine, much more likely to move against poorly performing managers when problems begin to surface.

An even more significant impact has been made on corporate executives. Today, managers are generally more concerned with maintaining "core competencies" than expanding lines of business, with maximizing economic values than with building corporate empires, with promoting entrepreneurial behavior than with reinforcing bureaucratic compliance. Corporate budgeting has become more rigorous, organizations less fat, and restructuring more routine throughout the corporate economy. All this has occurred as managers have relearned the virtue of hitching their personal fortunes to those of their shareholders. The use of stock options as a significant part of executive pay packages has increased dramatically.[17] In 1997, the Business Roundtable's new "Statement on Corporate Governance" reflected a profound change in the collective thinking of the nation's more prominent senior executives: "[T]he principal objective of a business enterprise is to generate economic returns to its owners . . . . [I]f the CEO and the directors are not focused on shareholder value, it may be less likely the corporation will realize that value."[18] That corporate profits and productivity have been rising for the first time in decades is due in part to these changing attitudes and behavior among owners and managers alike.[19]

As for the financial community, an important lesson from KKR's experience is that there is no easy path to long-term success through financial engineering. The mere use of leverage to acquire the "undervalued" equity of companies was never a formula for getting rich quick. KKR's equity investors had to be as patient as the debt in its deals was impatient. Only through a carefully nurtured combination of flexible financing, strong management talent, well-structured incentives, active board monitoring, and constant attention to details could KKR earn consistently good returns on its investments – 28.2 percent per annum in gross terms from 1977 through 1997. In pure cash terms, KKR's limited partners have realized $22 billion on a total cumulative equity investment of $10.9 billion, with an estimated $18.1 billion still unrealized.

In a more fundamental historical sense, KKR's legacy is this: its management buyouts breathed new life into a moribund system of financial capitalism, which in turn stimulated a new era of sustained economic growth, vibrant securities markets, and at this writing, nearly full levels of employment. Many macro- and microeconomic factors have contributed to these happy circumstances, to be sure. Yet the catalytic role of the management buyout cannot be denied. Once scorned as a dangerous form of paper capitalism, it demonstrated the beneficial effects of linking managerial and ownership interests in the common pursuit of value. It showed how creative financial strategies could impel and assist corporate reform and how varied, rather than formulaic, were the paths to value creation. It attested to the importance of rigorous board oversight and the utility of allowing businesses to float on their own bottoms, unencumbered by the overhead and entanglements of more traditional corporate bureaucracy. As both prod to action and example, the management buyout has helped restore American business to its vital promise.

Appendix

Chronology of KKR Buyouts: Transaction Values, Leverage, and Returns for 1976–1993 Funds[a]

Fund	Transaction	Year of Investment	Pre-Buyout Status	Transaction Value	Leverage Ratio	Holding Period[b]	Pre-KKR ROI[b]
1976	AJ Industries	1977	NYSE	$ 26M	66%	8.32	57.3%
	LB Foster	1977	Private	$ 94M	88%	12.38	15.1%
	USNR	1977	ASE	$ 23M	60%	7.28	39.9%
	Houdaille	1979	NYSE	$ 380M	86%	8.45	33.9%
	Sargent Industries	1979	ASE	$ 39M	81%	5.47	40.4%
	Eagle/F-B Truck Line	1979	OTC	$ 13M	67%	5.87	−100.0%
	Idex	1988	Division	$ 202M	N/A	9.92	58.8%
	Total Fund Investment						$32.6M
	Current Value before KKR Carry and Management Fee[b,c]						$539.6M
	Fund Return before KKR Carry and Management Fee						39.9%
	Fund Return after KKR Carry and Management Fee:						35.6%
1980	Eaton Leonard	1980	Private	$ 14M	81%	5.54	−100.0%
	Rotor Tool	1981	Division	$ 26M	86%	5.95	43.2%
	The Marley Company	1981	NYSE	$ 330M	88%	16.60	26.4%
	Lily-Tulip	1981	Division	$ 160M	80%	4.72	57.9%
	PT Components	1981	Division	$ 135M	91%	4.87	52.7%
	Norris Industries	1981	NYSE	$ 440M	88%	3.21	87.1%
	Fred Meyer, Inc.	1981	OTC	$ 229M	93%	15.33	19.5%
	Fred Meyer Real Estate	1981	N/A	$ 304M	59%	16.06	21.2%
	Total Fund Investment						$356.8M
	Current Value before KKR Carry and Management Fee[b,c]						$1,825.9M
	Fund Return before KKR Carry and Management Fee						29.0%
	Fund Return after KKR Carry and Management Fee:						25.7%
1982	PacTrust	1983	ASE	$ 55M	64%	5.47	15.1%
	Dillingham	1983	NYSE	$ 500M	80%	4.56	21.9%
	Golden West	1983	Private	$ 300M	76%	2.92	76.7%

Appendix *(continued)*

Fund	Transaction	Year of Investment	Pre-Buyout Status	Transaction Value	Leverage Ratio	Holding Period[b]	Pre-KKR ROI[b]
1982	Amstar	1984	NYSE	$ 520M	79%	2.79	80.5%
	Wometco Companies	1984	NYSE	$ 1,075M	76%	3.83	37.2%
	Total Fund Investment						$403.9M
	Current Value before KKR Carry and Management Fee[b,c]						$1,360.8M
	Fund Return before KKR Carry and Management Fee						47.6%
	Fund Return after KKR Carry and Management Fee:						40.2%
1984	Malone & Hyde	1984	NYSE	$ 700M	81%	3.89	34.4%
	AutoZone	1984	Division	N/A	N/A	13.29	42.3%
	Cole National	1984	NYSE	$ 330M	71%	2.96	44.3%
	Pace Industries	1984	Division	$ 1,620M	83%	11.18	31.2%
	Motel 6	1985	Division	$ 945M	72%	5.55	37.9%
	M&T	1985	Private	$ 110M	56%	3.41	20.7%
	Union Texas Petroleum	1985	Division	$ 1,760M	82%	12.51	13.7%
	Storer Communications	1985	NYSE	$ 2,430M	89%	2.91	60.4%
	Total Fund Investment						$1,058.5M
	Current Value before KKR Carry and Management Fee[b,c]						$6,144.4M
	Fund Return before KKR Carry and Management Fee						33.4%
	Fund Return after KKR Carry and Management Fee:						28.7%
1986	Beatrice	1986	NYSE	$ 8,730M	84%	6.16	52.5%
	Safeway	1986	NYSE	$ 4,800M	86%	11.35	42.7%
	Owens-Illinois	1987	NYSE	$ 4,680M	95%	10.80	20.6%
	Walter Industries	1987	NYSE	$ 3,260M	96%	10.29	−1.3%
	Total Fund Investment						$856.8M
	Current Value before KKR Carry and Management Fee[b,c]						$9,457.5M
	Fund Return before KKR Carry and Management Fee						36.1%
	Fund Return after KKR Carry and Management Fee:						31.4%
1987	Seaman Furniture	1987	NASDAQ	$ 390M	88%	5.48	−47.0%
	Stop & Shop	1988	NYSE	$ 1,530M	92%	8.33	31.9%
	First Interstate	1988	NYSE	$ 230M	N/A	7.49	28.4%
	Duracell/Gillette	1988	Division	$ 2,060M	83%	9.53	39.3%
	RJR Nabisco/Borden	1989	NYSE	$31,430M	80%	8.90	2.8%
	K-III/Primedia	1989	Startup	$ 1,130M	58%	8.52	14.9%
	Fleet/BNE	1991	RTC	$ 280M	N/A	6.48	34.6%
	Granum Communications	1991	Startup	$ 62M	57%	4.57	30.4%
	K.C. Cable Associates	1992	Division	$ 140M	68%	4.28	5.9%
	American Re Corp	1992	Division	$ 1,500M	73%	4.18	57.3%

Fund	Transaction	Year of Investment	Pre-Buyout Status	Transaction Value	Leverage Ratio	Holding Period[b]	Pre-KKR ROI[b]
1987	Flagstar Companies, Inc.	1992	NASDAQ	$ 1,900M	84%	5.12	−100.0%
	Alden Press (WCP)	1993	NYSE	$ 145M	N/A	4.85	25.2%
	KSL Recreation	Various	Startup	$ 530M	55%	4.50	12.1%
	Total Fund Investment						$6,240.4M
	Current Value before KKR Carry and Management Fee[b,c]						$17,439.1M
	Fund Return before KKR Carry and Management Fee						16.1%
	Fund Return after KKR Carry and Management Fee:						13.8%
1993	World Color Press	Various	Private	$ 250M	N/A	4.03	34.0%
	Primedia	Various	Division	$ 270M	N/A	3.29	15.3%
	Canadian General	1995	Division	$ 160M	27%	2.97	47.7%
	Neway Anchorlok	Various	Private	$ 100M	51%	2.89	N/A
	Walter Industries	1995	NYSE	$ 58M	N/A	2.78	17.1%
	Granum Holdings	1995	Private	$ 180M	N/A	1.29	114.5%
	Reltec	Various	Division	$ 634M	65%	2.48	58.5%
	Bruno's	1995	OTC	$ 1,220M	75%	2.37	−100.0%
	Merit Behavioral Care	1995	Division	$ 370M	63%	2.27	36.2%
	Newsquest	Various	Division	$ 813M	72%	1.99	86.4%
	Evenflo & Spalding	1996	Private	$ 1,000M	63%	1.26	3.1%
	KinderCare	1997	NYSE	$ 609M	72%	0.89	N/A
	Amphenol	1997	NYSE	$ 1,500M	69%	0.63	N/A
	Total Fund Investment						$1,958.0M
	Current Value before KKR Carry and Management Fee[b,c]						$3,308.9M
	Fund Return before KKR Carry and Management Fee						27.7%
	Fund Return after KKR Carry and Management Fee:						21.6%
	Aggregate Fund Investments, 1976–1993 Funds						$10,906M
	Aggregate Realized and Unrealized Value as of 12/31/97						$40,076M
	Total Fund Returns before KKR Carry and Management Fee						28.2%
	Total Fund Returns after KKR Carry and Management Fee						23.7%

[a]KKR has essentially sold off its interests in the 1980 and 1982 Funds. Only Idex remains from the 1976 Fund; only Union Texas Petroleum from the 1984 Fund.

[b]Holding periods, returns and valuations are calculated as of 12/31/97.

[c]Includes realized and unrealized value before KKR carry and management fee. Realized value is the net cash and consideration received by the Fund. Unrealized value is determined by KKR, which values investments at cost for at least one year after they are made, unless there are transactions involving third parties. Privately held companies are increased in value by KKR only if positive events, such as higher than anticipated operating earnings, debt reduction, or asset sales occur. Such increases in valuation are discounted for illiquidity from the prevailing values of comparable assets whose market prices are known.

Note on Sources for Financial Data

All data and related information on acquisition financings – including equity prices, final financing costs, and balance sheet structures – have been culled from such basic financing documents as Acquisition Financing Confidential Memoranda, Prospecti, Offering Memoranda, and other standard SEC filings required for mergers and acquisitions. They are a matter of public record; to avoid mind-numbing annotations, we refer those who seek information on a particular transaction to such documents. Data on the postacquisition performance of KKR-controlled companies were gathered and calculated from standard annual and other interim financial reports, which for public companies are also readily accessible for verification. For proprietary information, the reader can assume that we are drawing upon the data that KKR provides to its limited partners, unless specific notes are provided.

We accessed documents for all the transactions described herein from KKR's archival storage facilities or, in the case of companies still in KKR's portfolio, from the firm's active files. Since numbers inevitably vary from one document to the next, we checked our final calculations with KKR's accounting department, which verified and/or corrected our findings (corrections were typically minor) using data consistent with reports KKR has made to its limited partners.

Notes

Chapter 1. The Rebirth of Financial Capitalism

1. The film, produced in England, appeared in 1951.
2. *Capitalism, Socialism, and Democracy* (New York: Harper & Brothers, 1942), esp. ch. 7.
3. See ibid., p. 132, in which Schumpeter observes that "the environment resists in many ways that vary, according to social conditions, from simple refusal either to finance or to buy a new thing, to physical attack on the man who tries to produce it." This problem is also implied throughout the sweeping overview of technological change and social response in Nathan Rosenberg and L.E. Birdzell, *How the West Grew Rich: The Economic Transformation of the Industrial World* (New York: Basic Books, 1986). For a case in point, a detailed recounting of the social and political repression of entrepreneurial activity in Chinese history, see Sterling Seagrave, *Lords of the Rim: The Invisible Empire of the Overseas Chinese* (G.P. Putnam's Sons, 1995).
4. Jonathan Hughes, *The Vital Few* (New York: Oxford University Press, expanded edition, 1986), conveys this dynamic in U.S. history very effectively through a series of biographies, including those of people who try to effect change within highly resistant bureaucratic environments.
5. For overviews of the history of financial innovation see George David Smith and Richard Sylla, *The Transformation of Financial Capitalism: An Essay on the History of Capital Markets*, in Salomon Center, *Financial Markets, Institutions and Instruments* (Cambridge, MA: Blackwells, 1993); and Vincent P. Carosso, *Investment Banking in America: A History* (Cambridge, MA: Harvard University Press, 1970). Good biographies of Gould and Morgan that transcend the simplistic muckraking accounts of their financial practices are Maury Klein, *The Life and Legend of Jay Gould* (Baltimore: Johns Hopkins University Press, 1986); and Ron Chernow, *The House of Morgan: An American Banking Dynasty and the Rise of Modern Finance* (New York: Atlantic Monthly Press, 1990).

6. J.P. Morgan would bring back Vail in 1906, when the Morgan interests took control of AT&T, which was struggling at the time to meet an onslaught of competition. See Robert W. Garnet, *The Telephone Enterprise: The Evolution of the Bell System's Horizontal Structure, 1879–1909* (Baltimore: Johns Hopkins University Press, 1985).

7. For our discussion of merger waves we have relied on a vast literature. Some useful references include Ralph Nelson, *Merger Movements in American History: 1895–1956* (Princeton, N.J.: Princeton University Press, 1959); Peter O. Steiner, *Mergers: Motives, Effects and Public Policies* (Ann Arbor: University of Michigan Press, 1975); and Alan Auerbach, ed., *Mergers and Acquisitions* (Chicago: University of Chicago Press, 1988). Patrick A. Gaughan, *Mergers, Acquisitions and Corporate Restructurings,* provides a useful overview of the sequential history of the great merger waves.

8. Smith and Sylla, *Transformation of Financial Capitalism,* pp. 2–5; Vincent Carosso, *The Morgans: International Private Bankers, 1854–1913* (Cambridge, MA: Harvard University Press, 1987), pp. 487–90.

9. "Financial capitalism" or "finance capitalism" has been associated with a particular period in U.S. history, spanning roughly the years from 1896 through 1913. See, for example, the typologies employed by N.S.B. Gras and Henrietta Larson, *Casebook in American Business History* (New York: Appleton Century-Crofts, Inc., 1939), and Alfred D. Chandler, Jr., *The Visible Hand* (Cambridge, MA: Harvard University Press, 1977), on the phases of U.S. business development.

10. Walter Lippmann, *Drift and Mastery: An Attempt to Diagnose the Current Unrest* (Englewood Cliffs, NJ: Prentice Hall, reprint 1961), pp. 42–43.

11. Alfred D. Chandler, Jr., echoed this view in a series of influential works on the history of big business that shaped a generation of studies on the history of managerial enterprise. See *Visible Hand,* op. cit., along with his *Strategy and Structure* (MIT Press, 1960) and *Scale and Scope* (Cambridge: Harvard University Press, 1992).

12. Smith and Sylla, *Transformation of Financial Capitalism,* pp. 27–29; Mark Roe, "Political and Legal Constraints on Ownership and Control of Public Companies," *Journal of Financial Economics,* 27 (1990), pp. 7–41.

13. *The Modern Corporation and Private Property* (New York: Macmillan, 1933), p. 122.

14. The literature on principal-agent problems burgeoned in the 1970s and is discussed in more detail below; see note 62.

15. See Michael Jensen's classic statement on this point: "Agency Costs of Free Cash Flow, Corporate Finance, and Takeovers," *American Economic Review*, 76, no.2 (May 1986), p. 323. "Free cash flow is cash flow in excess of that required to fund all projects that have positive net present values when discounted at the relevant cost of capital. . . . The problem is how to motivate managers to disgorge the cash rather than investing it at below the cost of capital or wasting it on organization[al] inefficiencies."

16. Nowhere is the contrast between Ford and Sloan better illustrated than in the two men's autobiographies. See Henry Ford, *My Life and Work* (Garden City: Doubleday & Company, 1923); Ford with Samueal Crowther, *Moving Forward* (Garden City: Doubleday & Company, 1930); and Alfred P. Sloan, Jr., *My Years with General Motors* (New York: Doubleday, 1963).

17. Peter Drucker, *The Concept of the Corporation* (New York: John Day Co., 1946).

18. Useful books on the labor problems are David Brody, *Workers in Industrial America: Essays on the 20th-Century Struggle* (New York: Oxford University Press, 1980), esp. chs. 5–6; and Richard C. Edwards, *Contested Terrain: The Transformation of the Workplace in the Twentieth Century* (New York: Basic Books, 1985).

19. John Kenneth Galbraith, *The New Industrial State* (Boston: Houghton-Mifflin, 1967); Jean-Jacques Servan-Schreiber, *The American Challenge* (New York: Atheneum, 1968).

20. These trends are the subject of a voluminous literature. Some of the historical literature is summarized and interpreted in George David Smith and Davis Dyer, "The Rise and Transformation of the Modern Corporation," in *The Corporation Today*, ed. Karl Kaysen (New York: Oxford University Press, 1996). That the relative decline of U.S. firms was not simply due to lower labor costs but rather to serious declines in technological and organizational competencies is illustrated in numerous specialized studies. See, for example, Paul Tiffany, *The Decline of American Steel: How Management, Government and Labor Went Wrong* (New York: Oxford University Press, 1988); David Halberstam, *The Reckoning* (New York: Morrow, 1986); and Alfred D. Chandler, Jr., "The Competitive Performance of U.S. Industrial Enterprises since the Second World War," *Business History Review*, 68 (Spring 1994), pp. 1–72.

21. Mark Roe, *Weak Owners, Strong Managers* (Princeton University Press, 1994); Joseph Grundfest, "Subordination of American Capital," *Journal of Financial Economics*, 27 (1990), pp. 89–114.

22. Jonathon Barron Baskin and Paul J. Miranti, Jr., *A History of Cor-*

porate Finance (New York: Cambridge University Press, 1997), p. 288. By the late 1970s the "combined effect of antitrust laws, federal rules governing stock tenders and state anti-takeover legislation made it difficult to oust entrenched managements. . . . Fiduciary responsibilities also compelled trust and insurance companies, mutual funds and pension funds to avoid the risks associated with a concentration of ownership in a few firms. Moreover the Employment Retirement Safety Act of 1974 (ERISA) prohibited pension fund representatives from serving on the corporate boards unless they possessed competence in the underlying businesses. Finally, besieged managements were able to mount 'poison pill' defenses. . . ."

23. Roe, "Political and Legal Restraints on Ownership and Control of Public Companies," pp. 7–41.
24. John Pound, "Shareholder Activism and Share Values," *Journal of Law and Economics* (October 1989), pp. 357–379.
25. Gaughan, *Mergers, Acquisitions,* chapter 2.
26. "The Enduring Logic of Economic Success," *Harvard Business Review*, March-April, 1990.
27. Harold Geneen, *Managing* (New York: Avon Publishing Company, 1984).
28. Steven N. Kaplan and Michael N. Weisbach, "The Success of Acquisitions: Evidence from Divestitures," *Journal of Finance*, no. 1 (March 1992), pp. 107–138. Other useful studies of conglomerate organization include Richard P. Rumelt, *Strategy, Structure, and Economic Performance* (Cambridge, MA: Harvard University Press, 1974); and Milton T. Leontiades, *Managing the Unmanageable: Strategies for Success within the Conglomerate* (Reading, MA: Addison Wesley, 1986.)
29. Robert Sobel, *The Rise and Fall of the Conglomerate Kings* (New York: Stein and Day, 1984), p. 190.
30. Ann Fisher, "The Decade's Worst Mergers," *Fortune*, April 30, 1984.
31. Gaughan, *Mergers, Acquisitions,* pp. 39–40, provides a useful summary of these three 1970s hostile takeovers.
32. T. Boone Pickens, *Boone* (Boston: Houghton Mifflin, 1987); T. Boone Pickens, "The Restructuring of the Domestic Oil and Gas Industry," in Daniel Yergin and Kate Garnick, *Reshaping of the Oil Industry: Just Another Commodity?* (Cambridge, MA: Cambridge Research Energy Associates, 1985).
33. Martin Feldstein, *American Economic Policy in the 1980s* (Chicago: University of Chicago Press, 1994), pp. 600–01.

34. The NBER Digest, "Takeovers Busted Up Conglomerates, Boosted Efficiency," National Bureau of Economic Research, August 1990.

35. Jerry Sterner, *Other People's Money: The Ultimate Seduction* (New York, 1991), pp. 28, 82.

36. A recent biography is Roger Lowenstein, *Buffett: The Making of an American Capitalist* (New York: Doubleday, 1996).

37. It was not for lack of potential interest. There were intermediate publications, such as the *Harvard Business Review*, where scholars publicized their findings to business audiences. Michael Jensen's "The Eclipse of the Public Corporation," *Harvard Business Review, 5* (1989), pp. 61–74 – an indictment of the managerial corporation that hailed the restructuring efforts of those acting on behalf of shareholders – generated more letters to the editor than any *HBR* article in history.

38. A September 24, 1979, *Barron's* article, "High-Wire Finance: Leverage Buyouts Offer Plenty of Reward, Risk," offered an excellent survey of some of the early buyouts, noting the patience required to achieve rewards and the importance that KKR in particular attached to tying managerial incentives to equity performance. A recent discussion of mergers and acquisitions in *The Economist* (March 1998) restates that magazine's consistent view over the years that the LBOs have resulted in more value creation than ordinary mergers.

39. See, for example, N. R. Kleinfield, "Kohlberg Collects Companies," *New York Times*, December 12, 1983; Irwin Ross, "How the Champs Do Leveraged Buyouts," *Fortune*, January 23, 1984; Stephen Maita, "Kohlberg, Kravis, Roberts Lets Its Deals Do the Talking," *San Francisco Chronicle*, November 25, 1985; "King of the Buyouts . . . ," *Wall Street Journal*, April 11, 1986; and Carol J. Loomis, "Buyout Kings," *Fortune*, July 4, 1988.

40. Anxieties about the state of the debt markets run through commentaries from the late 1970s to the end of the following decade. Such fears seem always to exist, even among experts, making it harder to discern when real crises are at hand. A recent *Forbes* article sounds the alarm anew: see Matthew Schifrin, "LBO Mania" (March 9, 1998), pp. 128–134. Schifrin argues that pension funds and other institutions are rushing heedlessly to invest in "a game of leverage," succumbing to the blandishments of LBO firms whose manipulative reporting of returns somehow fools sophisticated investors into pouring good money after bad.

41. Connie Bruck, *The Predator's Ball: The Junk-Bond Raiders and the Man Who Staked Them* (New York: Simon and Schuster, 1988);

James B. Stewart, *Den of Thieves* (New York: Simon and Schuster, 1991), p. 467. Stewart's reportage provides an almost classic example of populist hyperbole. In his prologue (pp. 16–17), Stewart sees the crimes of many individuals as part of a wholesale "crime wave" on Wall Street in which "the ownership of entire corporations changed hands often forcibly, at a clip never before witnessed." He goes on to note that thousands of employees lost jobs and that many businesses were restructured and forced into bankruptcy. All this, he says, "shows how the nation's financial markets were in fact corrupted from within, and subverted for criminal purposes."

42. "The Reckoning: Safeway LBO Yields Vast Profits but Exacts a Heavy Human Toll," *Wall Street Journal*, May 16, 1990.

43. Sarah Bartlett, *The Money Machine* (New York: Warner Books, 1992).

44. George Anders, *The Merchants of Debt: KKR and the Mortgaging of American Business* (New York: Basic Books, 1992). Anders wrote a much more sympathetic account of leveraged buyout financing for the *Harvard Business Review* (July-August 1992, pp. 79–87).

45. Brian Burrough and John Helyer, *Barbarians at the Gate* (New York: Harper & Row, 1990). A colorful and highly fictionalized made-for-television movie was made from the book for Home Box Office.

46. Both Jensen's remark and that of Joseph Grundfest, "Just Vote or Just Don't Vote," Stanford Law School working paper (1990), are quoted from Michael Jensen, "Corporate Control and the Politics of Finance," *Journal of Applied Corporate Finance* (Summer, 1991), vol. 4, no. 2, p. 14.

47. Yakov Amihud, ed., *Leveraged Management Buyouts: Causes and Consequences* (New York, 1989), p. 214.

48. Greenspan's view on altering the tax code was lukewarm. See his testimony before the Committee on Finance, Leveraged Buyouts and Corporate Debt, January 26, 1989, S361–31, p. 4ff.

49. Le Baron also argued that for pension fund managers, the long-term returns on LBO equity participation helped to offset the risk of their high debt portfolios. See his testimony, U.S. House of Representatives, Subcommittee on Labor-Management Relations, Committee on Education and Labor, Oversight Hearings on the Role of Pension Funds in Corporate Takeovers, February 9, 1989, H341–63, p. 176ff.

50. Testifying a year earlier, Goodyear's Dennis Rich, perhaps not yet sensing which way the tide of managerial theory was running, complained that his company had been forced to reverse its strategies for diversification by the takeover attempt, all in the name of generating

higher share prices. Both lamented what they saw as the increasing pressure to manage their businesses for short-term stock prices rather than for the longer term interests of their shareholders and other corporate constituencies. See the U.S. House of Representatives Subcommittee on Economic Stabilization of the Committee on Finance, and Urban Affairs, Oversight Hearings on Mergers and Acquisitions, May 12, 1987, H241–39, pp. 13ff and 185ff.

51. Testimony before U.S. House of Representatives, Subcommittee on Oversight and Investigations, Committee on Energy and Commerce, Corporate Takeovers, February 8, 1988, H361–85, p. 312ff. See also Business Roundtable Ad Hoc Task Force, *Analysis of the Issues in the National Industrial Policy Debate: Working Papers,* rev. 15 May 1984.

52. Business Roundtable Ad Hoc Task Force, *Analysis of the Issues in the National Industrial Policy Debate: Working Papers,* rev. 15 May 1984.

53. "Corporate Takeovers: A Search for the Public Interest," *The Corporate Board* (September-October, 1989).

54. Testimony, U.S. House of Representatives, Subcommittee on Labor-Management Relations, Committee on Education and Labor, Oversight Hearings on the Role of Pension Funds in Corporate Takeovers, February 9, March 2 and 7, 1989, H341–63, p. 10ff.

55. Max Holland, *When the Machine Stopped* (New York: McGraw-Hill, reprint 1989).

56. Boyce and Holland sparred in their testimonies during the Oversight Hearings on the Role of Pension Funds . . . , March 7, 1989, H341–63, pp. 361ff, 371ff and 495ff.

57. Testimony, Oversight Hearings on Mergers and Acquisitions, May 12, 1987, H241–39, p. 98ff.

58. These issues are adumbrated in more detail by Allen Kaufman and Ernest Englander, "Kohlberg Kravis Roberts & Co. and the Restructuring of American Capitalism," *Business History Review,* 67 (Spring 1963), p. 85ff. For a typical view of the charge that LBOs unfairly manipulated the tax code, see "How the Government Subsidizes Leveraged Takeovers," *Forbes,* November 1988, pp. 192–96.

59. The methodology was criticized by a pair of academic experts, William Long and David Ravenscraft, regarding its broader applicability and the lack of long-term data on particular firms. Deloitte's defense of the data pointed out some errors in the critics' analysis and noted that the KKR data applied only to KKR deals. See the testimonies of William Long of the Brookings Institution and Emil Sunley of Deloitte, Haskins & Sells before the Subcommittee on Telecommunications, Committee on Energy and Commerce, Management

and Leveraged Buyouts, May 25, 1989, H361–62, pp. 170ff and 201ff.

60. The KKR data in updated and strengthened form were reissued as Kohlberg Kravis Roberts, "Presentation on Leveraged Buyouts," 1990, private printing, KKR files.

61. Testimony, Oversight Hearings on the Role of Pension Funds . . . , February 9, 1989, H.341–63, p. 10ff.

62. Henry G. Manne, "The 'Higher Criticism' of the Modern Corporation," *Columbia Law Review* 62 (1962), pp. 399–432, and "Tender Offers and the Firm Market," *Mergers & Acquisitions* 2 (1966), pp. 91–95. Agency theory was taken up by a number of influential scholars in the 1970s and 1980s, reflecting, and in turn influencing, the new market for corporate control. Some leading examples: Stephen A. Ross, "The Economic Theory of Agency: The Principal's Problem," *American Economic Review*, 63 (May 1973), pp. 134–39; William H. Meckling and Michael C. Jensen, "Theory of the Firm: Managerial Behavior, Agency Costs and Ownership Structure," *Journal of Financial Economics*, vol. 3 (1976), pp. 305–70; Eugene Fama, "Agency Problems and the Theory of the Firm," *Journal of Political Economy*, no. 2 (April 1980), pp. 288–307.

63. Allen Kaufman and Lawrence Zacharias, "From Trust to Contract: The Legal Language of Managerial Ideology, 1920–1980," *Business History Review*, vol. 66 (Autumn, 1992), pp. 547–59.

64. Jensen, "Eclipse of the Public Corporation."

65. On an industry adjusted basis, employment among rank-and-file workers remained relatively stable, in the summary view of various studies using various methodologies to measure the effects of LBOs on employment. Productivity grew significantly, according to a report undertaken by the National Bureau of Economic Research. "In addition, . . . plant closings – often viewed as a particularly disruptive source of job loss – are actually lower in frequency after LBOs than is typical for the industries in which they are located." On the other hand, management employment typically declined, as overgrown bureaucracies were reformed. Wages and productivity tended to increase on average, while the evidence on benefits was inconclusive. See Steven Kaplan, "The Effects of Management Buyouts on Operations and Value," *The Journal of Financial Economics,* 24 (1989), pp. 217–54; Chris J. Muscarella and Michael Vetsuypens, "Efficiency and Organizational Structure: A Study of Reverse LBOs," *Journal of Finance,* 45 (1990), pp. 1389–1414; Abbie Smith, "Corporate Ownership Structure and Performance: The Case of Management Buyouts," *Journal of Finan-*

cial Economics, 27 (1990), pp. 143–64; and Frank R. Lichtenberg and Donald Siegel, "The Effects of Leveraged Buyouts on Productivity and Related Aspects of Firm Behavior," working paper, National Bureau of Economic Research, 1989. The evidence on capital and R&D spending was mixed. "Two other studies report slight reductions in both R&D and capital spending," noted a report issued by the Massachusetts Pension Reserves Management Board (see *LBOs, Public Pension Funds, and Public Policy*, pp. 2, 15–16). The report went on to say that "larger LBOs are more often undertaken at firms in stagnant industries where strategic realignment is necessary. In these industries, higher payout rates to investors and reduced R&D are likely to lead to efficiency gains."

66. Michael C. Jensen, Steven Kaplan, and Laura Stiglin, "Effects of LBOs on Tax Revenues of the U.S. Treasury," *Tax Notes*, February 6, 1989, pp. 727–33.

67. Steven N. Kaplan and Jeremy Stein, "Evolution of Buyout Pricing and Capital Structure in the 1980s," *Quarterly Journal of Economics* (1993), pp. 313–57. The evidence on capital spending was mixed, but it was likely that many companies had been overspending before their buyouts.

68. Andrei Shleifer and Robert Vishny, "The Takeover Wave of the 1980s," *Science*, 249 (August 1990), pp. 745–49; Dennis Mueller, "Mergers," in *New Palgrave Dictionary of Finance*, ed. Peter Newman et al. (New York: Stockton Press, 1992); Bronwyn H. Hall, "Corporate Restructuring and Investment Horizons in the United States, 1976–1987," *Business History Review*, 68 (Spring, 1994), pp. 110–43.

69. Baskin and Miranti, *History of Corporate Finance*; Roe, *Weak Owners, Strong Managers*; Grundfest, "Subordination of American Capital"; Kaufman and Englander, "Kohlberg Kravis Roberts & Co. and the Restructuring of American Capitalism," Allen Kaufman, Lawrence Zacharias and Marvin Karson, *Managers vs. Owners: The Struggle for Corporate Control in American Democracy* (New York: Oxford University Press, 1995), esp. chap. 10.

70. Kaplan and Stein, "Evolution of Buyout Pricing and Capital Structure in the 1980s," pp. 313–57.

71. Lawrence White, *The S&L Debacle* (New York: Oxford University Press, 1992), pp. 180–93.

72. Jensen, "Corporate Control and the Politics of Finance," pp. 13–33.

73. *Mergers and Acquisitions, Almanac and Index* (1987, 1991).

74. According to the Securities Data Corporation database.

75. This point was well made by one critic of the LBO movement: see Albert Rappaport, "The Staying Power of the Public Corporation," *Harvard Business Review* 1 (1990), pp. 96–104.
76. Steven N. Kaplan, "The Evolution of U.S. Corporate Governance: We Are All Henry Kravis Now," University of Chicago and NBER working paper, February 1997.

Chapter 2. Recasting the Role of Debt: Creative Leverage and Buyout Financing

1. "[T]hink what you do when you go in debt; you give to another power over your liberty." See *The Complete Works . . . of the Late Dr. Benjamin Franklin . . .* Vol. 3 (London: J. Johnson,1806), p. 453ff. Sovereigns borrowed heavily, of course, often for no better purpose than to finance military adventures or courtly extravagance; what distinguished lords from common borrowers was their power to command credit and to evade responsibility for repayment.
2. See the excellent discussion of Jefferson's views on debt in Joseph J. Ellis, *American Sphinx: The Character of Thomas Jefferson* (Alfred A. Knopf, 1997), p. 194ff.
3. *Lombard Street* (New York: E.P. Dutton, 1920), pp. 8–10.
4. *An Introduction to Political Economy* (New York: Eaton & Mains, rev. ed. 1889), p. 198. Ely did not mean to say that credit per se was bad. He also explained that debt played a useful role in value creation.
5. George David Smith and Richard Sylla, *The Transformation of Financial Capitalism: An Essay on the History of Capital Markets,* in Salomon Center, *Financial Markets, Institutions and Instruments* (Cambridge, MA: Blackwells, 1993); Vincent P. Carosso, *Investment Banking in America: A History* (Cambridge, MA: Harvard University Press, 1970).
6. See for example, Franco Modigliani and Merton Miller, "Corporate Income Taxes and the Cost of Capital: A Correction," *American Economic Review* 53 (June 1963), pp. 433–43; Michael C. Jensen and William H. Meckling, "Theory of the Firm: Managerial Behavior, Agency Costs and Ownership Structure," *Journal of Financial Economics*, vol. 3 (1976), pp. 305–70; Edward Altman, R. Haldeman, and P. Narayanan, "Zeta Analysis: A New Model to Identify Bankruptcy Risk of Corporations," *Journal of Banking and Finance* (June 1977).
7. George David Smith and Robert Sobel, *Dover Corporation: A History, 1955–1989* (The Winthrop Group, Inc., 1991). Originally pri-

vately printed, this book is registered with the Library of Congress and can be accessed through the authors or through The Winthrop Group, Inc. in Cambridge, Massachusetts.

8. There is very little literature available on bootstrap acquisitions, which are memorialized mainly in Wall Street folklore. Brief summaries can be found in Roy C. Smith, *The Money Wars* (New York: Truman Talley Books, 1990), p. 183ff; and Barrie A. Wigmore, *Securities Markets in the 1980s: The New Regime, 1979–1984* (Oxford University Press, 1977), p. 339.

9. W. Carl Kester and Timothy A. Luehrman, "Rehabilitating the Leveraged Buyout," *Harvard Business Review* (May-June, 1995), pp. 119–30.

10. There is a wealth of scholarly literature on this point. See, for example, Allen Kaufman, Lawrence Zacharias, and Marvin Karson, *Managers vs. Owners: The Struggle for Corporate Control in American Democracy* (Oxford, 1995), p. 148: "Buyers presumably decide the price they are willing to pay today [by discounting earnings as the immediate future], so artists of the [buyout] would sell themselves short by being myopic." However, there is ample room for debate, at least on a case-by-case basis. That many managers of buyout firms may have felt pressure to forgo investment in innovation in favor of short-term operating results is certain. Jonathon Barron Baskin and Paul J. Miranti, *A History of Corporate Finance* (Cambridge University Press, 1996) generalize about this tendency. More specialized financial studies (which we cite throughout) are more favorable to the long-term effects of leveraged buyouts. We argue in Chapter 3 that KKR buyouts worked generally to promote the longer-term health of their portfolio companies.

11. "Buyout Pioneer Quitting the Fray," *New York Times*, June 19, 1987.

12. George Anders, *Merchants of Debt: KKR and the Mortgaging of American Business* (New York: Basic Books, 1992), p. 8.

13. Ibid., pp. 7–8; interview with Henry Kravis, 5/12/94.

14. Interview with Jerome Kohlberg, 1/6/98.

15. Kohlberg interview, 1/6/98.

16. Interview with George Roberts, 6/13/94.

17. Interview with George Roberts, 5/17/96.

18. Kohlberg interview, 1/6/98.

19. Roberts interview, 5/17/96.

20. Kohlberg interview, 1/6/98. "They weren't sure that they wouldn't be held responsible for the company going under with all this tremendous leverage."

21. Interview with Henry Kravis, 10/5/95.
22. Kohlberg interview, 1/6/98.
23. Kravis interview, 5/12/94.
24. Ibid.; Kohlberg interview, 1/6/98; Anders, *Merchants of Debt*, pp. 44–45.
25. Kravis interview, 5/12/94; Anders, *Merchants of Debt*, p. 46.
26. The leverage ratios of KKR's deals have in fact fluctuated significantly over the past 25 years. See figure, p. 81.
27. This model is consistent with calculations on data from KKR's acquisitions, from 1977 to 1990. The average change in the book value of assets from the time of acquisition to the time of divestiture for all KKR portfolio companies that have been sold is just about zero, even though equity values in those companies increased by an average of more than 30 percent per year.
28. Interview with Joseph A. Grundfest, 6/27/96.
29. Interviews with Raymond O'Keefe, 6/16/94, and George Roberts, 4/18/94.
30. See the Note on Sources preceding the endnotes.
31. Roberts interview, 4/18/94.
32. Cf. Anders, *Merchants of Debt*, pp. 26–36. Much of our insight into the Houdaille transaction comes from interviews with the following: Donald Boyce, 7/14/94; George Roberts, 4/18/94; Henry Kravis, 5/12/94; Thomas Hudson, 6/6/94 and 5/17/95.
33. Kohlberg interview, 1/6/98.
34. Roberts interview, 4/18/94; Boyce interview, 7/14/94.
35. Roberts interview, 4/18/94; interview with Michael Tokarz, 6/6/94.
36. Saltarelli retired, as expected, after the deal was consummated. He departed complaining about KKR's acquisition fees. He certainly would not have been comfortable in the new order; but he had made his stockholders, and himself, much richer. He took with him a lump sum payment of $1,062,432 as well as $5.2 million from the sale of his own Houdaille stock, along with a generous retirement package. O'Reilly became the new CEO and was awarded a salary increase from $110,000 to $200,000. Boyce, who would eventually succeed O'Reilly in the top job, became the CFO, with an increase from $60,000 to $100,000. That, along with their ownership participation, was the carrot. The stick was built right into the company's financial structure in the form of more than $300 million in debt. See Anders, *Merchants of Debt*, pp. 26–36; Kravis interview, 5/12/94.
37. Hudson interview, 6/6/94.
38. Anders, *Merchants of Debt*, p. 34.

39. As with steel and automobiles, Japanese machine-tool companies made a decisive move on the U.S. market when American producers were most vulnerable – this time taking advantage of a strong dollar and an economic recession. In November 1982 orders for machine tools dropped 55 percent from the previous year, and Japanese companies' share of the U.S. market increased to 60 percent. The Minneapolis-based Di-Acro, a Houdaille subsidiary, went under; another small-machine subsidiary, the once highly profitable Burgmaster Corporation of Los Angeles, was hemorrhaging $1 million a month. KKR and Houdaille's management were convinced that Japanese machine-tool companies were "dumping" – that is, selling below cost – but there would be no help from the federal government. Boyce interview, 7/14/94; Kravis interview, 5/12/94.

40. Crane had been acquired in a kind of "LBO within an LBO," as Donald Boyce called the transaction. In keeping with the strict spirit of a leveraged buyout, Crane was not allowed by KKR to "commingle" its finances with Houdaille; its debt would be paid out of its own earnings. This enabled Crane, free of Houdaille's cash-flow problems, to grow nicely under Houdaille's management. Boyce interview, 7/14/94; Tokarz interview, 6/6/94.

41. Though KKR buyouts numbered fewer than 40 during this period, the firm's transactions led all U.S. firms in total market value of acquisitions. This was even true for the period from 1977 through 1987, *before* the acquisition of the giant RJR Nabisco.

42. Interview with Jamie Greene, 6/27/96.

43. Interviews with Henry Kravis, 5/17/95, and Thomas Hudson, 5/17/95.

44. Fred Meyer Real Estate Properties, Ltd. was formed in a complicated manner best understood by tax accountants and lawyers. It acquired outright FMI's wholly owned real properties, leasehold interests and improvements, and capitalized store leases. It also acquired FMI's ownership interests ranging from 34 to 74 percent, in seven affiliated real estate companies which leased land and buildings to the Fred Meyer operating company. Interview with Thomas Hudson, 5/14/95.

45. Interview with George Roberts, 2/9/95; interview with Michael Michelson, 5/16/95.

46. The joint venture in this case was designed to hedge KKR's risk in a deal it would otherwise have avoided. Six years later, KKR would craft a joint venture buyout in a different context when it teamed up with Fleet Financial Group to bid on the failed Bank of New England, which had been taken over by the Federal Deposit Insurance Corporation (FDIC). This alliance helped KKR to overcome regula-

tory resistance to its entry into the banking field. The vehicle for investing in BNE and Fleet also involved an innovative use of preferred stock, in this case a dual convertible issue, which KKR could convert into shares of either the parent company or the subsidiary. (See Chapter 6.) In this case, as with UTP, the joint venture and the particulars of the deal financing were designed to maximize KKR's flexibility in the face of various contingencies. Interview with George Roberts, 10/24/95.

47. By late 1989, about half of all large public pension funds in the United States were authorized to invest in LBOs, along with other specialized "high-return, high-risk" investments. See *LBOs, Public Pension Funds, and Public Policy, Final Report, November 28, 1989,* A Report Sponsored by the Massachusetts Pension Reserves Investment Management Board. Though LBO investments represented only a small fraction of pension fund portfolios – typically around 1 percent – their participation provided large sums of money in absolute terms to LBO partnerships, enabling them to expand their activities significantly.

48. Michelson interview, 5/16/95, and Roberts interview, 5/16/95.

49. Interview with Paul Raether, 8/10/95.

50. Interview with Saul Fox, 8/17/95.

51. Interview with Jerome Kohlberg, 1/29/98.

52. The CEO of Motel 6 along with some former managers of CIC – the company that had sold the business to KKR – had set up beneficially owned corporations under different names to contract with Motel 6 on developments around the country. They had used these construction vehicles to channel money supposedly intended for dubious construction projects into their own pockets. Fox interview, 8/17/95; KKR Fund reports; KKR active files.

53. As Saul Fox explained it, while Motel 6 repaid its bank loans, "there was always some other financing source coming in to replace it." In this way KKR could continue to apply all the proceeds to growth. Interview, 8/17/95.

54. Ibid. The tax feature was especially important under the then-current federal code. The conversion had been formally effected as a liquidation of Motel 6 and then a reconstitution of its assets in the partnership. Section 333 of the tax code allowed for the tax-free liquidation for "small" corporations (Motel 6 qualified), provided that one liquidated all the business within a month. Still, taxes had to be paid on cash, securities, or other marketable assets distributed to the owners. KKR, however, received a ruling from the IRS that the distributed limited partnership interests would not be counted as

securities. Thus no tax was paid upon conversion. Afterward, Motel 6 could continue to avoid taxes while building value, as depreciation and interest would continue on an asset basis that had been stepped up in the conversion.

55. This account of the Beatrice transaction draws mainly on George P. Baker, "Beatrice: A Study in the Creation and Destruction of Value," *Journal of Finance*, 47, no. 3 (July, 1992), pp. 1081–1119.

56. During the final negotiation and revision of the KKR offer, Martin Siegel and Robert Freeman, who were advisors to KKR, had access to information about the process of the negotiations. Both subsequently pled guilty to trading illegally on insider information relating to the Beatrice LBO. Although KKR was thoroughly investigated as part of the Siegel and Freeman cases, no improprieties on KKR's part were discovered. Interview with Michael Tokarz, 4/17/96.

57. As part of its agreement with Drexel, KKR agreed to sell to Drexel (for $8 million) warrants to purchase 33 million shares of common stock, as an inducement to investors to get them to buy the bonds. In the event, Milken was able to sell the bonds without the warrants; the warrants were kept by Milken and other managers at Drexel, a fact unknown to KKR at the time or for some time thereafter. When KKR's partners learned that Milken and others had kept the warrants for their own personal accounts (as had also happened in the financing for Storer), they were upset; but they recognized that there was nothing in the contract with Drexel that required that they return the undistributed securities. In future transactions, KKR explicitly contracted with Drexel for the return of unused warrants.

58. Effectively included in the leverage was redeemable preferred stock that was convertible into debt. See Baker, "Beatrice," p. 1109.

59. Between 1979 and 1987, Beatrice led all U.S. firms in number of divestitures. Margaret Blair, Sarah Lane and Martha Schary, "Patterns of Corporate Restructuring," Brookings Institution discussion paper, 1991.

60. Interview with Henry Kravis, 10/18/95.

61. Lazard-Frères' Felix Rohatyn, who was advising RJR Nabisco's nonmanagement directors, may have helped tipped the scales when he pronounced the bids "essentially equivalent . . . from a financial point of view" but pointed out nonprice factors that seemed to favor KKR. KKR offered to leave 25 percent of the stock in shareholders' hands, while the Johnson-Shearson offer was for less. KKR also proposed to retain more of the company following the acquisition and to guarantee certain employee benefits. RJR Nabisco's board of di-

rectors also had to take into account the bad public relations Johnson had engendered in his flamboyant initial attempt to buy out the company for a mere $75 per share. See Brian Burrough and John Helyer, *Barbarians at the Gate* (New York: Harper & Row, 1990); Anders, *Merchants of Debt,* pp. 126–30.

62. The PIK securities – in this case, preferred stock and a convertible debenture – paid interest and dividends, not in cash, but in more of the same kind of securities for a number of years. The preferred stock was ultimately redeemable at $25 per share plus dividends. The convertible debentures (due in 2009) were ultimately redeemable as common stock – 25 percent of outstanding shares on a fully diluted basis.

63. *Mergerstat Review,* 1997.

64. RJR Nabisco's bondholders were not so fortunate. The high-yield "junk bonds" used to finance the transactions would so lower the credit rating of the company that Metropolitan Life Insurance Company led bondholders in bringing suit against KKR, seeking to stop the buyout. *Metropolitan Life Insurance Co. et al. v. RJR Nabisco, Inc.* was filed in late 1988 in the federal court for the Southern District of New York. It failed to stop the proceeding. Most buyout targets had relatively lower credit ratings to begin with. Steven N. Kaplan and Jeremy Stein, "Evolution of Buyout Pricing and Capital Structure in the 1980s," *Quarterly Journal of Economics* (1993), pp. 313–57, found that this was a relatively rare case in which bondholders suffered as the result of a leveraged buyout financing.

65. Upon the merger of the RJR Acquisition Corporation into the target company, all outstanding common shares of RJR Nabisco were converted into the right to receive the aforementioned PIK preferred stock of an acquisition entity known as RJR Holdings Group, and PIK converting debentures.

66. The more than $11 billion loan for the tender offer was paid off in the form of an "asset sale bridge facility" (to be paid in full by August 9, 1991), a "refinancing bridge facility" (to be paid in full by 1991), a revolving credit and term loan (any revolving credit to be converted to term loans in February 1991), and excess cash.

67. These included: PIK subordinated debentures due in 2001; subordinated discount debentures due in 2001; $225 million principal amount of subordinated debentures due in 2001; $225 million principal amount of subordinated extendible reset debentures; and $250 million principal amount of subordinated floating rate notes due in 1999. The purchasers of these various bonds also got equity kickers; and Drexel and Merrill Lynch, retained to place the securities they

had helped to design, also held warrants. In toto, those warrants would amount to 14 percent of fully diluted equity.

68. Kravis interview, 10/18/95.

69. KKR normally collected a fee of 1 percent at the time of a deal's closing, although in the case of Houdaille and RJR Nabisco, the transaction fee was lowered. KKR also charged its investment funds for its fund management activities (1.5 percent of the funds committed) and for postdeal monitoring (directors' fees).

70. Kravis interview, 5/12/94.

Chapter 3. Redefining Value in Owner-Managed Corporations

1. Interview with Robert Kidder, 7/24/96.

2. Interview with Michael Tokarz, 6/6/94.

3. Susan Faludi, "The Reckoning: Safeway LBO Yields Vast Profits but Exacts a Heavy Human Toll," *Wall Street Journal*, May 16, 1990.

4. Magowan and his mother both denied that this conversation had taken place. See Steve-Anna Stevens and Karen Wruck, *Safeway, Inc.'s Leveraged Buyout (C): Media Response* (Boston, MA: Harvard Business School, 1994), which provides source materials and an in-depth analysis and critique of the *Journal* article.

5. More than a year earlier, in February, 1985, the Belzberg Brothers, a pair of Canadian financiers, appeared to have put the company into play when they purchased a large block of Safeway's stock in the open market. Their expected offer for the company did not materialize, but they drove Safeway's share price upwards sufficiently to reap a good profit and to put the company's management on notice.

6. If anything, the evidence from Faludi's own files and other sources suggests that the LBO was born of necessity. Magowan's efforts had been undertaken in response to "speculation that the Belzberg brothers of Canada were preparing to make a tender offer" that would result in the liquidation of "large chunks of the company, for the very simple reason that Safeway's assets – primarily the real estate value of our store locations – are worth more than the stores are worth as performing assets...." See Magowan's address to the United Food and Commercial Workers Union, February 15, 1985 in Steve-Anna Stevens and Karen Wruck, *Leveraged Buyouts and Restructuring: The Case of Safeway, Inc.* (Boston, MA: Harvard Business School, 1992), pp. 1–2. Soon afterward, the Dart Group mounted its raid, leaving KKR to enter the fray as a white knight. The Hafts most certainly would have liquidated Safeway. The alter-

native would have been for Safeway either to pay greenmail, a temporary reprieve at best, or to recapitalize by borrowing and/or selling off assets, but "the risk . . . is that you end up with a much weaker company in terms of the leverage . . . with the continuing disadvantage of being a public company." Ibid., p. 3, which cites a transcript of Faludi's interview of Magowan, May 2, 1990.

7. Faludi noted that prior to the buyout Safeway had suffered from underperforming businesses and bloated payrolls. She reported the company's denials of employee contentions about managerial mistreatment, citing KKR's George Roberts to make the point that in the current economic environment workers were being asked to do more, to be more accountable, certainly "if they are going to be more competitive with the rest of the world." And she quoted Roberts in defense of KKR's investment interest, noting that the firm's "limited partners represent retired teachers, sanitation workers, and firemen, and [that] 80 percent of our profits go to them." *Wall Street Journal,* May 16, 1995.

8. Ibid. Kroger, in fact, had a preexisting labor cost advantage; Safeway's labor costs were upwards of 33% above the industry average.

9. By 1990, Safeway was actually employing more man-hours of work than it had in 1985 before the buyout, albeit at lower wages. Interview with Jerome Kohlberg, 1/29/98.

10. Interview with Michael Tokarz, 4/17/96.

11. "The principals of KKR believe," noted KKR in a 1982 document "that the ownership and financial structure [of a buyout] significantly improve the ability of the new corporation to succeed as an ongoing venture in that there are common goals through the equity interest shared by the parties involved." This basic notion appears in different language throughout KKR prospectuses and fund memoranda over the years. Kohlberg Kravis Roberts & Co., 1982 Investment Fund, KKR files.

12. Ibid.

13. Interview with Henry Kravis, 5/12/94.

14. KKR, 1982 Investment Fund.

15. Interview with Michael Cook, 8/5/96.

16. In the case of Motel 6, the problem was fraud (see Chapter 2).

17. Contrary to industry rumors that Peter Storer had been forced out, his decision to leave seems to have caught KKR by surprise. Interview with Paul Raether, 8/16/95.

18. Interview with Perry Golkin, 5/28/96.

19. Interviews with Don Boyce, 7/14/94; Charles Perrin and Wade Lewis, 8/21/95; Scott Stuart, 8/19/96.

20. Interview with George Roberts, 5/7/94.
21. Kidder interview, 7/24/96.
22. Stevens and Wruck, *Leveraged Buyouts and Restructuring,* esp. p.11.
23. Ibid., pp. 6–7.
24. Ibid., pp. 3–4.
25. Interview with Steven Burd, 9/22/95.
26. Safeway financial reports; KKR files.
27. Safeway's management enlisted the cooperation of the United Food and Commercial Workers Union "to preserve the employee base" as much as possible in asset sales. In vulnerable divisions where the union was able to make concessions, it was possible to sell assets for higher prices; hence fewer assets had to be sold. And by getting wage concessions in stores that were to be sold, buyers were more likely to preserve existing jobs. See Peter Magowan and executive vice president Harry Sunderland's discussion of Safeway's attempts to cooperate with the UFCW in Stevens and Wruck, p. 10.
28. Ibid; interview with Jamie Greene, 6/27/96. Safeway took an 80 percent interest in PDA, and 20 percent in Pac Realty .
29. Burd interview, 9/22/95. Calculating this ratio required a market valuation of each of Safeway's stores.
30. In November 1991, Safeway sold $300 million of 10 percent senior subordinated notes to redeem the $300 million of 11.75 percent senior subordinated notes. It also redeemed the remaining $565 million of 14.5 percent junior subordinated debentures. This cycle continued in January 1992, when another $300 million of 9.65 percent senior subordinated debentures were sold to redeem the 11.75 percent notes. In March 1992 the company sold another $400 million in debt: $250 million of 9.35 percent senior subordinated notes and $150 million of 9.875 percent senior subordinated debentures, the proceeds from which were used to redeem the remaining $150 million of 11.75 percent senior subordinated notes and $250 million of 12 percent subordinated debentures.
31. Greene interview, 6/27/96.
32. Ibid.
33. 1995 *Annual Report;* 1995 KKR Portfolio Company Employment Statistics; KKR files.
34. Perrin and Lewis interview, 8/21/95. Perrin was impressed by Kravis's solicitation of Duracell's management after KKR had won the bidding. As he recalled it, "Henry took us to breakfast. He was pretty straight. 'We've won, and we'd really like to have you on board. But if you don't want to be on board, that's fine too. I know that you didn't support me, but let's go forward together.' I don't

think at that point he knew that some of us had not supported Forstmann. But he did not appear to hold a grudge. He was very direct
and I thought, very fair."

35. In structuring the acquisition, KKR used its usual array of accounting
    and tax techniques, which would enable Duracell to take higher de-
    preciation and amortization deductions in the U.S. Such step-ups in
    valuation were also used in some foreign locations. Debt was stra-
    tegically placed, where possible, in higher-tax countries to further
    improve cash savings.
36. Perrin and Lewis interview, 8/21/95.
37. Ibid., Kidder interview, 7/24/96.
38. Ibid., interview with Paul Raether, 8/16/95; Kidder interview, 7/24/
    96.
39. Ibid.
40. Ibid.
41. This number includes $2.8 billion of unrealized cash in the form of
    Gillette stock as of December 31, 1997 (KKR files).

Chapter 4. When Risk Becomes Real: Managing Buyouts in Distress

1. Carol Loomis, *Fortune*, 1990. See also, "The Best and Worst Deals
   of the 1980s," *Business Week*, January 15, 1990, p. 52.
2. See Steven Kaplan, "Campeau's Acquisition of Federated: Value Created or Value Destroyed?" *Journal of Financial Economics,* 25
   (1989), pp. 119–212; "Campeau's Acquisition of Federated: Post-
   bankruptcy Results," ibid., 35 (1994). More liberal estimates approached $3 billion.
3. Kaplan found that in pure financial terms, the net costs in fees and
   restructuring costs were minimal. Ibid, pp. 128–29.
4. "How Costly Is Financial (Not Economic) Distress? Evidence from
   Highly Leveraged Transactions that Became Distressed," working
   paper, November 3, 1996. The authors also found that the net effect
   of highly leveraged transactions and distress in their sample was to
   leave value "slightly higher."
5. See Karen Wruck, "Financial Distress, Reorganization, and Organizational Efficiency," *Journal of Financial Economics*, 27 (1990), pp.
   419–44. Wruck takes care, as we do, not to confuse "distress" with
   insolvency on a stock basis – i.e., a business with a negative net
   worth. "A firm in financial distress is insolvent on a flow basis . . .
   unable to meet current obligations." This definition is important to

our understanding (more fully articulated below) that under conditions of high leverage well-managed, well-performing assets can run into distress.

6. Jensen, *Eclipse of the Public Corporation.* We are not suggesting, nor was Jensen, that all companies would be better off with high leverage. The point is that large public corporations typically lack any corresponding alarm mechanism to prompt shareholders or their representatives to early action.

7. Steven Kaplan and Jeremy Stein, "The Evolution of Buyout Pricing and Financial Structure in the 1980s, *Quarterly Journal of Economics* (1993), pp. 313–57.

8. We are not taking into account the default of SCI-TV, which in some of the bankruptcy literature has been attributed to KKR. See, for example, Gregor Andrade and Steven N. Kaplan, "How Costly Is Financial (Not Economic) Distress?" SCI-TV's problems came after KKR had divested its control in an unintendedly convoluted deal. In October 1987, KKR agreed to sell to George Gillett, Jr., a group of television stations it had acquired when it bought Storer Communications, Inc., in 1985. The proposed all-cash sale was for $1.3 billion, the cash portion of which (some $1.1 billion) represented more than 13 times cash flow. When financing stalled in the 1987 stock market crash, KKR and Storer took back $223 million in stock and other securities, retaining a 45 percent interest in the assets to get the deal done. SCI-TV subsequently faltered, as the markets that had recently been so kind to television properties reversed direction. Advertising revenues flattened, as cable made incursions into television's more traditional markets. On September 30, 1989, the company missed a mandatory principal payment on its bank debt, and in October it failed to make scheduled interest payments on its bonds. After many complex iterations with debtholders KKR reduced its ownership to 15 percent in a restructuring. SCI-TV filed for bankruptcy protection in June 1993. The original sale of the television properties combined with the sale of Storer's cable properties for $3.1 billion in 1988, enabled KKR Fund investors to realize a return of 51.8 percent on their original investment. (See also Chapter 2.)

9. Charles J. Fombrun, *Reputation: Realizing Value from the Corporate Image* (Boston: Harvard Business School Press, 1996), p. 13, notes how investment bankers bear "extraordinary *reputational* risks that threaten their very existence." We extend the argument further than most assessments of reputational risks in financial services – which typically deal with dishonest behavior – to consider how a firm's

reputation is linked to perceptions of how well expectations for performance are met or exceeded.

10. Jensen would later alter his view of this issue in the face of experience. See, for example, "The Eclipse of the Public Corporation," pp. 61–74.

11. Interview with Robert MacDonnell, 2/19/95. The principal bondholders were Northwestern National Life and two of its subsidiaries.

12. Ibid.

13. Ibid.

14. Interview with George Roberts, 4/19/94.

15. MacDonnell interview, 2/9/95.

16. Ibid. There was also a plan to set up a small subsidiary to perform maintenance R&D along with research into tube mill and laser scanner technologies.

17. Notes from a conversation with George Roberts, 9/10 /97.

18. In 1986, Rotor Tool, which had been acquired five years earlier, was sold to another LBO firm for more than $40 per share, on an original investment of $5 per share.

19. MacDonnell interview, 2/9/95.

20. Seaman, Inc., Confidential Financing Memorandum, KKR files.

21. Morton's brother, Carl, and his nephew, Jordon, were not invited to invest in the post-buyout ownership of the business. Out of deference to his family, Morton would continue to provide his brother with a title and an office, while Jordon departed for greener pastures. Interviews with Paul Raether, 9/23/94, and Henry Kravis, 7/23/94.

22. Morton Seaman personally had owned approximately 11 percent of Seaman at the time of the buyout; total family holdings exceeded 40 percent.

23. KKR's projections for sales growth at Seaman were aggressive enough. With 1987 sales at $224.8 million, the company was expected to realize $338.8 million in sales in 1989 and $567.1 million by 1993. EBIT, which had been at about 14 percent of sales in 1986 and 1987 was expected to increase gradually to 16.6% by 1993. Summary of Historical and Projected Financial Statistics, Seaman Furniture Company, Inc., KKR Files.

24. Kravis interview, 7/23/94.

25. Raether's statement to investors, KKR files.

26. Seaman financial reports, KKR files. Interview with Paul Raether, 9/23/94. Following the restructuring the banks became Seaman's biggest shareholders; they collectively owned 47.5 percent of the stock. KKR now held 44.5 percent, and subordinate debtholders 8 percent. It was estimated that the company's lenders were likely to get 50 to

60 cents on the dollar, while holders of the company's "junk bonds" would receive less than 17 cents on the dollar.

27. Seaman's sales in 1989 were $271.2 million. In 1990 sales had declined to $259 million, despite an increase of seven stores; in 1991, same-store sales fell to $256 million. EBIT for those years declined from $23 million in 1989, to $10.8 million in 1990, to $2.1 million in 1991. Seaman financial reports, KKR files.
28. Seaman news clippings, KKR files.
29. Raether interview, 9/23/94. Serra's strategy was literally to grow Seaman out of its problems; Seaman 1991 Strategic Plan, KKR files. The following year's plan reversed the strategy, emphasizing instead improved efficiencies through cost reductions. The 1991 and 1992 plans are also in the KKR files.
30. Seaman financial reports, KKR files.
31. Seaman Furniture Company continued to operate while reorganizing its finances under bankruptcy protection, having obtained an additional $25 million in debtor-in-possession (DIP) financing from GE Capital Corporation. See Andrade and Kaplan, "How Costly Is Financial (Not Economic) Distress?," p. 37.
32. "KKR's Dream Financing," *Institutional Investor*, January 1989, pp. 64–67. The buyout included the "largest collateralized mortgage obligation ever issued," which is discussed more fully below.
33. In the buyout, the new parent company was Hillsborough Holdings, Inc.; later the company would become Walter Industries. For consistency we use the name Walter throughout.
34. Conversation with Henry Kravis, 9/10/97.
35. Interview with Michael Tokarz, 8/17/95.
36. Walter Industries financial reports, KKR files.
37. Tokarz interview, 8/17/95.
38. Interview with Perry Golkin, 9/18/97.
39. Conversation with Kravis, 9/10/97.
40. See Andrade and Kaplan, "How Costly Is Financial (Not Economic) Distress?", p. 39. In its last year of distress, Jim Walter's EBITDA to sales ratio had increased by 24 percent over that of its pre-buyout fiscal year. There was a corresponding increase of 34 percent in the ratio of net cash flow to sales.
41. Kaplan and Stein, "Evolution of Buyout Pricing and Financial Structure in the 1980s," pp. 314–56.
42. See "Michael Milken – My Story," *Forbes Magazine,* March 16, 1992.
43. Kaplan and Stein, "Evolution of Buyout Pricing and Financial Structure in the 1980s," pp. 326–28. For their sample buyouts, "the me-

dian ratio of EBITDA to cash obligations is always above one before 1986, but falls to between 0.76 and 0.66 for the 1986–1988 period. . . . Similarly, the median ratio of net cash flow to cash obligations, which was always above 0.56 before 1986, does not exceed 0.41 from 1986 to 1988."

44. Brian Burrough and John Helyer, *Barbarians at the Gate* (New York: Harper & Row, 1990), pp. 394–95. Burrough and Helyer also reported (p.395) that KKR was uncomfortable operating in the intense media spotlight. "Do we really need this aggravation?" George Roberts was reported to have asked his partners.

45. Andrade and Kaplan, "How Costly Is Financial (Not Economic) Distress?", p. 36.

46. See George Anders, *Merchants of Debt, KKR and the Mortgaging of American Business* (Basic Books, 1992), p. 250ff., for a fuller account. Anders makes much of the fact that the reset had no provision for an upper limit.

47. Interview with George Roberts, 10/24/95.

48. Anders, *Merchants of Debt*, p. 252.

49. Roberts interview, 10/24/95.

50. *Forbes*, March 16, 1992. No one at KKR recalls Milken expressing any opinion on the equity investment at the time of the deal. Milken had for some time been expressing his view that the corporate economy had become "over-leveraged."

51. Although the dilution was significant, Henry Kravis maintained that at the time of the buyout, doubling the equity investment might have made financial sense. Paul Raether agreed, but noted that KKR would not have committed such a large portion of its 1987 Fund to a single deal. Conversations with Henry Kravis and Paul Raether, 7/24/97.

52. The cost basis for the original 1989 equity investment was $5.00 per share. The cost basis of the 1991 equity investment was $6.25. On a blended basis, the shares had cost $5.61. (KKR files.)

53. RJR Nabisco financial reports, KKR files.

54. Interview with Henry Kravis, 10/18/95.

55. Interview with Clifford Robbins, 10/27/95.

56. Kravis interview, 10/18/95. Such "fraudulent conveyance" might be implicit in a spin-off if it could be shown that KKR anticipated that the company's liabilities – e.g., those arising from judgments in tobacco litigation – would exceed its assets.

57. Ibid.

58. Roberts interview, 10/24/95; Robbins interview, 10/27/95.

59. Kravis interview, 10/18/95.

60. Ibid.

61. In response to the question why investors would not prefer to take a distribution to Borden, Roberts replied, "You have to remember that these are large institutions. Capital's not a problem for them. Getting it invested is." Roberts interview, 10/18/95.

62. Interview, 1/29/98.

63. KKR files.

64. At that time, the annual rate of return on RJR Nabisco from dividend flows and capital appreciation was only about 2.5 percent in nominal terms (KKR files).

65. Recall George Roberts's rhetorical question: "Which would you rather have: low leverage with no flexibility or high leverage with flexibility?" See above, Chapter 2, page 62.

66. Interview with Scott Stuart, 11/1/95.

Chapter 5. KKR as an Institutional Form: Structure, Function, and Character

1. Interview with David Chung, 6/28/96.

2. Interviews with Mark Lipschultz, 10/10/96, and Alexander Navab, 11/21/97.

3. "Conglomerates and LBO Associations: A Comparison of Organizational Forms," Harvard Business School working paper, November 4, 1994, p. 2.

4. Much of this analysis is drawn from Baker and Montgomery, ibid.

5. Michael Jensen, "The Market for Corporate Control and the Politics of Finance," *Journal of Applied Corporate Finance*, vol. 4, no. 2 (Summer 1991), p. 22.

6. Allen Kaufman and Ernest J. Englander, "Kohlberg Kravis Roberts & Co. and the Restructuring of American Capitalism," *Business History Review*, 67 (Spring 1993), pp. 52–97. Their characterizations of KKR are reflected in Jonathon Barron Baskin and Paul J. Miranti, Jr., *History of Corporate Finance* (Cambridge University Press, 1997), chap. 7.

7. Kaufman and Englander, "Kohlberg Kravis Roberts & Co.," pp. 92–95. "[Bank] ownership would provide additional sources of capital for . . . leveraged buyouts, and would provide economies of scope in dealing with the financial markets in arranging non-LBO acquisitions. A bank would also be able to provide commercial services to

KKR's other holdings, forming integral business ties among them and potentially structuring KKR's empire into an industrial group. If KKR is successful in carrying out this strategic goal, it will create a complex set of investor-controlled firms that find their closest analogue in the Japanese *keiretsu*."

8. Ibid., p. 95, note 16. The authors acknowledged that they were speculating: "Our history depends on public documents, which we tie together in a narrative by concepts taken from theoretical business disciplines."

9. In a few cases, as with the uniquely "tax advantaged" investments in forest products companies, the equity financing for KKR deals was raised independently of a fund; but the same principle applied.

10. Baker and Montgomery, "Conglomerates and LBO Associations," p. 9, note 9.

11. Ibid., pp. 10–11. This fit with the stated preferences of some outspoken conglomerate managers, who thought of themselves as institution builders and did not want their businesses to shrink. "I did not become Prime Minister of the British Empire to preside over its demise," one conglomerate CEO paraphrased Winston Churchill to make the point. Baker and Montgomery dismiss one of the more commonly cited reasons for the reluctance of conglomerate managers to sell: that selling units incurs tax disadvantages.

12. Note that in some cases, holding periods for equity exceeded 12 years, which required permission from the fund investors.

13. W. Carl Kester and Timothy A. Luehrman, "Rehabilitating the Leveraged Buyout," *Harvard Business Review* (May-June, 1995), pp. 119–30.

14. Henry Kravis explained that by offering the CEOs of its constituent companies a high degree of independence, along with substantial equity investments in their own individual businesses, KKR could more easily persuade CEOs to consider buyouts as an alternative to selling to strategic or financial buyers who were more likely to change managers. Interview with Henry Kravis, 4/24/96.

15. Eric Ipsen, "The Master of Junkyard Capitalism," *Institutional Investor*, vol. 22 (1988), pp. 132–37.

16. Interview with Henry Kravis, 2/25/98.

17. Interview with Paul Raether, 4/9/96. George Roberts recalled that at the time KKR started, the three partners were intent on creating a durable firm, albeit one of small scale. Roberts had thought of Henry Hillman's Wilmington Securities as something of a model. "We had no idea that we would do one-millionth of what we wound up ac-

complishing," he said (telephone conversation with George Roberts, 1/22/98).

18. This was the way Kohlberg himself described his role; interview with Jerome Kohlberg, 1/22/98.

19. Interview with Jerome Kohlberg, 1/6/98.

20. Interview with Raymond O'Keefe, 6/16/94.

21. Raether interview, 4/9/96.

22. Ibid.; interview with Michael Michelson, 7/26/95.

23. Interview with Michael Chu, 10/6/97. Pace had been sold to KKR in 1984 by City Investing Company, which was in the process of liquidating its assets. Chu had worked at City Investing and had experience with acquisitions.

24. Three books on KKR dealt with this episode in some detail, closer to the events. Brian Burrough and John Helyer in *Barbarians at the Gate* (New York: Harper and Row, 1990) attributed Kohlberg's departure largely to his poor health and advancing age (he turned sixty in 1985). Sarah Bartlett, *The Money Machine* (New York: Warner Books, 1992), relied largely on conversations with Kohlberg and sources close to him and painted a starkly different picture. In her telling, Kravis and Roberts had been taking the firm in a direction Kohlberg could not live with for ethical reasons – their financings were beginning to border on the hostile, and their refinancings were often undertaken to the detriment of other equity partners. Kohlberg, in her view, was harried out of the firm. The third, George Anders, *Merchants of Debt: KKR and the Mortgaging of American Business* (New York: Basic Books, 1992), offers the most complete account, relying largely on interviews with Kravis, Roberts, and Paul Raether (though not Kohlberg). In his treatment of the episode Anders searches for a middle ground, reporting the positions of both sides in some detail. Whereas Anders and Bartlett focus largely on the personal and financial disputes (which are important), we have focused on the more basic policy issues at stake for the firm.

25. A more detailed account of this proposal is provided in Anders, *Merchants of Debt*, pp. 139–41.

26. Telephone conversation with George Roberts, 1/20/98.

27. Anders, *Merchants of Debt*, p. 143.

28. Conversation with Paul Raether, 2/2/98.

29. Kohlberg's announcement was accompanied by a critique of the ethics of Wall Street, which many commentators took to be a criticism of KKR's buyouts. James Sterngold, "Buyout Pioneer Quitting Fray," *New York Times*, June 19, 1987, was the first to write that

"philosophical differences" had been a factor in Kohlberg's decision and that he was off to pursue the kinds of LBO transactions "where reason still prevails." From our interviews with Kohlberg and KKR principals, we find no evidence that Kohlberg was fundamentally unhappy with the trajectory of KKR's investments before his resignation. The differences appear to have been more closely related to how the partnership should be structured and run.

30. In *Jerome Kohlberg Jr. v. Kohlberg Kravis Roberts & Co.*, New York State Supreme Court, August 21, 1989, Kohlberg charged KKR with violating its fiduciary duty toward its equity investors and misappropriating their assets. His complaint was essentially this: that KKR, rather than selling off assets for their highest current market value, had refinanced several of its buyouts in the mid-1980s to its own advantage, buying shares back from other investors that KKR knew were likely to increase in value. KKR saw things very differently: the firm recapitalized companies at opportune times to improve their balance sheets, in the expectation of realizing longer-term gains, and when that happened, it normally offered all equity investors the opportunity either to cash out (some were impatient) or to stay invested on equal terms. Kohlberg's equity positions in recapitalized companies reflected his current, rather than historic, shares in the firm. Kravis and Roberts settled with their former mentor out of court, in an agreement that adjusted some terms of Kohlberg's participation.

31. Anders, *Merchants of Debt*, p. 276.

32. Telephone conversation with George Roberts, 1/22/98.

33. Kravis interview, 4/24/96.

34. Interview with Nils Brous, 12/11/97.

35. Roberts, telephone conversation, 2/2/98.

36. Raether interview, 4/9/96.

37. Kravis interview, 4/24/96.

38. When associates were asked to join the firm as partners, their percentages in the pool increased somewhat, but the main distinction was that partners were formally brought into discussions about the governance of the firm and became privy to all the firm's financial results. Conversation with Henry Kravis, 2/24/98.

39. The literature on the internal operations of investment banks is scant. A useful work is Robert G. Eccles and Dwight Crane, *Doing Deals: Investment Banks at Work* (Boston: Harvard Business School Press, 1988), chaps. 6–8.

40. Michelson interview, 7/26/95. "If you meet an employee from another Wall Street firm, and he's a jerk, one might conclude that everyone at that firm is a bunch of jerks. At KKR, we've got 21 people

doing deals. That's not very many. One person can really affect how we're perceived. There are plenty of times when we have very young people out there operating independently, and we want to be sure that these are people that are going to represent us well. You want to be sure that these are people who are confident, but who have the judgment to understand when they're about to go too far. We're looking for values, judgment, maturity, as well as technical competence and sheer intellectual brain power."

41. Ibid.
42. Interview with Michael Tokarz, 4/17/96.
43. Burrough and Helyer, *Barbarians at the Gate*, p. 450.
44. Michelson interview, 7/26/95.
45. Grimm to George Roberts, 12/30/96, KKR files.
46. Kravis interview, 4/24/96.
47. Navab interview, 11/21/97.
48. Ammon, who wanted to run a business, became head of Big Flower Press; Bousquette became the CFO of Sotheby's.
49. Navab interview, 11/21/97.
50. Michelson interview, 7/26/95.

Chapter 6. Into the Mainstream: KKR in the 1990s

1. Telephone conversation with George Roberts, 1/30/98.
2. Bennet Stewart, in "Remaking the Public Corporation from Within," *Harvard Business Review* (July, 1990), pp. 126–37, advocates the use of "internal LBOs" by which corporations can simulate the discipline and incentives of divisional LBOs without actually putting the equity of the divisions up for sale or borrowing large sums.
3. Interview with Michael Michelson, 7/26/95.
4. Jay R. Allen, "LBOs – The Evolution of Financial Strategies and Structures," *Journal of Applied Corporate Finance* (Winter, 1996), pp. 26–28, provides a more detailed discussion of various LBO firm strategies.
5. K-III evolved as a set of limited partnerships – three in all – that had been organized to pursue specific industry-related acquisitions. But the separate partnerships erected for different acquisitions had limits on debt and credit and hence limited the ability of K-III to make further acquisitions. Thus in 1992, partnerships were replaced by K-III Communications Corp., a new corporate parent that would run and own the three units: education, information, and magazines. To put the new corporate structure on its feet, K-III refinanced its units' debt, raising a total of $940 million, comprised of $590 million in

new bank loans, $250 million in 10.625 percent senior secured notes, and $100 million of senior exchangeable preferred stock (Series B). The proceeds were used largely to pay down previous bank debt. As a result of this restructuring KKR held 88.4 percent of K-III, with management and employees holding the rest.

6. K-III was able to take advantage of section 197 of the tax code, which permitted companies making asset purchases to amortize the cost of intangible assets like franchises, trademarks, customer lists, and information databases against taxes. Many of K-III's acquisitions included a large chunk of intangible assets. The law permitted companies to write these costs down over a forty-year period, but K-III chose to amortize most of its acquired intangible assets over three to five years. This had the effect of cleaning up the company's balance sheet more quickly and reducing the company's tax liability. In 1992, K-III took $171.6 million in depreciation and amortization, and in 1993 it took $143.3 million in depreciation and amortization. As a result, K-III paid $0.3 million in taxes in 1992 and no taxes in 1993.

7. The money for the investment came from the 1987 Fund, which was, of course, set up for the purpose of funding LBOs. The Fund's agreement, however, gave KKR discretionary authority to place the assets of the fund in interim investments before all of its resources were drawn down. Once the investment in First Interstate was made, KKR had two options: it could use its equity stake as a basis for proposing a friendly takeover of First Interstate, or it could simply hold its investment until an attractive leveraged buyout target presented itself. With the declining number of good buyout opportunities following the RJR buyout, KKR decided to hold onto its investment.

8. In the spring of 1989, KKR proposed to the Federal Reserve Board that it be allowed to acquire a bank holding company on the condition that neither KKR nor the participants in its fund agreement become a bank holding company. KKR proposed that it be allowed to make the acquisition by arranging a private placement of equity securities to its fund investors on a discretionary basis (i.e., each investor would determine whether or not to participate); that the equity securities be held directly by investors; that KKR's interest be limited to 1 percent, and that KKR and representatives of management be allowed to seek election to minority seats on the board. "No potential investor . . . should be offered more than 9.9% of any class of voting securities of [the bank] nor account for more than 24.9 percent of [its] total capitalization, and should any bank holding company affiliates be considered as investors they individually would be limited to 4.9 percent of any such class." KKR also expected to

serve as the financial advisor to the acquired bank. "Presentation to Federal Reserve Board, March, 1989," KKR files.

9. The transaction cost $616 million. In addition to KKR's $283 million of dual convertible preferred stock, Fleet contributed an equal amount in the form of common equity. The FDIC invested an additional $50 million in the form of nonconvertible preferred stock.

10. Under the terms of the financing, KKR could either convert its dual convertible preferred stock into 50 percent of BNE or into 16 million shares of Fleet at $17.65 per share – for what then amounted to an 11.2 percent stake in the parent company. In addition, KKR received rights to purchase an additional 6.5 million shares of Fleet common stock for $17.65 each. Fleet's willingness to structure the transaction had also given KKR the confidence to increase its offer for the Bank of New England, which enabled it and Fleet to overcome a competing bid from the Bank of America. The information on KKR's underlying concerns in the Fleet transaction comes from the Fleet and Bank of New England records, KKR files, and a telephone conversation with Paul Raether, 4/7/98.

11. Kravis is quoted in Anders, *Merchants of Debt*, pp. 275–76. Anders comes to a very different and more pessimistic conclusion about the fate of the LBO business; the trends were unclear to him.

12. Venture Economics, *Buyouts* Yearbook, 1997, pp. 30–31.

13. Securities Data Co., *Buyouts* Newsletter [1997]. The publication reported twenty-two total U.S. buyouts with a value of more than $1 billion for the 1990s. KKR is credited with four. Its $1.8 million financing of Flagstar is missing from the list; Borden was not, strictly speaking, an LBO – an extension of the RJR Nabisco investment, it had been acquired with RJR Nabisco stock. See Chapter 4.

14. Kohlberg Kravis Roberts & Co., 1996 Fund, April 1996. For instance, KKR's 1.5 percent management fee would be reduced as commitments exceeded $3 billion. Its deal transactions fees would be negotiated so that at some upper limit, fees would be shared with the limited partners on an 80 percent (LPs) to 20 percent (KKR) basis.

15. Matthew Schifrin, "LBO Mania," *Forbes* (March 9, 1998), pp. 128–134.

16. Taking note of these developments, the SEC has reinforced these trends in a pair of 1992 rulings. One removed onerous proxy procedures and thereby lowered the cost of coordinated shareholder action. The other required more candid disclosure of the details of executive compensation, which has led to more widespread understanding of the potential abuses of conventional bonus and stock

option programs that protect managers against the downside risks of their own behavior.

17. Brian Hall and Jeffrey Liebman, "Are CFOs Really Paid Like Bureaucrats," forthcoming in *The Quarterly Journal of Economics*.

18. Business Roundtable White Paper, "Statement on Corporate Governance" (September 1997), pp. 1–2.

19. Steven Kaplan, "We Are All Henry Kravis Now: Evolution of U.S. Corporate Governance," University of Chicago and NBER working paper, February 1997, p. 13 and figure 3. Cf. Mark Roe, *Weak Owners, Strong Managers* (Princeton, NJ: Princeton University Press, 1994); Joseph A. Grundfest, "Subordination of American Capital," *Journal of Financial Economics*, 27 (1990), pp. 89–114, for more pessimistic views of the longer-term prospects for effective shareholder activism. The authors note the potential recidivist effects of antitakeover legislation and judicial affirmation of "poison-pill" defenses.

Index

earnings before interest and taxes (EBIT), 52
earnings growth, 98, 112
earnings per share, 48, 98
Eastern Europe, 201
Eaton Leonard, 128, 132–4, 160, 161
"Eclipse of the Public Corporation, The" (Jensen), 215n37
economic expansion, "golden age" of, 10
economic value added (EVA), 117–18
Economist, The, 29
economy (U.S.), 11–12, 24–5, 42, 206; local, 139; overleveraged, 33
Edison, Thomas, 2
EFB Truck Lines, 105, 129–32, 159, 161, 162
efficiency(ies), 4, 6, 15, 97; Duracell, 116–17, 119; RJR Nabisco, 149; Safeway, 113
Ely, Richard, 46
Emerson Electric, 17
empire building, 6, 9, 10, 14
employee ownership: Duracell, 120
employment, 22, 29, 35, 106; effect of buyouts on, 37, 39, 218n65; full, 206; retrenchments in, 40
Employment Retirement Security Act (ERISA), 13
employment structures, 11
Englander, Ernest, 167
entrepreneurs, 1–2, 6, 195; use of debt, 46
equity: changing terms of, 201–3; distributed to management, 96; structuring of, and management incentives, 116; use of, to reform underperforming corporations, 205
equity fund(s), 25, 56, 58, 59, 80, 85, 89, 175, 176, 177, 192, 202; limited partnerships organized as, 167–8; 1978, 68; 1979, 74; 1996, 202–3
equity holders, 125, 171; and distress, 130; Duracell, 120; Eaton Leonard, 134; interests of, 144, 160
equity investors, 4, 10, 89, 94, 95, 169; buyout partnership and, 97; relations with, 79, 193; Safeway buyout, 95
equity kicker, 53, 226n67
equity markets: change in structure of, 12–13
equity pools, 26, 79–80, 87
equity structure: KKR buyout companies, 171
ESB Corporation, 19

Esmark, 84
ethical standards, 188, 191
Europe, 201
European banks, 87
Eveready, 117
excess capacity, 5, 6, 22, 36
Executive Life, 143
executive managers; *see* managers
executive pay: linked to performance, 205
expertise, 195, 196; growing, 186; managerial/advisory, 172; outside, 204; specialized, 101, 171–2, 176–7
Exxon, 18, 27

F.B. Truck Line Company, 61, 129, 130; *see also* EFB Truck Lines
failure, learning from, 159–60
Faludi, Susan, 31, 92, 94
family firms, 61, 135, 180
Federated Department Stores, 124–5, 126
Federal Deposit Insurance Corporation (FDIC), 199, 223–4n46
Federal Reserve Board, 23, 199, 240n8
Federal Trade Commission, 23
fees, 94, 203, 227n69
fiduciary oversight/responsibility, 14, 15, 53, 89, 99
finance: anti-heroes of, 27
financial capitalism, 5–7, 22, 35, 42–3, 206; rebirth of, 1–43
financial community, 206
financial economists, 49
financial engineering, xii
financial incentives (KKR), 184–6
Financial Institutions Reform, Recovery and Enforcement Act (FIRREA), 41
financial intermediaries, 7, 8, 31; KKR as, 165
financial management: conventions of, 52
financial restructuring, 128; RJR Nabisco buyout, 151–3, 160, 161; Walters Industries, 146
financial schemes, 2, 3
Financial Security Assurance, 141
financial services industry, 200
financial strategies, 105, 206
financial structure, 26, 80, 159; of buyouts, 57, 58, 97; crafting, 127; creative, 69; importance in corporate value creation, xii; Jim Walter, Inc., buyout, 140–1, 143; and managerial performance, xi; RJR Nabisco